THE TOP 10 OF EVERYTHING 1991

For Caroline, as always

THE TOP 10 OF EVERYTHING 1991

RUSSELL ASH

Macdonald
Queen Anne Press

A QUEEN ANNE PRESS BOOK

© Queen Anne Press and Russell Ash 1990

First published in Great Britain in 1990 by
Queen Anne Press, a division of
Macdonald & Co (Publishers) Ltd
Orbit House
1 New Fetter Lane
London EC4A 1AR

A member of Maxwell Macmillan Pergamon Publishing Corporation

Design: Bridgewater Design Limited

British Library Cataloguing in Publication Data
The Top 10 of everything.
  1991–
  1. Records of achievement
  032.02

  ISBN 0–356–19211–3

Typeset by August Filmsetting, Haydock, St Helens
Printed and bound in Great Britain by BPCC Paulton Books Ltd,
Paulton, Bristol (Member of BPCC Ltd)

Contents

Introduction

Welcome to **THE TOP 10 OF EVERYTHING** – or, if you were one of the readers who helped get the first edition into the Top 10 bestsellers, welcome back – and thanks! Thanks also to the many readers who sent in comments, corrections, and suggestions for new lists. Keep the ideas coming, please.

In compiling this new edition, I have been continually amazed at how helpful some organizations and individuals can be: it would not be fair to single out any one in particular, but take, for example, the *Oxford English Dictionary*. After years of work in putting the world's greatest dictionary onto a massive computer database, I came along and asked questions like 'what 10 letters of the alphabet are most used?' and 'what are the 10 words with the most meanings?' Instead of telling me to push off, they went away and found out! Similarly, *Forbes Magazine*, the prime source of data on rich Americans and entertainers, came up trumps as usual.

Discovering short-cuts to key information sources is very rewarding – such as finding that the American Forestry Commission operates something evocatively called 'The Register of Big Trees', or that one of my neighbours runs a company that collates the most detailed statistical information available on the British retail trade. In fact, it's the latter type of source, private individuals, experts and enthusiasts, which provides some of the most fascinating and otherwise quite unobtainable information. As in the previous edition, where The 10 Longest-named British Pubs, or The 10 Highest-scoring Scrabble Words came from such specialists, many lists could not have been compiled without them. In keeping with the procedure followed by most books of records and yearbooks, sources are not generally given, unless it is important to know where the data came from or where a source has been particularly helpful, although all the individuals and organizations who supplied information are credited on page 254.

How accurate are the Top 10 lists? The answer is that they are as accurate as the sources I use. Clearly, with figures such as The Top 10 Pig Countries, I have not been to the countries and counted them – but then, neither has anyone else. Figures like these are estimated nationally by means ranging from accurate returns to wild guesses. They are then collected internationally by organizations such as the Food and Agriculture Organization of the United Nations. The results represent the best guesstimates anyone can make, and, though they may be questionable, there's often no better source available. Many of the lists are unique to **THE TOP 10 OF EVERYTHING**, others, in this ecology-conscious age, have been recycled from official publications that I trust (though my degree of trust sometimes varies).

Somewhere in the Lake District there is a foot-weary surveyor who is probably cursing me: while I was preparing a list of The 10 Largest National Parks for this edition, I noticed that, depending on which source one used, the area in square miles of the Lake District was given two completely different figures. When I queried this, the Countryside Commission realized that they had one figure and the National Park itself had been giving out a different one for 30 years without anyone spotting the discrepancy. They eventually got back to me and said the correct figure was 885 square miles. I asked them if they'd simply calculated it from a map: 'Oh no', was the answer. 'We sent someone out to measure it!' If nothing else, we can thus claim to have been instrumental in enhancing the accuracy of one official statistic.

The information is the most up-to-date available for a complete year, which in most instances is 1989, but in the case of some official statistics, which are a long time coming, they may be as old as 1988. Where figures such as 'annual sales' are presented, they are the latest known (or estimated by reliable authorities – many firms refuse to divulge them, citing 'commercial confidentiality').

The form of presenting some lists has been changed: the inevitable problem in using absolute figures is that it usually results in China and the USSR coming out on top. The Top 10 Film-going Countries, for example, previously shown by total number of visits, is now given by visits per head, which brings in a country such as Iceland. There are still occasional oddities caused by rounding-off and converting certain figures, especially those of art prices where dollar/sterling conversions often cause an otherwise neat list of 10 to assume an apparently confused order.

Some gremlins invaded the previous edition: there was obviously an 'l' shortage at the printers – it was amazing that no one spotted the one that went missing from the 1,185-letter longest word; one was also dropped from the World Trade Center, thus making it the *Word Trade Center* – which sounds like the sort of institution many writers could find useful!

Certain lists have continued to defeat me: I'm still looking for a reliable way of compiling lists of, for instance, The 10 Largest Cemeteries in the UK or The 10 Tallest Statues in the World. Can anyone out there help?

In the new edition, there are some 'fixed' lists (tallest mountains, etc) which remain scarcely changed. A larger number of Top 10s have been completely revised and updated with latest figures and new descriptive text. Some changes have even been made to historical subjects, such as those lists relating to ballooning and twentieth-century marine disasters, where more accurate information has come to light. A lot of trivia lists (such as The Top 10 Smith's Crisp Flavours) have been replaced – but with other total trivia lists (such as The 10 Bestsell-ing Heinz Soups). Most of the lists, however, are completely new. As we head for 1992 and the European open market, there is more on Europe. There are also more varied sports lists, more on consumer products and popular culture, such as videos and comics, and more on environmental issues. I've added 'lists of the decade' – The 10 Bestselling Books, Most Successful Groups, Films, etc of the 1980s – and there are celebratory (if that's the right word) lists relating to the 50th anniversaries of the Battle of Britain and the Blitz. Finally, I've included thematic quizzes which, I hope, will add to the entertainment value of the book.

I suppose the 'Book of Lists' concept is the starting-off point for **THE TOP 10 OF EVERYTHING**, but its fundamental point of departure is that my lists are all of things that can be measured: they are not my favourites, or lists of what I say are the best or worst, but represent a definitive, quantitative list of 10. It's a way of measuring one achievement against another, and perhaps it appeals to our sympathy for underdogs by rehabilitating some of history's also-rans. I've always felt sorry for people like Elisha Gray, who was beaten to the US Patent Office by a matter of hours in registering his patent for the telephone. The man who got there first was a representative of Alexander Graham Bell, who is consequently regarded as the inventor of the phone. And can you imagine how disappointing it must have been to be the *second* person to fly, or the *third* person on the Moon? The same, in a strangely anthropomorphic way, applies to animals and even to inanimate features, the lakes and rivers, mountains and deserts that are big, but never quite got into the record books – until **THE TOP 10 OF EVERYTHING**.

Russell Ash

If you have any comments or suggestions for new Top 10 lists, please write to:

Russell Ash
c/o Queen Anne Press
Orbit House
1 New Fetter Lane
London EC4A 1AR

ABOUT THE AUTHOR

Photo by Susan Greenhill

Russell Ash was born in Surrey and went to school in Bedford. After obtaining a Joint Honours degree in Geography and Anthropology at the University of Durham, he worked briefly as an aviation insurance broker before his move into book publishing, which has occupied him for over 20 years, latterly as a director of several major publishing companies. He is a contributor to numerous publications, among them *Punch* and the *Observer*, and has weekly columns in the *Kent Messenger* and the London magazine *Midweek*. He has written over 40 books in the diverse fields of art (particularly on the Impressionists and other nineteenth-century painters such as Sir Lawrence Alma-Tadema), animals real and fictitious (he is the official biographer of Paddington Bear, the author of *The Pig Book* and, most recently, a book on the 'Sloane Ranger' teddy bears, Henry & Caroline), reference books including *The Londoner's Almanac* as well as many humorous books, such as *The Cynic's Dictionary* and, as co-author, *Bizarre Books*. He compiles **THE TOP 10 OF EVERYTHING** with the indispensable help of his wife, Caroline, an Apple Macintosh computer and a fax – and despite his two-year-old son, Alexander.

The Universe

THE 10 LARGEST ASTEROIDS IN THE SOLAR SYSTEM

Name	Year discovered	Diameter km	miles
1 Ceres	1801	936	582
2 Pallas	1802	607	377
3 Vesta	1807	519	322
4 Hygeia	1849	450	279
5 Euphrosyne	1854	370	229
6 Interamnia	1910	349	217
7 Davida	1903	322	200
8 Cybele	1861	308	192
9 Europa	1858	288	179
10 Patienta	1899	275	171

Asteroids are fragments of rock orbiting between Mars and Jupiter. There are perhaps 45,000 of them, but fewer than 10 per cent have been named. The first (and largest) to be discovered was Ceres, which was found by Giuseppi Piazzi, director of the observatory in Palermo, Sicily, on New Year's Day, 1801. All have been numbered according to the order in which they were discovered. Some have only code numbers, but most also have names: girls' names are especially popular and include Marilyn (No. 1,486), Sabrina (No. 2,264) and Samantha (No. 3,147). Among asteroids named after men are Mark Twain (No. 2,362) and Brian (No. 3,254). Nos. 3,350–3,356 were named after the seven astronauts killed in the 1986 *Challenger* space shuttle disaster, No. 2,309 is called Mr Spock after the character in 'Star Trek' and Nos. 453, 1,896 and 2,683 have the odd names, respectively, of Tea, Beer and Bus.

The planet Jupiter and two of its 16 moons photographed from 28,400,000 km/17,646,940 miles by *Voyager 1*.

THE PLANETS

Based on apparent visual magnitude as viewed from Earth. At its brightest, the star Betelgeuse is brighter than some of these, but as it is variable its average brightness disqualifies it from the Top 10. If the Sun is excluded, the 10th brightest star is Hadar.

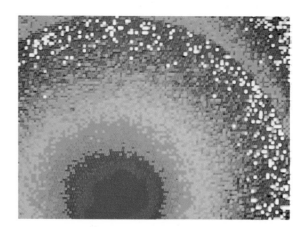

Sirius, the second brightest star visible from Earth.

THE 10 STARS NEAREST TO EARTH

Star	Light years	Distance km	miles
1 Proxima Centauri	4.22	33,923,310,000,000	24,805,160,000,000
2 Alpha Centauri	4.35	41,153,175,000,000	25,569,300,000,000
3 Barnard's Star	5.98	56,790,790,000,000	35,150,440,000,000
4 Wolf 359	7.75	73,318,875,000,000	45,554,500,000,000
5 Lalande 21185	8.22	77,765,310,000,000	48,317,160,000,000
6 Luyten 726–8	8.43	79,752,015,000,000	49,551,540,000,000
7 Sirius	8.65	81,833,325,000,000	50,844,700,000,000
8 Ross 154	9.45	89,401,725,000,000	55,547,100,000,000
9 Ross 248	10.40	98,389,200,000,000	61,131,200,000,000
10 Epsilon Eridani	10.80	102,173,400,000,000	63,482,400,000,000

A spaceship travelling at 56,327 kph/35,000 mph – which is faster than any human has yet reached in space – would take over 80 years to reach Earth's closest star, Proxima Centauri.

THE 10 LARGEST PLANETARY MOONS

Moon	Planet	Diameter km	miles
1 Ganymede	Jupiter	5,262	3,270

Discovered by Galileo in 1609–10 and believed to be the largest moon in the Solar System, Ganymede – one of Jupiter's 16 satellites – is thought to have a surface of ice about 97 km/60 miles thick. The 1979 *Voyager 1* and *2* space probes failed to detect evidence of an atmosphere.

2 Titan	Saturn	5,150	3,200

Titan, the largest of Saturn's 20 or more moons, is actually larger than two of the planets in the Solar System, Mercury and Pluto. It was discovered by the Dutch astronomer Christian Huygens in 1655. We have no idea what its surface looks like because it has a dense atmosphere containing nitrogen, ethane and other gases which shroud its surface – not unlike that of Earth 4 billion years ago – but data sent back by *Voyager 1* during 1980 and recent radio telescope observations suggest that it may have ethane 'oceans' and 'continents' of ice or other solid matter.

3 Callisto	Jupiter	4,820	2,995

Possessing a similar composition to Ganymede, Callisto is heavily pitted with craters, perhaps more so than any other body in the Solar System.

4 Io	Jupiter	3,632	2,257

Most of what we know about Io was reported back by the 1979 *Voyager* probe, which revealed a crust of solid sulphur with massive volcanic eruptions in progress, hurling sulphurous material 300 km/186 miles into space.

| 5 Moon | Earth | 3,475 | 2,159 |

Our own satellite is a quarter of the size of the Earth, the 5th largest in the Solar System and, to date, the only one to have been explored by Man.

| 6 Europa | Jupiter | 3,126 | 1,942 |

Although Europa's ice-covered surface is apparently smooth and crater-free, it is covered with mysterious black lines, some of them 64 km/40 miles wide and resembling canals.

| 7 Triton | Neptune | 2,500 | 1,553 |

Discovered on 10 October 1846 by brewer and amateur astronomer William Lassell, 17 days after he had discovered Neptune itself, Triton is the only known satellite in the Solar System that revolves around its planet in the opposite direction to the planet's rotation. It is getting progressively closer to Neptune, and it is believed that in several million years the force of the planet's gravity may pull it apart, scattering it into a form like the rings of Saturn. Recent studies have more than halved Triton's estimated size, relegating it from 1st to 7th position in the Top 10 Moons, and removing it altogether from its place in the 10 largest bodies in the Solar System. Information sent back to Earth by *Voyager 2* during August 1989 showed that Triton has an atmosphere composed largely of methane and a surface covered with methane ice glaciers.

THE 10 LARGEST BODIES IN THE SOLAR SYSTEM

Name	Maximum diameter km	miles
1 Sun	1,392,140	865,036
2 Jupiter	142,984	88,846
3 Saturn	120,536	74,898
4 Uranus	51,118	31,763
5 Neptune	49,600	30,820
6 Earth	12,756	7,926
7 Venus	12,103	7,520
8 Mars	6,794	4,222
9 Ganymede	5,262	3,270
10 Titan	5,150	3,200

Ganymede is the largest of Jupiter's 16 satellites. The diameter of Mercury is 4,880 km/3,032 miles; that of Pluto, the only other planet not large enough to rank in the Top 10, is uncertain, but is thought to be approximately 2,284 km/1,419 miles. Triton, one of Neptune's two moons (the other is the much smaller Nereid), was formerly ranked 9th, but its diameter has recently been re-estimated (*see* The 10 Largest Planetary Moons).

| 8 Titania | Uranus | 1,610 | 1,000 |

The largest of Uranus's 15 moons, Titania was discovered by William Herschel in 1787 and has a snowball-like surface of ice.

| 9 Oberon | Uranus | 1,550 | 963 |

Also discovered by Herschel, it was given the name of the fairy king husband of Queen Titania, both characters in *A Midsummer Night's Dream*.

| 10 Rhea | Saturn | 1,530 | 951 |

Saturn's second-largest moon was discovered by seventeenth-century Italian-born French astronomer Giovanni Cassini. *Voyager 1*, which flew past Rhea in November 1980, confirmed that its icy surface is pitted with craters, one of them 225 km/140 miles in diameter.

Planets **Q**uiz

1 Which planet was the most recently discovered?
2 Which was the first planet on which a space probe landed?
3 Which was the first planet to be discovered by means of a telescope?
4 Which planet has a highland zone called Ishtar Terra in which the Maxwell Mountains are located?
5 Which planet is nearest the Sun?
6 Is the distance from the Earth to the Moon approximately equivalent to 10, 100 or 1,000 times the distance round the Earth at the equator?
7 Which planet has the shortest day?
8 Which planets are not named after classical gods?
9 How long is a year on Neptune?
10 In Gustav Holst's orchestral work, *The Planets*, which planet is called 'The Bringer of Old Age'?

Saturn with just six of its 20 moons, including Dione (foreground), Titan (top right) and Rhea (top left).

Planet Earth

THE 10 LONGEST RIVERS IN THE WORLD

River	Length	
	km	miles
1 Nile (Tanzania, Uganda, Sudan, Egypt)	6,670	4,145
2 Amazon (Brazil)	6,448	4,007
3 Mississippi–Missouri–Red Rock (USA)	5,970	3,710
4 Yenisey–Angara–Selenga (USSR)	5,540	3,442
5 Yangtze Kiang (China)	5,530	3,436
6 Ob'–Irtysh (USSR)	5,410	3,362
7 Huang Ho (Yellow River) (China)	4,830	3,001
8 Zaire (Congo)	4,700	2,920
9 Lena–Kirenga (USSR)	4,400	2,734
10 Amur–Argun (China, USSR)	4,345	2,700

A village on the Nile, the longest river in the world and Egypt's principal source of water for irrigation.

THE 10 LONGEST RIVERS IN THE USA

River	Length km	miles
1 Missouri–Red Rock	4,088	2,540
2 Mississippi	3,779	2,348
3 Missouri	3,726	2,315
4 Yukon	3,185	1,979
5 Rio Grande	2,832	1,760
6 Arkansas	2,348	1,459
7 Colorado	2,334	1,450
8 Ohio–Allegheny	2,102	1,306
9 Red	2,076	1,290
10 Columbia	2,000	1,243

The Mississippi, Missouri and Red Rock rivers are often combined, thus becoming the third longest river in the world at 5,970 km/3,710 miles.

A high altitude aerial infra-red photograph of the Mississippi, the second longest river in the USA.

THE 10 LONGEST RIVERS IN THE UK

River	Length km	miles
1 Severn	354	220
2 Thames	346	215
3 Trent	298	185
4 Aire	259	161
5 Great Ouse	230	143
6 Wye	217	135
7 Tay	188	117
8 Nene	161	100
9 Clyde	159	98.5
10 Spey	158	98

During their courses, some rivers change their names, for example, Trent/Humber, Thames/Isis.

THE 10 LONGEST RIVERS IN EUROPE*

River	Countries	Length km	miles
1 Danube	West Germany/Austria/Czechoslovakia/Hungary/Yugoslavia/Romania/Bulgaria	2,842	1,766
2 Rhine	Switzerland/West Germany/Holland	1,368	850
3 Elbe	Czechoslovakia/East Germany/West Germany	1,167	725
4 Loire	France	1,014	630
5 Tagus	Portugal	1,009	627
6 Meuse	France/Belgium/Holland	950	590
7 Ebro	Spain	933	580
8 Rhône	Switzerland/France	813	505
9 Guadiana	Spain/Portugal	805	500
10 Seine	France	776	482

*Excluding USSR.

Without excluding those rivers in the USSR in Europe, all 10 rivers would be in that country, with the 3,687-km/2,291-mile Volga heading the list.

THE 10 HIGHEST WATERFALLS IN THE UK

	Waterfall	Country	Drop m	ft
1	Eas Coul Aulin	Scotland	201	658
2	Falls of Glomach	Scotland	113	370
3	Pystyll y Llyn	Wales	91	300
4	Pistyll Rhaeadr	Wales	73	240
5	Falls of Foyers	Scotland	62.5	205
6	Falls of Clyde	Scotland	62.2	204
7=	Caldron Snout	England	61	200
7=	Falls of the Bruar	Scotland	61	200
7=	Grey Mare's Tail	Scotland	61	200
10	Falls of Measach	Scotland	46	150

LEFT Venezuela's Angel Falls, the world's highest waterfall.

ABOVE Grey Mare's Tail waterfall cascades 61 m/200 ft.

THE 10 HIGHEST WATERFALLS IN THE WORLD

	Waterfall	River	Location/ country	Drop m	ft
1	Angel	Carrao	Venezuela	979	3,212
2	Tugela	Tugela	South Africa	948	3,110
3	Utigård	Jostedal Glacier	Nesdale, Norway	800	2,625
4	Mongefossen	Monge	Mongebekk, Norway	774	2,540
5	Yosemite	Yosemite Creek	California, USA	739	2,425
6	Østre Mardøla Foss	Mardals	Eikisdal, Norway	657	2,154
7	Tyssestrengane	Tysso	Hardanger, Norway	646	2,120
8	Cuquenán	Arabopo	Venezuela	610	2,000
9	Sutherland	Arthur	South Island, New Zealand	580	1,904
10	Kjellfossen	Naero	Gudvangen, Norway	561	1,841

THE 10 HIGHEST ACTIVE VOLCANOES IN THE WORLD

Volcano	Country	Height	
		m	ft
1 Antofalla	Argentina	6,450	21,161
2 Guallatiri	Argentina/Chile	6,060	19,882
3 Cotopaxi	Ecuador	5,897	19,347
4 Sangay	Ecuador	5,320	17,454
5 Kluchevskaya	USSR	4,850	15,912
6 Wrangell	Alaska	4,269	14,006
7 Mauna Loa	Hawaii	4,171	13,684
8 Galeras	Ecuador	4,083	13,392
9 Cameroon	Cameroon	4,070	13,353
10 Acatenango	Guatemala	3,959	12,989

ON TOP OF THE WORLD

THE 10 HIGHEST MOUNTAINS IN THE USA

Mountain	m	ft
1 McKinley	6,194	20,320
2 St Elias	5,489	18,008
3 Foraker	5,304	17,400
4 Bona	5,044	16,550
5 Blackburn	4,996	16,390
6 Kennedy	4,964	16,286
7 Sanford	4,949	16,237
8 South Buttress	4,842	15,885
9 Vancouver	4,785	15,700
10 Churchill	4,766	15,638

All 10 tallest mountains in the United States are in Alaska or on the Alaska/Canada border. Mt Logan in Canada is the second tallest peak in the North American continent at 6,050 m/19,850 ft. Colorado and California also have a number of mountains of over 4,267 m /14,000 ft. Only one other state – Washington – has a mountain in the Top 80: Mt Rainier at 4,392 m/14,410 ft.

THE 10 HIGHEST MOUNTAINS IN THE WORLD

Mountain	Country	m	ft
1 Everest	Nepal/Tibet	8,848	29,028
2 K2 (Chogori or Godwin-Austen)	Kashmir/China	8,611	28,250
3 Kanchenjunga	Nepal/Sikkim	8,598	28,208
4 Lhotse	Nepal/Tibet	8,501	27,890
5 Makalu	Nepal/Tibet	8,470	27,790
6 Dhaulagiri I	Nepal	8,172	26,810
7 Manaslu	Nepal	8,156	26,760
8 Cho Oyu	Nepal	8,153	26,750
9 Nanga Parbat	Kashmir	8,126	26,660
10 Annapurna I	Nepal	8,078	26,504

All 10 of the world's highest mountains are in the Himalayas, but the peak of Chimborazo in Ecuador, which is not even one of the Top 30 highest mountains in the world, is 2,151 m/7,057 ft further from the centre of the Earth than Everest's. This is because it is nearer the Equator, where the earth bulges more. No two sources agree on the precise heights of the world's tallest mountains, partly because of the inaccuracy of measuring instruments, which are affected by the gravitational attraction of the mountains, partly because the ice caps on their peaks vary in depth from season to season, and partly because many of them are inaccessible. In recent years, satellite surveys have provided some new data, but even this is hotly disputed, especially when the result of one recent survey suggested that K2 was actually 8,859 m/29,064 ft, some 11 m/36 ft higher than Everest!

THE 10 HIGHEST MOUNTAINS IN SCOTLAND

Mountain	m	ft
1 Ben Nevis, Highland	1,344	4,408
2 Ben Macdhui, Grampian	1,309	4,296
3 Braeriach, Grampian/Highland	1,296	4,252
4 Cairn Toul, Grampian	1,293	4,241
5 Cairn Gorm, Grampian/Highland	1,245	4,084
6 Aonach Beag, Highland	1,236	4,054
7 Carn Mór Dearg, Highland	1,223	4,012
8 Aonach Mór, Highland	1,219	3,999
9 Ben Lawers, Tayside	1,214	3,984
10 Beinn a' Bhùird, Grampian	1,196	3,924

THE 10 HIGHEST MOUNTAINS IN IRELAND

	Mountain	Height m	ft
1	Carrauntual, Kerry	1,041	3,414
2	Beenkeraugh, Kerry	1,010	3,314
3=	Caher, Kerry	975	3,200
3=	Ridge of the Reeks, Kerry	975	3,200
5	Brandon, Kerry	953	3,127
6	Lugnaquilla, Wicklow	926	3,039
7	Galtymore, Tipperary	920	3,018
8=	Slieve Donard, Co Down	852	2,796
8=	Baurtregaum, Kerry	852	2,796
10	Mullaghcleevaun, Wicklow	850	2,788

Slieve Donard is the highest mountain in Northern Ireland. All the others are in the Irish Republic.

THE 10 HIGHEST MOUNTAINS IN WALES

	Mountain	Height m	ft
1	Snowdon	1,085	3,560
2	Carnedd Llewelyn	1,062	3,484
3	Carnedd Dafydd	1,044	3,426
4	Glyder Fawr	999	3,279
5	Glyder Fâch	994	3,262
6	Y Garn	946	3,104
7	Foel Fras	942	3,091
8	Elidir Fawr	923	3,029
9	Tryfan	917	3,010
10	Aran Fawddwy	905	2,970

All the tallest Welsh peaks are in the Snowdonia region of the county of Gwynedd. Several also have sub-peaks that are similarly tall, but are not included as separate mountains.

THE 10 HIGHEST MOUNTAINS IN ENGLAND

	Mountain	Height m	ft
1	Scafell Pike	977	3,206
2	Sca Fell	964	3,162
3	Helvellyn	949	3,113
4	Skiddaw	931	3,054
5	Bow Fell	902	2,960
6	Great Gable	899	2,949
7	Cross Fell	893	2,930
8	Pillar	892	2,927
9	Esk Pike	885	2,903
10	Fairfield	873	2,863

All 10 of England's highest peaks are in Cumbria.

Mountains Quiz

1 What was the greatest achievement of English mountaineer Edward Whymper?
2 What was the exceptional achievement of English mountaineer Geoffrey Winthrop Young?
3 What did Japanese mountaineer Junko Tabei achieve on 16 May 1975?
4 What is the longest mountain range in the world?
5 Who had a No.1 hit in 1961 with 'Climb Ev'ry Mountain'?
6 What is the tallest mountain in Africa?
7 Mount Kosciusko is the highest mountain in which country?
8 What is the highest mountain in the UK that can be climbed by railway?
9 What is the name of the mountain in the USA that has gigantic carvings depicting US presidents?
10 What 1975 film starring Clint Eastwood has the name of a Swiss mountain in its title?

At 899 m/2,949 ft Great Gable is approximately one-tenth of the height of Mount Everest.

THE 10 DRIEST PLACES IN GREAT BRITAIN

	Weather station	Average annual rainfall	
		mm	in
1	Shoeburyness, Essex	539	21.22
2	Cambridge	556	21.89
3=	Pontefract, West Yorkshire	593	23.35
3=	Raunds, Northamptonshire	593	23.35
3=	Scarborough, North Yorkshire	593	23.35
6	Redcar, Cleveland	594	23.39
7	Skegness, Lincolnshire	596	23.46
8	Nottingham	602	23.70
9	Gorleston, Norfolk	604	23.78
10	Nairn, Highland	613	24.13

THE 10 WARMEST PLACES IN GREAT BRITAIN

	Weather station	Average annual temperature	
		°C	°F
1	St Mary's, Isles of Scilly	11.6	52.9
2	Penzance, Cornwall	11.3	52.3
3	Ilfracombe, Devon	11.0	51.8
4=	Torbay, Devon	10.9	51.6
4=	Sandown, Isle of Wight	10.9	51.6
6=	London	10.7	51.3
6=	Newquay, Cornwall	10.7	51.3
6=	Plymouth, Devon	10.7	51.3
6=	Southampton, Hampshire	10.7	51.3
6=	Swansea, West Glamorgan	10.7	51.3

THE 10 COLDEST PLACES IN GREAT BRITAIN

	Weather station	Average annual temperature	
		°C	°F
1	Braemar, Grampian	6.4	43.5
2	Lerwick, Shetland	7.1	44.8
3	Eskdalemuir, Dumfries and Galloway	7.2	45.0
4	Buxton, Derbyshire	7.6	45.7
5=	Wick, Highland	7.7	45.9
5=	Aberdeen, Grampian	7.7	45.9
7	Kirkwall, Orkney	7.8	46.0
8=	Lake Vyrnwy, Powys	7.9	46.2
8=	Cape Wrath, Highland	7.9	46.2
10=	Duntulm, Highland	8.3	46.9
10=	Glentee, Dumfries and Galloway	8.3	46.9
10=	Nairn, Highland	8.3	46.9
10=	Stornoway, Western Isles	8.3	46.9

THE 10 WETTEST PLACES IN GREAT BRITAIN

	Weather station	Average annual rainfall	
		mm	in
1	Achnashellach, Highland	2,161	85.08
2	Onich, Highland	2,029	79.88
3	Ambleside, Cumbria	1,902	74.88
4	Lake Vyrnwy, Powys	1,633	64.29
5	Tredegar, Gwent	1,559	61.38
6	Glentee, Dumfries and Galloway	1,507	59.33
7	Eskdalemuir, Dumfries and Galloway	1,506	59.29
8	Duntulm, Highland	1,366	53.78
9	Buxton, Derbyshire	1,284	50.55
10	Benbecula, Western Isles	1,204	47.40

THE 10 LARGEST ISLANDS IN THE WORLD

Island	Approx. area* sq km	sq miles
1 Greenland (Kalaatdlit Nunaat), Denmark Arctic Ocean	2,175,590	840,000
2 New Guinea, West Pacific	789,900	304,980
3 Borneo, Indian Ocean	751,000	289,961
4 Madagascar (Malagasy Republic), Indian Ocean	587,041	226,657
5 Baffin Island, Canada Arctic Ocean	507,451	195,926
6 Sumatra, Indonesia Indian Ocean	422,200	163,011
7 Honshu, Japan Northwest Pacific	230,092	88,839
8 Great Britain North Atlantic	218,041	84,186
9 Victoria Island, Canada Arctic Ocean	217,290	83,896
10 Ellesmere Island, Canada Arctic Ocean	196,236	75,767

Mainlands, including areas of inland water, but excluding offshore islands.

Australia is regarded as a continental land mass rather than an island; otherwise it would rank first, at 7,618,493 sq km/2,941,517 sq miles, or 35 times the size of Great Britain.

BOTTOM LEFT Sailing off the Needles, Isle of Wight, one of the UK's Top 10 islands.

ABOVE Gateway to the frozen north: an ice arch in Greenland, the largest island in the world.

THE 10 LARGEST ISLANDS IN GREAT BRITAIN

Island	sq km	sq miles	Population
1 Lewis with Harris, Outer Hebrides	2,225.30	859.19	23,390
2 Skye, Hebrides	1,666.08	643.27	8,139
3 Mainland, Shetland	967.00	373.36	22,184
4 Mull, Inner Hebrides	899.25	347.20	2,605
5 Anglesey	713.80	275.60	68,500
6 Islay, Inner Hebrides	638.79	246.64	3,997
7 Isle of Man	571.66	220.72	64,679
8 Mainland, Orkney	536.10	206.99	14,299
9 Arran	435.32	168.08	4,726
10 Isle of Wight	380.99	147.10	120,400

THE 10 LARGEST METEORITE CRATERS IN THE WORLD

Name	Location	Diameter km	miles
1 = Sudbury	Ontario, Canada	140	87
1 = Vredefort	South Africa	140	87
3 = Manicouagan	Quebec, Canada	100	62
3 = Popigai	USSR	100	62
5 Puchezh-Katunki	USSR	80	50
6 Kara	USSR	60	37
7 Siljan	Sweden	52	32
8 Charlevoix	Quebec, Canada	46	29
9 Araguainha Dome	Brazil	40	25
10 Carswell	Saskatchewan, Canada	37	23

Unlike on the Solar System's other planets and moons, many astroblemes (collision sites) on Earth have been weathered over time and obscured. One of the great debates in geology is thus whether or not certain crater-like structures are of meteoric origin, or the remnants of long-extinct volcanoes. All the giant meteorite craters in the Top 10 are believed to be so, and are listed as such (along with 106 others) by the International Union of Geological Sciences Commission on Comparative Planetology. The relatively small Barringer Crater in Arizona (1.265 km/0.79 miles) is, however, the largest that all scientists agree is indisputably an astrobleme. Recently, by using photographs taken from space, many new possible astroblemes have been discovered, including a massive 320 km/199 mile diameter site centred on Prague, Czechoslovakia, which has been named the Praha Basin. It has been postulated that what may turn out to be Europe's biggest crater was caused 15,000,000 years ago by a meteorite of some 80 km/50 miles diameter which impacted with a force a million times more powerful than the atomic bomb that destroyed Hiroshima.

The Hoba meteorite, reduced to perhaps half its original size after 1,000,000 years of weathering.

THE 10 LARGEST METEORITES EVER FOUND

	Location	Estimated weight (tonnes)
I	Hoba West, Grootfontein, South Africa	54.4
2	Ahnighito ('The Tent'), Cape York, West Greenland	30.9
3	Bacuberito, Mexico	27
4	Mbosi, Tanganyika	26
5	Agpalik, Cape York, West Greenland	20.1
6	Armanti, Western Mongolia	20
7=	Chupaderos, Mexico	14
7=	Willamette, Oregon	14
9	Campo del Cielo, Argentina	13
10	Mundrabila, Western Australia	12

The Hoba meteorite, the largest in the world, was found on a farm in 1920. A 2.73 m/9 ft × 2.43 m/8 ft slab, it consists of 82 per cent iron and 16 per cent nickel. 'The Tent', known by its original Eskimo name, Ahnighito, was discovered in 1897 by the American Arctic explorer Admiral Robert Peary and is now in the Hayden Planetarium at the New York Museum of Natural History. It is the largest meteorite in the world on exhibition.

THE 10 LARGEST METEORITES FOUND IN THE UK

	Location	Date found	Approx. weight kg	lb
I	Barwell, Leicestershire	24 Dec 1965	46	101
2=	Appley Bridge, Lancashire	13 Oct 1914	33	73
2=	Hatford, Berkshire (3 rocks)	9 Apr 1628	33	73
4	Wold Cottage, Yorkshire	13 Dec 1795	25.4	56
5	Strathmore, Tayside (4 rocks)	3 Dec 1917	13	29
6	Strechleigh, Devon	10 Jan 1623	12	26
7	Perth	17 May 1830	11	24
8	High Possil, Strathclyde	5 Apr 1804	4.5	10
9	Crumlin, Antrim	13 Sep 1902	4.1	9
10	Rowton, Shropshire	20 Apr 1876	3.2	7

TOP A Leonid meteor shower photographed in 1966.

THE 10 HEAVIEST ELEMENTS

	Element	Year discovered	Density (grams per cubic cm at 20°C)
1	Osmium	1804	22.59
2	Iridium	1804	22.56
3	Platinum	1748	21.45
4	Rhenium	1925	21.01
5	Neptunium	1940	20.47
6	Plutonium	1940	20.26
7	Gold	Prehistoric	19.29
8	Tungsten	1783	19.26
9	Uranium	1789	19.05
10	Tantalium	1802	16.67

ABOVE A micrograph of atoms of iridium, the second heaviest element.

BELOW The view to the south west near Dores on Loch Ness, the UK's fourth largest lake.

OPPOSITE An aerial view of the Great Lakes Superior and Michigan.

The two heaviest elements, the metals osmium and iridium, were discovered at the same time by the British chemist Smithson Tennant (1761–1815), who was also the first to prove that diamonds are made of carbon. A cubic foot (0.0283 cu m) of osmium weighs 640 kg/1,410 lb – equivalent to 10 people each weighing 10 stone.

THE 10 LARGEST LAKES IN THE WORLD

	Lake	Location	Approx. area sq km	sq miles
1	Caspian Sea	Iran/USSR	371,800	143,552
2	Superior	Canada/USA	82,350	31,795
3	Victoria	Kenya/Tanzania/Uganda	69,500	26,834
4	Aral Sea	USSR	65,500	25,290
5	Huron	Canada/USA	59,600	23,012
6	Michigan	USA	58,000	22,394
7	Tanganyika	Burundi/Tanzania/Zaire/Zambia	32,900	12,703
8	Great Bear	Canada	31,800	12,278
9	Baikal	USSR	30,500	11,776
10	Nyasa (Malawi)	Malawi/Mozambique/Tanzania	29,600	11,429

THE 10 LARGEST LAKES IN THE UK

	Lake	Country	Area sq km	sq miles
1	Lough Neagh	Northern Ireland	381.74	147.39
2	Lower Lough Erne	Northern Ireland	105.08	40.57
3	Loch Lomond	Scotland	71.22	27.50
4	Loch Ness	Scotland	56.64	21.87
5	Loch Awe	Scotland	38.72	14.95
6	Upper Lough Erne	Northern Ireland	31.73	12.25
7	Loch Maree	Scotland	28.49	11.00
8	Loch Morar	Scotland	26.68	10.30
9	Loch Tay	Scotland	26.39	10.19
10	Loch Shin	Scotland	22.53	8.70

The largest lake in England is Windermere, 14.74 sq km/5.69 sq miles.

THE 10 LARGEST OCEANS AND SEAS IN THE WORLD

Ocean/sea	Approx. area	
	sq km	sq miles
1 Pacific Ocean		
(with adjacent seas)	181,343,000	70,017,000
(without adjacent seas)	166,241,000	64,186,000
2 Atlantic Ocean		
(with adjacent seas)	94,314,000	36,415,000
(without adjacent seas)	86,557,000	33,420,000
3 Indian Ocean		
(with adjacent seas)	74,118,000	28,617,000
(without adjacent seas)	73,426,000	28,350,000
4 Arctic Ocean		
(with adjacent seas)	12,256,000	4,732,000
(without adjacent seas)	9,485,000	3,662,000
5 Coral Sea	4,791,000	1,850,000
6 Arabian Sea	3,864,000	1,492,000
7 South China Sea	3,686,000	1,423,000
8 Caribbean Sea	2,753,000	1,063,000
9 Mediterranean Sea	2,515,000	971,000
10 Bering Sea	2,305,000	890,000

RIGHT Ever-deeper sections of the world's deepest caves are being explored.

ABOVE An island in the Maldives group – a very small dot in the very large Indian Ocean.

For comparison, the North Sea is 660 m/2,165 ft at its deepest point, and has an average depth of 94 m/308 ft.

THE 10 DEEPEST OCEANS AND SEAS

Ocean/sea	Greatest depth		Average depth	
	m	ft	m	ft
1 Pacific Ocean	10,918	35,820	4,028	13,215
2 Indian Ocean	7,455	24,460	3,963	13,002
3 Atlantic Ocean	9,219	30,246	3,926	12,880
4 Caribbean Sea	6,946	22,788	2,647	8,685
5 South China Sea	5,016	16,456	1,652	5,419
6 Bering Sea	4,773	15,659	1,547	5,075
7 Gulf of Mexico	3,787	12,425	1,486	4,874
8 Mediterranean Sea	4,632	15,197	1,429	4,688
9 Japan Sea	3,742	12,276	1,350	4,429
10 Arctic Ocean	5,625	18,456	1,205	3,953

Sources disagree on the depths of the Top 10 and the rest of the world's great cave systems since measurements are undergoing constant revision as new branches are discovered and mapping improved. The deepest cave in the UK is the 308 m/1,010 ft Ogof Ffynnon Ddu in Wales. The most extensive cave system in the world is that of the limestone Mammoth Cave, Kentucky, which extends some 530 km/329 miles.

THE 10 DEEPEST CAVES IN THE WORLD

	Cave system	Location	Depth m	ft
1	Résneau Gouffe Jean Bernard	France	1,535	5,036
2	Atea Kananda	Papua New Guinea	1,500	4,920
3	Snezhnaya	USSR	1,470	4,823
4	Sima de las Puertas de Illamina	Spain	1,338	4,390
5	Gouffe de la Pierre-Saint-Martin	France	1,332	4,370
6	Sistema Huautla	Mexico	1,246	4,088
7	Mammuthöhle	Austria	1,219	3,999
8	Sumidero de Cellagua	Spain	970	3,182
9=	Antro di Corchia	Italy	950	3,117
9=	Kievskaya	USSR	950	3,117

THE 10 LARGEST DESERTS IN THE WORLD

	Desert	Location	Approx. area sq km	sq miles
1	Sahara	North Africa	9,000,000	3,474,920
2	Australian	Australia	3,830,000	1,478,771
3	Arabian	Southwest Asia	1,300,000	501,933
4	Gobi	Central Asia	1,295,000	500,002
5	Kalahari	Southern Africa	520,000	200,772
6	Turkestan	Central Asia	450,000	173,745
7	Takla Makan	China	327,000	126,255
8=	Sonoran	USA/Mexico	310,000	119,691
8=	Namib	Southwest Africa	310,000	119,691
10=	Thar	Northwest India/ Pakistan	260,000	100,386
10=	Somali	Somalia	260,000	100,386

Plants & Crops

THE 10 MOST POPULAR BULBS

	Plant	Annual sales
1	Daffodil	150,000,000
2	Crocus	105,000,000
3	Tulip	80,000,000
4	Gladioli	61,000,000
5	Iris	50,000,000
6	Snowdrop	20,000,000
7	Allium (ornamental onion)	14,000,000
8	Grape hyacinth	13,000,000
9 =	Lily	10,000,000
9 =	Scilla	10,000,000

These are the Agricultural Development and Advisory Service's estimates for bulbs grown domestically in the UK, and do not include those used commercially and for forced cut flowers.

'A host of golden daffodils', as popular now as when William Wordsworth wrote his famous poem.

TREE TOPS

THE 10 BIGGEST TREES IN THE USA BY SPECIES

	Species	State	Points
1	General Sherman Giant Sequoia	Sequoia National Park, California	1,300
2	Coast Redwood	Humboldt Redwoods State Park, California	1,010
3	Western Redcedar	Forks, Washington	924
4	Sitka Spruce	Olympic National Forest, Washington	922
5	Coast Douglas Fir	Olympic National Park, Washington	762
6	Common Baldcypress	Cat Island, Louisiana	748
7	Sycamore	Jeromesville, Ohio	737
8	Port-Orford Cedar	Siskiyou National Forest, Oregon	680
9	Incense Cedar	Marble Mountains Wilderness, California	626
10	Bluegum Eucalyptus	Fort Ross State Historic Park, California	622

The American Forestry Association operates a National Register of Big Trees which is constantly updated as new 'champion trees' are nominated. Their method of measurement, which gives this Top 10 by species, is based not solely on height, but also takes account of the thickness of the trunk and spread of the upper branches and leaves, or crown. The formula adds the circumference in inches of the tree at breast height ($4\frac{1}{2}$ feet above the ground) to the total height of the tree in feet and to $\frac{1}{4}$ of the average crown spread in feet. The General Sherman Giant Sequoia is 998 inches in circumference, 275 feet tall and with an average crown spread of 107 feet, hence $998 + 275 + 27 = 1,300$ points. However it is measured, it comes out not only at the top of this list, but is also the largest tree – and the largest living object – on the planet.

A Giant Redwood in Mariposa Grove, California.

THE 10 COUNTRIES WITH THE LARGEST AREAS OF FOREST

	Country	Hectares	Acres
1	USSR	944,000,000	2,232,671,200
2	Brazil	557,990,000	1,378,821,189
3	Canada	354,000,000	874,751,700
4	USA	265,188,000	655,292,807
5	China	116,565,000	288,037,943
6	Australia	106,000,000	261,931,300
7	Peru	69,150,000	170,873,108
8	India	67,100,000	165,807,455
9	Argentina	59,500,000	147,027,475
10	Bolivia	55,770,000	137,810,458
	UK	2,324,000	5,742,720
	World total	4,068,536,000	10,005,355,588

The subject of massive international conservation campaigns, the Amazonian rainforest places Brazil in second position in the world's Top 10 forests.

Planting in progress: the Forestry Commission undertaking its important task of conserving Britain's woodland.

THE 10 LARGEST FORESTS IN GREAT BRITAIN

Forest	Area hectares	acres
1 Kielder	39,380	97,310
2 Newton Stewart	35,275	87,166
3 Dornoch	35,180	86,932
4 Ayrshire and Arran	29,189	72,127
5 Castle Douglas	27,415	67,774
6 Kintyre	26,287	64,956
7 Loch Awe	25,202	62,275
8 Aberfoyle	24,431	60,370
9 Easter Ross	23,795	58,799
10 Cowal	23,521	58,122

The Kielder Forest is in Northumberland, but the other nine largest forests under the aegis of the Forestry Commission are all located in Scotland. The total area of forest in Great Britain is 2,135,000 hectares/5,275,692 acres.

THE TOP 10 TREES PLANTED IN GREAT BRITAIN

1 Sitka spruce
2 Scots pine
3 Lodgepole pine
4 Larch
5 Norway spruce
6 Corsican pine
7 Douglas fir
8 Beech
9 Oak
10 Birch

In 1988–89, the Forestry Commission planted 4,100 hectares/ 10,131 acres, and private woodland owners a further 25,400 hectares/ 62,765 acres. The total number of trees planted is equivalent to approximately one tree for every person in Great Britain.

THE 10 MOST FORESTED COUNTRIES IN THE WORLD

	% forest cover
1 Surinam	92
2 Solomon Islands	91
3 Papua New Guinea	84
4 Guyana	83
5 French Guiana	82
6 Gabon	78
7 Finland	76
8 Kampuchea	75
9 North Korea	74
10 Bhutan	70

These are the 10 countries with the greatest area of forest and woodland as a percentage of their total land area. The world average is 31 per cent, and that of the UK less than 10 per cent, with Ireland just 4 per cent. The least-forested large countries in the world are the desert lands of the Middle East and North Africa, such as Libya with under 0.4 per cent.

Trees Quiz

1 What was known as 'Tyburn Tree'?
2 Which group had a No. 1 hit in 1973 with the song, 'Tie A Yellow Ribbon Round The Old Oak Tree'?
3 What tree belongs to the *Fraxinus* family?
4 What was the date of the Great Storm of 1987 which destroyed approximately 15,000,000 trees in Great Britain?
5 What is the name of the wood that comes to Dunsinane in Shakespeare's *Macbeth*?
6 What tree's name derives from the Spanish word for 'raft'?
7 A Christmas tree is presented annually by Norway to Great Britain and erected in Trafalgar Square. Why?
8 Who was the American author of the poem, *The Village Blacksmith*, which begins, 'Under the spreading chestnut-tree/The village smithy stands'?
9 What tree was traditionally grown in English churchyards?
10 Where was the oak tree under which Princess Elizabeth was sitting when she heard she had been proclaimed Queen Elizabeth I?

THE TOP 10 BANANA-GROWING COUNTRIES

	Country	Annual production (tonnes)
1	Brazil	5,139,000
2	India	4,600,000
3	Philippines	3,645,000
4	China	2,350,000
5	Ecuador	2,238,000
6	Indonesia	1,860,000
7	Thailand	1,606,000
8	Burundi	1,480,000
9	Vietnam	1,450,000
10 =	Colombia	1,300,000
10 =	Tanzania	1,300,000
	World total	*41,913,000*

The tobacco harvest in North Carolina: the USA's huge tobacco output is just one-quarter that of China.

THE TOP 10 TOBACCO-GROWING COUNTRIES

Country	Annual production (tonnes)
1 China	2,353,000
2 USA	604,000
3 Brazil	439,000
4 USSR	340,000
5 India	320,000
6 Turkey	212,000
7 Italy	161,000
8 Indonesia	147,000
9 Greece	142,000
10 Bulgaria	117,000
World total	*6,531,000*

THE TOP 10 WHEAT-GROWING COUNTRIES

Country	Annual production (tonnes)
1 China	87,505,000
2 USSR	84,500,000
3 USA	49,295,000
4 India	45,096,000
5 France	29,677,000
6 Turkey	20,500,000
7 Canada	15,655,000
8 Australia	14,102,000
9 Pakistan	12,675,000
10 UK	11,605,000
World total	*509,952,000*

Despite their vast size, the wheatlands of the Great Plains of the USA rank third in the world's Top 10.

THE TOP 10 APPLE-GROWING COUNTRIES

Country	Annual production (tonnes)
1 USSR	5,700,000
2 China	4,268,000
3 USA	4,037,000
4 West Germany	2,467,000
5 France	2,357,000
6 Italy	2,326,000
7 Turkey	1,954,000
8 Poland	1,393,000
9 Argentina	1,078,000
10 Iran	1,067,000
World total	*40,860,000*

The UK's production steadily declined during the 1980s in the face of cheap imports and is now put at about 241,000 tonnes.

THE TOP 10 SUGAR PRODUCERS

Country	Annual production (tonnes)
1 USSR	9,240,000
2 India	9,100,000
3 Brazil	8,500,000
4 Cuba	7,548,000
5 USA	6,260,000
6 China	5,925,000
7 France	4,424,000
8 Mexico	3,822,000
9 Australia	3,580,000
10 West Germany	3,130,000
UK	*1,413,000*

Food for more than one billion: harvesting rice, the world's largest single crop, near Longsheng, China.

An apple orchard in New York state. The USA is the third largest apple producer in the world.

THE TOP 10 COFFEE-GROWING COUNTRIES

Country	Annual production (tonnes)
1 Brazil	1,321,000
2 Colombia	780,000
3 Indonesia	358,000
4 Mexico	283,000
5 Ivory Coast	187,000
6 Uganda	184,000
7 Ethiopia	180,000
8 Guatemala	162,000
9 El Salvador	152,000
10 Costa Rica	145,000
World total	*5,515,000*

Perhaps surprisingly, Kenya does not appear in the Top 10 as its annual production is only 125,000 tonnes, ranking it equal with India at No. 14 in the world league.

THE TOP 10 RICE-GROWING COUNTRIES

Country	Annual production (tonnes)
1 China	172,365,000
2 India	101,950,000
3 Indonesia	41,769,000
4 Bangladesh	21,900,000
5 Thailand	20,813,000
6 Vietnam	15,200,000
7 Burma	14,000,000
8 Japan	12,419,000
9 Brazil	11,804,000
10 Philippines	8,971,000
World total	*483,466,000*

THE TOP 10 ORANGE-GROWING COUNTRIES

Country	Annual production (tonnes)
1 Brazil	15,319,000
2 USA	7,751,000
3 China	3,272,000
4 Spain	2,225,000
5 Italy	1,968,000
6 Mexico	1,942,000
7 Egypt	1,400,000
8 India	1,370,000
9 Pakistan	1,100,000
10 Morocco	913,000
World total	*46,738,000*

In the past decade, orange production has progressively increased from a world total of less than 40,000,000 tonnes. China's, in particular, has rocketed up, more than quadrupling from under 800,000 tonnes to its present third position in the world league table.

THE TOP 10 POTATO-GROWING COUNTRIES

Country	Annual production (tonnes)
1 USSR	62,700,000
2 Poland	34,707,000
3 China	29,550,000
4 USA	15,875,000
5 India	14,138,000
6 East Germany	11,473,000
7 Romania	8,000,000
8 West Germany	7,353,000
9 UK	6,812,000
10 Netherlands	6,742,000
World total	*269,702,000*

It should be noted that dividing a country's population by the weight of potatoes grown will not reveal who eats the most, since a great deal of the world's potato harvest is used in the manufacture of alcohol and other products.

THE TOP 10 TEA-GROWING COUNTRIES

Country	Annual production (tonnes)
1 India	690,000
2 China	566,000
3 Sri Lanka	225,000
4 Kenya	164,000
5 USSR	160,000
6 Indonesia	144,000
7 Turkey	140,000
8 Japan	96,000
9 Iran	46,000
10 Bangladesh	41,000
World total	*2,499,000*

The top three producers are responsible for nearly 60 per cent and the Top 10 for over 90 per cent of the total world tea production.

Harvest-time in Darjeeling, north-east India. The high-quality tea from the region is a major export crop.

Animals & Birds

This list is based on research conducted by Edward O. Wilson, Professor of Zoology at Harvard University, who defined intelligence as speed and extent of learning performance over a wide range of tasks, also taking account of the ratio of the animal's brain size to its body bulk. It may come as a surprise that the dog does not make the Top 10, and that if Man is excluded, No. 10 becomes the pig.

THE 10 MOST INTELLIGENT MAMMALS

1	Man
2	Chimpanzee
3	Gorilla
4	Orang-utan
5	Baboon
6	Gibbon
7	Monkey
8	Smaller toothed whale
9	Dolphin
10	Elephant

Arguably the two most intelligent animals on Earth: Man and chimpanzee – from *Bedtime for Bonzo* (1951), starring Ronald Reagan and Diana Lynn.

TOP CATS

THE TOP 10 CAT-OWNING REGIONS OF THE UK

Region*	Homes owning cats
1 London	919,000
2 Midlands	740,000
3 Southern	505,000
4 Lancashire	443,000
5 Wales and the West	433,000
6 East of England	416,000
7 Yorkshire	364,000
8 South West	201,000
9 Southern Scotland	187,000
10 North East	141,000

*Based on research undertaken in the UK's television regions on behalf of catfood manufacturers, to help plan their advertising campaigns.

TOP LEFT Whiskas, the UK's bestselling catfood.

THE 10 MOST POPULAR CATS' NAMES IN GREAT BRITAIN

1	Sooty
2	Tiger
3	Smokey/Smoky
4	Tigger
5	Whiskey/Whisky
6	Kitty
7	Lucky
8	Susie
9	Fluffy
10	Snowy

A Gallup Survey commissioned by Kattomeat asked 4,000 owners about their pets and revealed this list, with Suky, Thomas and Tabby in equal 11th place.

THE TOP 10 BRANDS OF CATFOOD IN THE UK

1	Whiskas
2	Kattomeat
3	Kit-e-Kat
4	Felix
5	Choosy
6	Katkins Chunks
7	Sheba
8	Savour
9	Go-Cat Gourmet
10	Katkins Mariner

Specific sales figures for the Top 10 brands are a trade secret, but it is estimated that in 1988 cat-owners spent a total of £400,000,000 on 496,000 tonnes of canned catfood. Non-canned catfood accounted for a further 28,500 tonnes at a retail value of £43,000,000, while cat biscuits and 'treats' added 760 tonnes worth £3,500,000.

RIGHT Seal, red and blue point Siamese cats, in second place but far below Persians in popularity.

THE 10 MOST POPULAR CATS' NAMES IN THE USA

Female		Male
Samantha	1	Tiger/Tigger
Misty	2	Smokey
Patches	3	Pepper
Cali/Calico	4	Max/Maxwell
Muffin	5	Simon
Angel/Angela	6	Snoopy
Ginger	7	Morris
Tiger/Tigger	8	Mickey
Princess	9	Rusty/Rusti
Punkin/Pumpkin	10	Boots/Bootsie

THE 10 MOST POPULAR PEDIGREE CAT BREEDS IN THE USA

Breed	Total registered
1 Persian	56,847
2 Siamese	3,743
3 Abyssinian	2,669
4 Maine Coon Cat	2,449
5 Burmese	1,206
6 Oriental Shorthair	1,179
7 Exotic Shorthair	1,124
8 American Shorthair	1,104
9 Scottish Fold	983
10 Birman	918

Cat Quiz

What are the names of the following fictitious cats?

1 Alice's cat in *Alice in Wonderland?*
2 The comic-strip cat named after the grandfather of its creator, Jim Davis?
3 The star in 1927 of one of the first cartoon talkies?
4 Tom Kitten's mother in Beatrix Potter's *The Tale of Tom Kitten?*
5 The Marmalade Cat in Kathleen Hale's books?
6 The cat created by Robert Crumb, who in 1972 appeared in the first ever X-rated cartoon?
7 Meg the witch's cat in Jan Pienkowski's stories?
8 The cartoon cat created in 1945 by 'Friz' Freleng, whose would-be victim is Tweety Pie?
9 The cat that, with Ripley (Sigourney Weaver), is a survivor in the film *Alien?*
10 Holly Golightly's cat in the film of Truman Capote's *Breakfast at Tiffany's?*

The Cat Fanciers' Association of the USA is the world's largest pedigree cat registry. In 1989 it registered 79,145 cats of 35 different breeds, of which Traditional, Pointed Pattern and Colorpoint Carrier Persians were by far the most popular breed, with Oriental Longhair the rarest (just 14 registrations). Of the total, females outnumbered males (46,487 compared with 32,558).

THE 10 MOST POPULAR TYPES OF PET IN GREAT BRITAIN

1 Dog

2 Cat

3 Goldfish

4 Budgerigar

5 Rabbit

6 Tropical fish

7 Hamster

8 Guinea pig

9 Canary

10 Horse/pony/donkey

German shepherds (Alsatians), the most popular pedigree dogs in Great Britain.

THE 10 MOST POPULAR BREEDS OF DOGS IN GREAT BRITAIN

Breed	No. registered by Kennel Club
1 German Shepherd (Alsatian)	14,650
2 Labrador Retriever	13,674
3 Golden Retriever	10,278
4 Yorkshire Terrier	9,368
5 Cavalier King Charles Spaniel	8,658
6 Rottweiler	7,958
7 Cocker Spaniel	6,278
8 Staffordshire Bull Terrier	5,940
9 English Springer Spaniel	5,703
10 West Highland White Terrier	5,385

This list represents only those dogs that were registered by the Kennel Club in 1988. During that year, the order of the first seven remained the same as in 1987, but the Dobermann dropped from 8th to 11th position, the Staffordshire Bull Terrier and English Springer Spaniel both moved up one place and the West Highland White Terrier entered the Top 10. The total number of dogs registered fell from 181,436 to 166,550, with West Highlands and Shih Tzus the only breeds in the Kennel Club's Top 20 showing increased registrations.

An alternative Top 10 is that produced by the Gallup National Dog Survey:

1 Labrador Retriever

2 German Shepherd (Alsatian)

3 Jack Russell

4 Border Collie

5 Golden Retriever

6 Yorkshire Terrier

7 English Springer Spaniel

8 Cocker Spaniel

9 Poodle

10 Cavalier King Charles Spaniel

THE 10 MOST POPULAR DOGS' NAMES IN THE USA

1	Lady
2	King
3	Duke
4	Peppy
5	Prince
6	Pepper
7	Snoopy
8	Princess
9	Heidi
10 =	Sam
10 =	Coco

A recent study of names appearing on dog licences in the USA produced a list that has only 'Prince' and 'Sam' in common with the British Top 10. The same American list also exposed a number of bizarre dogs' names, including Beowulf, Bikini, Fag, Rembrandt and Twit.

THE 10 MOST POPULAR BREEDS OF DOGS IN THE USA

Breed	No. registered by American Kennel Club
1 Cocker Spaniel	108,720
2 Labrador Retriever	86,446
3 Poodle	82,600
4 Golden Retriever	62,950
5 German Shepherd (Alsatian)	57,139
6 Chow Chow	50,781
7 Rottweiler	42,748
8 Beagle	41,983
9 Dachshund	41,921
10 Miniature Schnauzer	41,558

THE 10 MOST POPULAR DOGS' NAMES IN GREAT BRITAIN

Female		Male
Penny	1	Sam
Gemma	2	Patch
Sally	3	Ben
Bella	4	Max
Bess	5	Jamie
Sasha	6	Charlie
Bea	7	Barney
Kim	8	Roly
Holly	9	Prince
Meg	10	Toby

In the past decade, there has been a definite move away from traditional dogs' names. Ten years ago, the Top 10 list included such evergreen (and specifically canine) names as Shep, Brandy, Whisky, Patch, Butch, Rex, Lassie and, of course, Rover, although among names given to bitches there was a tendency to use names that might be given to girls: Rosie, Mandy and Tessa, for example. Nowadays, virtually any of the names could equally be those of people.

THE 10 BESTSELLING BRANDS OF CANNED DOGFOOD IN THE UK

1	Pedigree Chum
2	Pal
3 =	Chappie
3 =	Prime
5	Bounce
6	Chunky
7	Bonus
8	Choice
9	Mr Dog
10	Big Value

The total UK dogfood market – over 700,000 tonnes of it – is worth around £500,000,000 a year. One can in three that is sold is Pedigree Chum. Like Pal, Chappie, Bounce and Mr Dog it is manufactured by the Mars group, which accounts for some 55 per cent of the total petfood market and is dominant in the canned dogfood sector. In dry dogfood, Spillers' Winalot is the bestseller, with nearly 50 per cent of the market.

TOP A cocker spaniel, in seventh place in Great Britain but the top dog in the USA.

RIGHT Pedigree Chum, the bestselling dogfood in the UK.

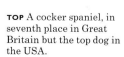

Australia's sheep population is not only the world's largest –
it outnumbers the human population 10 to one.

THE WORLD'S TOP 10 EGG-PRODUCING COUNTRIES

Country	Annual hen egg production
1 China	111,417,000,000
2 USSR	77,600,000,000
3 USA	67,427,000,000
4 Japan	40,150,000,000
5 Brazil	21,133,000,000
6 India	16,500,000,000
7 Mexico	15,467,000,000
8 France	15,200,000,000
9 UK	13,167,000,000
10 Spain	12,625,000,000

World annual total hen egg production is
estimated to be in excess of 580,000,000,000.

THE TOP 10 CATTLE COUNTRIES

Country	Cattle
1 India	193,000,000
2 Brazil	134,133,000
3 USSR	120,593,000
4 USA	98,994,000
5 China	73,963,000
6 Argentina	50,782,000
7 Mexico	31,200,000
8 Ethiopia	31,000,000
9 Colombia	24,307,000
10 Bangladesh	22,789,000
World total	*1,263,584,000*

THE TOP 10 SHEEP COUNTRIES

Country	Sheep
1 Australia	164,000,000
2 USSR	140,783,000
3 China	102,655,000
4 New Zealand	64,970,000
5 India	51,684,000
6 Turkey	40,000,000
7 Iran	34,500,000
8 South Africa	29,800,000
9 Argentina	29,202,000
10 UK	27,820,000
World total	*1,172,828,000*

THE TOP 10 CHICKEN COUNTRIES

	Country	Chickens
1	China	1,849,000,000
2	USA	1,540,000,000
3	USSR	1,129,000,000
4	Brazil	550,000,000
5	Indonesia	410,000,000
6	Japan	334,000,000
7	India	260,000,000
8	Mexico	224,000,000
9	Nigeria	190,000,000
10	France	189,000,000
	World total	*10,215,000,000*

THE TOP 10 HORSE COUNTRIES

	Country	Horses
1	USA	10,720,000
2	China	10,691,000
3	Mexico	6,160,000
4	USSR	5,885,000
5	Brazil	5,850,000
6	Argentina	3,100,000
7	Mongolia	2,047,000
8	Colombia	1,950,000
9	Ethiopia	1,610,000
10	Poland	1,051,000
	World total	*65,292,000*

The estimated world total chicken population is about twice the human population. In the UK chickens – 127,000,000 of them – outnumber people more than twice over.

TOP Home on the range: the USA ranks first in the world's top horse-owning countries.

LEFT Holy cows in India: the country's cattle population approaches 200,000,000.

RIGHT Chicken takeaways in a market near Dali, China.

THE WORLD'S TOP 10 MILK PRODUCERS

Country	Annual production	
	litres	pints
1 USSR	105,950,000,000	186,445,830,300
2 USA	66,010,000,000	116,161,295,500
3 France	27,510,000,000	48,410,805,030
4 West Germany	23,978,000,000	42,195,357,430
5 India	22,500,000,000	39,594,442,500
6 Poland	15,420,000,000	27,135,391,260
7 UK	14,981,000,000	26,362,859,690
8 Brazil	13,200,000,000	23,228,739,600
9 Netherlands	11,315,000,000	19,911,605,190
10 Italy	10,869,000,000	19,126,755,350

THE TOP 10 PIG COUNTRIES

Country	Pigs
1 China	334,862,000
2 USSR	77,403,000
3 USA	42,845,000
4 Brazil	32,700,000
5 West Germany	23,670,000
6 Poland	19,605,000
7 Spain	16,941,000
8 Mexico	16,500,000
9 Romania	15,224,000
10 Netherlands	14,226,000
World total	*823,403,000*

THE TOP 10 FISHING COUNTRIES

Country	Annual catch (tonnes)
1 Japan	11,966,800,000
2 USSR	11,260,000,000
3 China	8,000,100,000
4 Chile	5,771,600,000
5 Peru	5,609,600,000
6 USA	4,943,200,000
7 South Korea	3,102,500,000
8 India	2,925,300,000
9 Indonesia	2,521,200,000
10 Thailand	2,119,000,000

The world total of fish caught in 1986 was 91,456,800 tonnes. The UK's contribution (No. 22 in the world list) was 847,800 tonnes.

THE 10 TYPES OF ANIMAL USED MOST IN EXPERIMENTS IN GREAT BRITAIN

1 Mice

2 Rats

3 Birds

4 Other rodents (hamsters, guinea pigs, gerbils, etc)

5 Fish

6 Rabbits

7 Ungulates (horses, pigs, cattle, sheep, etc)

8 Carnivores (dogs, cats, etc)

9 Reptiles and amphibians

10 Primates (monkeys, apes, etc)

A total of nearly 4,000,000 scientific procedures are performed on animals every year – more than half of them on specially-bred mice. Animals have long been used in medical research experiments, and under new EC legislation all new drugs *must* be tested on animals before being administered to humans. Although animal experimentation in Great Britain is subject to strict regulations under the 1986 Animals (Scientific Procedures) Act, it continues to arouse considerable controversy among animal-lovers and animal liberation organizations.

'This little piggy went to market' – and thereby became a reluctant part of China's vast pork industry.

The herbivorous diplodocus – long, stupid and extinct.

THE 10 LARGEST DINOSAURS

1 Seismosaurus
Length: 30–36 m/98–118 ft
Estimated weight: 80 tonnes

A single skeleton was found in 1985 near Albuquerque and is currently being studied by the New Mexico Museum of Natural History, which may establish its position as the largest dinosaur yet discovered. Its name means 'earthshaker'.

2 Ultrasaurus
Length: 30.5 m/100 ft
Height: 16–17 m/52–56 ft
Estimated weight: 50 tonnes

Ultrasaurus was discovered in Colorado in 1979 but has not yet been fully studied. Some authorities have claimed its weight as 100–140 tonnes.

3 Antarctosaurus
Length: 30 m/98 ft
Estimated weight: 80 tonnes

The thigh bone alone measures 2.3 m/7.5 ft.

4 Supersaurus
Length: 24–30 m/79–98 ft
Height: 15 m/49 ft
Estimated weight: 75–100 tonnes

The remains of supersaurus were found in Colorado in 1971.

5 Diplodocus
Length: 27 m/89 ft
Estimated weight: 10.6 tonnes

As he was long and thin, diplodocus was a relative lightweight in the dinosaur world. He was also probably one of the most stupid dinosaurs, having the smallest brain in relation to its body size. One skeleton was named *Diplodocus carnegii*, in honour of Scottish-American millionaire Andrew Carnegie, who financed the excavations that discovered it.

6 Brachiosaurus
Length: 23–27 m/75–89 ft
Height: 12 m/39 ft
Estimated weight: 78 tonnes

Some palaeontologists have put brachiosaurus's weight as high as 190 tonnes.

7 Barosaurus
Length: 22–27 m/72–89 ft

Barosaurus has been found in both North America and Africa, thus proving the existence of a land link in Jurassic times (205–140 million years ago).

8 Pelorosaurus
Length: 24 m/79 ft

The first pelorosaurus fragments were found in Sussex in 1850. Its name means 'monstrous reptile'.

9 Mamenchisaurus
Length: 22 m/72 ft

An almost complete skeleton discovered in 1972 showed it had the longest neck of any known animal, comprising half its total body length. It is named after the place in China where it was found.

10 Apatosaurus
Length: 20–21 m/66–69 ft
Estimated weight: 30 tonnes

Apatosaurus is better known as brontosaurus, or 'thunder reptile'. The bones of the first one ever found, in Colorado in 1879, caused great confusion for many years because its discoverer attached a head from a different species to the rest of the skeleton.

The first dinosaur bones were found in Sussex in 1822. The name 'dinosaur' was given to them by the naturalist Sir Richard Owen, and first appeared in print in 1841. It comes from two Greek words, *deinos*, fearful, and *sauros*, lizard.

Lengths have often been estimated from only a few surviving fossilized bones, and there is much dispute even among experts about the true lengths and weights of most dinosaurs. Everyone's favourite dinosaur, *Tyrannosaurus rex*, does not appear in the Top 10 because although it was the fiercest flesh-eating dinosaur, it was not as large as many of the herbivorous ones. However, measuring a probable 13.4 m/44 ft and weighing 8.5 tonnes certainly ranks it as the largest flesh-eating animal yet discovered. Bones of a dinosaur called epanterias were found in Colorado in 1877 and 1934, but incorrectly identified until compared with recent finds, which now suggest that this creature was almost as large and ferocious.

To compare these sizes with living animals, note that the largest recorded crocodile measured 6.2 m/20.3 ft and the largest elephant 10.7 m/35 ft from trunk to tail and weighed about 12 tonnes. The largest living creature ever measured is the blue whale at 33.6 m/110 ft – slightly smaller than the size claimed for seismosaurus.

THE 10 DEADLIEST SNAKES

	Species	Native region
1 =	**Taipan** Mortality is nearly 100% unless antivenin is administered promptly.	Australia and New Guinea
1 =	**Black mamba** Mortality nearly 100% without antivenin.	Southern and Central Africa
3	**Tiger snake** Very high mortality without antivenin.	Australia
4	**Common Krait** Up to 50% mortality even with antivenin.	South Asia
5	**Death adder** Over 50% mortality without antivenin.	Australia
6	**Saw-scaled or carpet viper** High mortality and, as it is relatively common, perhaps the cause of more deaths than any other snake.	Africa and Asia
7	**Yellow or Cape cobra** The most dangerous type of cobra; high mortality.	Southern Africa
8 =	**Boomslang** High mortality.	Africa
8 =	**Bushmaster** High mortality.	Central and South America
8 =	**Coral snake** High mortality.	North and South America

Measuring the strength of the venom of snakes is scientifically possible, but this does not indicate how dangerous they may be: the Australian smooth-scaled snake, for example, is believed to be the most venomous land snake, but no human victims have ever been recorded. The Top 10 takes account of the degree of threat posed by those snakes that have a record of causing fatalities – although it can only be approximate, since circumstances such as the amount of venom injected, speed of administering antivenin (an antitoxin that counteracts the venom), age and health of victim and so on, can vary enormously.

Deadliest of the deadly: without immediate treatment, the bite of the taipan snake is invariably fatal.

Although only the world's second fastest, the frigate bird is capable of a very impressive turn of speed.

THE 10 FASTEST BIRDS IN THE WORLD

	Bird	Maximum recorded speed	
		kph	mph
1	Spine-tailed swift	171	106
2	Frigate bird	153	95
3	Spur-winged goose	142	88
4	Red-breasted merganser	129	80
5	White-rumped swift	124	77
6	Canvasback duck	116	72
7	Eider duck	113	70
8	Teal	109	68
9 =	Mallard	105	65
9 =	Pintail	105	65

This does not include the speeds obtained by certain birds of prey in gravity-aided dives (such as the 362 kph/225 mph claimed for a peregrine falcon), or other exceptional circumstances, such as wind-assisted flight.

THE 10 FASTEST FISH IN THE WORLD

	Fish	Maximum recorded speed	
		kph	mph
1	Sailfish	110	68
2	Marlin	80	50
3	Wahoo	78	48
4	Tunny	74	46
5	Bluefish tuna	70	44
6	Great blue shark	69	43
7 =	Bonefish	64	40
7 =	Swordfish	64	40
9 =	Four-winged flying fish	56	35
9 =	Tarpon	56	35

Although a very fast fish, the striped marlin is relegated to second place by the even speedier sailfish.

THE 10 FASTEST MAMMALS IN THE WORLD

	Mammal	Maximum recorded speed	
		kph	mph
1	Cheetah	105	65
2	Pronghorn antelope	89	55
3 =	Mongolian gazelle	80	50
3 =	Springbok	80	50
5 =	Grant's gazelle	76	47
5 =	Thomson's gazelle	76	47
7	Brown hare	72	45
8	Horse	69	43
9 =	Greyhound	68	42
9 =	Red deer	68	42

Although some authorities have alleged higher speeds, this list is based on data from reliable sources using accurate methods of measurement. In addition to these speeds, estimated over distances of up to $0.4\,km/\frac{1}{4}$ mile, charging lions can achieve $80\,kph/50\,mph$ over very short distances, while various members of the antelope family, wildebeests, elks, dogs, coyotes, foxes, hyenas, zebras and Mongolian wild asses, have all been credited with unsustained spurts of $64\,kph/40\,mph$ or more.

London Zoo in Regent's Park, founded in1828 and still one of the UK's most-visited wildlife attractions.

THE 10 MOST-VISITED WILDLIFE ATTRACTIONS IN THE UK

	Attraction	Visitors per annum
1	London (Regent's Park) Zoo	1,221,000
2	Windsor Safari Park	1,049,722
3	Chester Zoo	904,251
4	Tropical World, Leeds	731,069
5	Edinburgh Zoo	555,000
6	Knowlsey Safari Park, Prescot	500,982
7	Bristol Zoo	450,908
8	Twycross Zoo, Atherstone	436,004
9	Blackpool Zoo	382,000
10	Whipsnade Park Zoo, Bedfordshire	380,000

Acinonyx jubatus, the cheetah – at full pelt it is the fastest of all mammals and an unbeatable adversary.

Human Body & Health

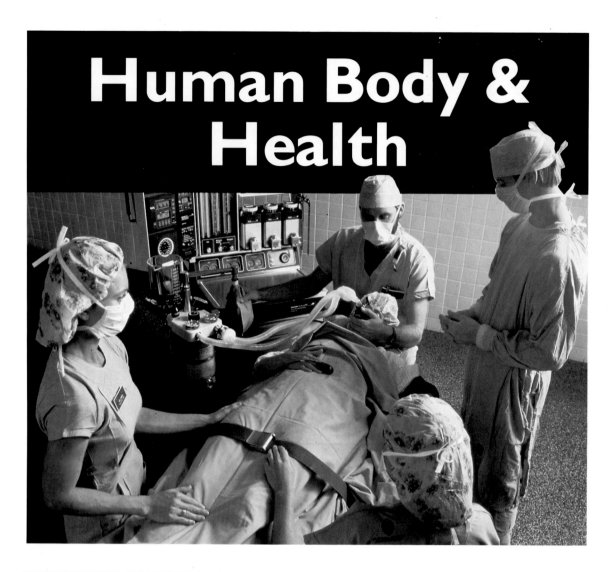

THE 10 COMMONEST REASONS FOR VISITS TO THE DOCTOR

	Condition	Consulting rate per 2,500 patients
1	Upper respiratory tract infections	600
2	Non-specific 'symptoms'	375
3	Skin disorders	350
4=	Psycho-emotional problems	250
4=	High blood pressure	250
4=	Minor accidents	250
7	Gastro-intestinal conditions	200
8	Rheumatic aches and pains	150
9=	Chronic rheumatism	100
9=	Acute throat infections	100
9=	Acute bronchitis	100
9=	Lacerations	100
9=	Eczema/dermatitis	100

The Royal College of General Practitioners considers that these statistics represent the average number of consultations per condition that a doctor with a typical practice of 2,500 patients might expect to deal with in a year. These relatively common complaints contrast with others that are extremely rare, so that on average a doctor might expect to see a person with a dislocated hip only once every 20 years, or a patient with phenylketonuria (a metabolic disorder) just once in 200 years.

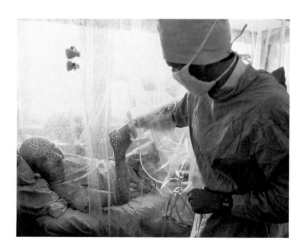

THE 10 COUNTRIES WITH THE HIGHEST DOCTOR–PATIENT RATIO

	Country	Doctors	Doctors per 1,000 population
1	Italy	245,116	42.4
2	USSR	1,170,000*	42.1
3	Czechoslovakia	55,871*	35.5
4	France	173,116	32.2
5	Spain	121,362	31.3
6	Hungary	34,758*	30.5
7	Belgium	29,776	30.2
8	Israel	11,895	29.0
9	Greece	28,212	28.5
10	Bulgaria	24,718	27.6
	USA	501,200	21.4
	UK	92,172	16.4

THE 10 COUNTRIES WITH THE MOST DENTISTS

	Country	Patients per dentist	Dentists
1	USA	1,769	137,817
2	USSR	2,696	105,000*
3	Japan	1,730	70,572
4	Brazil	2,176	65,000*
5	France	1,351	41,190
6	West Germany	1,812	33,751
7	Italy	1,864	30,767
8	UK	2,230	25,500
9	Argentina	1,575	20,000*
10	Philippines	3,019	19,000*

*Estimated figures.

The three countries marked * may not be as well off for doctors as the figures imply, since they include their dentists in the statistics (other countries list them separately). The worst ratios occur in Third World countries such as Ethiopia, where there are just 534 doctors – a ratio of 0.1 per 1,000 people.

BOTTOM LEFT One of the USSR's million-plus doctors.

BELOW Tooth extraction, eighteenth-century style.

HUMAN BODY & HEALTH

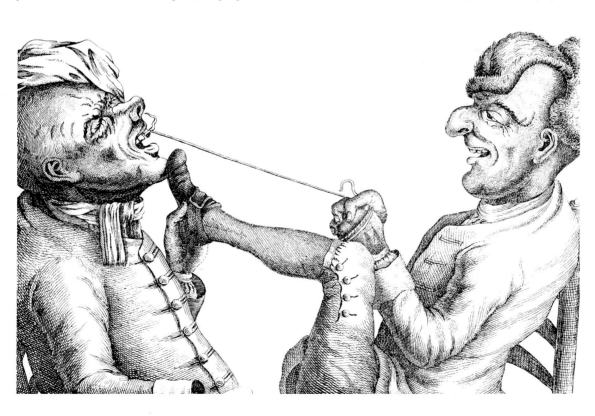

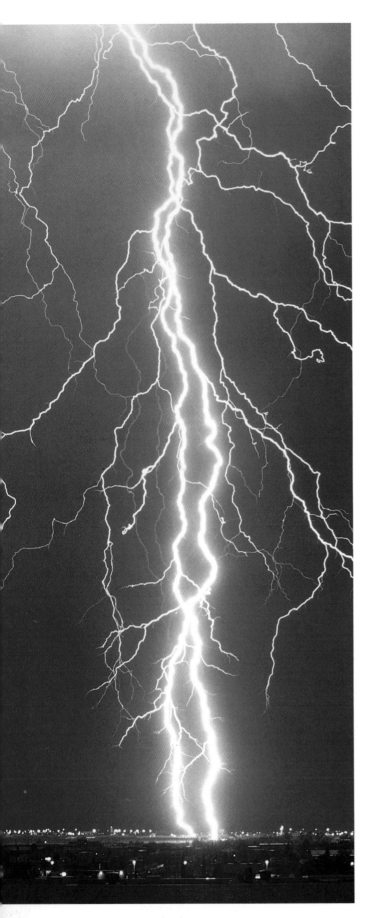

The fear of thunderstorms and related phenomena ranks eighth on a list of common and rare phobias that continues far beyond the Top 10.

THE 10 COMMONEST PHOBIAS

Object of phobia	Medical term
1 Spiders	Arachnephobia or arachnophobia
2 People and social situations	Anthropophobia or sociophobia
3 Flying	Aerophobia or aviatophobia
4 Open spaces	Agoraphobia, cenophobia or kenophobia
5 Confined spaces	Claustrophobia, cleisiophobia, cleithrophobia or clithrophobia
6 Heights	Acrophobia, altophobia, hypsophobia or hypsiphobia
7 Cancer	Carcinomaphobia, carcinophobia, carcinomatophobia, cancerphobia or cancerophobia
8 Thunderstorms	Brontophobia or keraunophobia; related phobias are those associated with lightning (astraphobia), cyclones (anemophobia) and hurricanes and tornadoes (lilapsophobia)
9 Death	Necrophobia or thanatophobia
10 Heart disease	Cardiophobia

A phobia is a morbid fear that is out of all proportion to the object of the fear. Many people would admit to being uncomfortable about these principal phobias, as well as others, such as snakes (ophiophobia), injections (trypanophobia) or ghosts (phasmophobia), but most do not become obsessive about them and allow such fears to rule their lives. True phobias often arise from some incident in childhood when a person has been afraid of some object and has developed an irrational fear that persists into adulthood. Nowadays, as well as the valuable work done by the Phobics Society and other organizations, phobias can be cured by taking special desensitization courses, for example, to conquer one's fear of flying.

There are many phobias that are much less common than those appearing in the Top 10. Even if only one person has ever been observed with a specific phobia, psychologists have often given it a name – some more bizarre than others:

Beards	Pogonophobia
Chickens	Alektorophobia
Chins	Geniophobia
Everything	Pantophobia, panophobia, panphobia or pamphobia
Opening one's eyes	Optophobia

Eggshells	No medical term
Gravity	Barophobia
Hair	Chaetophobia
Mirrors	Eisoptrophobia
Money	Chrometophobia
Satellites plunging to Earth	Keraunothnetophobia
Slime	Blennophobia or myxophobia
String	Linonophobia
Teeth	Odontophobia
The number thirteen	Terdekaphobia, tridecaphobia, triakaidekaphobia or triskaidekaphobia

THE 10 COMMONEST FOOD ALLERGENS*

1 Wheat
2 Milk
3 Yeast
4 Eggs
5 Corn
6 Chocolate
7 Coffee
8 Cheese
9 Beef
10 Oranges

Substances that cause allergies.

THE 10 COMMONEST ENVIRONMENTAL ALLERGENS*

1 House dust mites
2 House dust
3 Mould
4 Grass pollen
5 Domestic gas
6 Formaldehyde
7 Petrol fumes
8 Animal fur and danders (small particles of hair or feathers)
9 Perfume
10 Aerosols

HUMAN BODY & HEALTH

The words 'allergy' and 'allergen' date back only about 80 years. The definition of allergy provided by Dr Keith Mumby, founder of the Food and Environmental Allergy Clinic and author of *The Allergy Handbook*, is: 'an unpleasant reaction to foreign matter, specific to that substance, which is altered from the normal response and peculiar to the individual concerned'. The allergens that cause these reactions are commonly foods but also environmental agents, pollen as a cause of hay-fever being perhaps one of the best known. Reactions to them can result in a huge variety of symptoms ranging from severe mental or physical disability to more minor irritations – mild headache in the presence of fresh paint, for example. 'Elimination dieting' to identify and dispense with food allergens and the identification and avoidance of environmental allergens can result in complete cures from a wide variety of allergies.

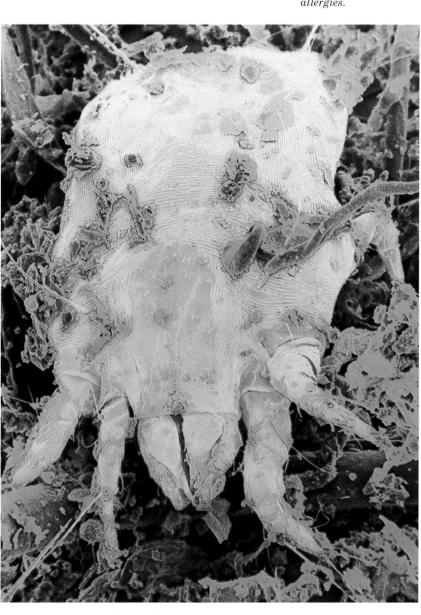

Collected from a sample in a domestic vacuum cleaner bag and here magnified to alarming size, *Glycyphagus sp.*, the dust mite, is the leading environmental allergen.

THE 10 HEAVIEST-SMOKING NATIONS IN THE WORLD

	Country	Cigarettes per adult per annum
1	Cyprus	4,050
2	Cuba	3,920
3	Greece	3,640
4	Poland	3,300
5 =	USA	3,270
5 =	Japan	3,270
7	Hungary	3,260
8	Canada	3,180
9	Iceland	3,100
10	Yugoslavia	3,000
	UK	*2,120*

In the Top 10 the *average* consumption of manufactured cigarettes by adults aged 15 and over ranges from the equivalent of 11 to 8 cigarettes per day. As each country's population also includes many non-smokers, light and occasional smokers, there must be large numbers of extremely heavy smokers to bring the average up to these levels. In Western countries, there has been an increasing trend towards non-smoking: in the UK, for example, smokers are now outnumbered by non-smokers, and since the World Health Organization last compiled these statistics, the average has probably declined in most countries – although it may even have increased in certain Third World territories. The lowest consumption was recorded in Burkina Faso, Guinea and Papua New Guinea, each averaging 30 cigarettes per person per annum.

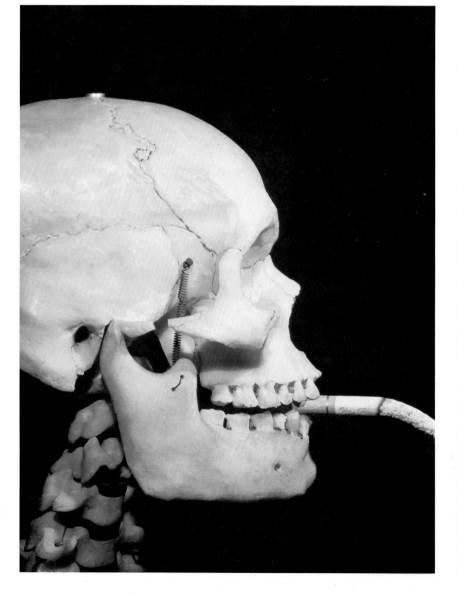

Cigarette end? Smokers are now outnumbered by non-smokers in the UK.

THE 10 MOST ABUSED DRUGS

1	Prescribed drugs
2	Cannabis
3	Heroin/opium
4	A mixture of drugs
5	Cocaine
6	Ecstasy
7	Amphetamines
8	Solvents
9	Hallucinogenics (LSD, etc)
10	Others

These are the 10 types of drug for which people most seek help from Release, Britain's largest drug-help agency. However, it could be argued that the most abused drugs are, in fact, alcohol and tobacco.

THE 10 COMMONEST CAUSES OF DEATH IN THE UK

Cause	England & Wales	Scotland	Northern Ireland	Total
1 Diseases of circulatory system	267,927	30,511	7,774	306,212
2 Cancer	144,260	14,889	3,409	162,558
3 Diseases of respiratory system	60,483	6,724	2,568	69,775
4 Accidents and violence	17,936	2,964	834	21,734
5 Diseases of digestive system	17,954	1,925	358	20,237
6 Mental disorders	13,234	1,005	35	14,274
7 Diseases of nervous system	11,220	864	152	12,236
8 Endocrine, nutritional and metabolic diseases and immunity disorders	10,106	691	73	10,870
9 Diseases of the genito-urinary sytem	7,589	810	250	8,649
10 Diseases of musculo-skeletal system	5,406	318	50	5,774
*Total deaths from all causes**	567,987	61,957	15,813	645,757

Heart disease is the principal cause of death in the UK.

Including some that do not appear in the Top 10.

The 10 principal causes of death remain the same and in the same order from year to year, with only slight fluctuations in total numbers. Total UK deaths in 1988 were 4,863 (0.76 per cent) higher than in the previous year. In category 1, heart attacks are the principal killer (a UK total of 175,794), and in category 2, lung cancer killed the most – 40,223 in 1988. In category 4, motor vehicle accidents accounted for most deaths (5,353).

THE TOP 10 CAUSES OF STRESS-RELATED ILLNESS

	Event	Value
1	Death of spouse	100
2	Divorce	73
3	Marital separation	65
4=	Death of close family member	63
4=	Detention in prison or other institution	63
6	Major personal injury or illness	53
7	Marriage	50
8	Losing one's job	47
9=	Marital reconciliation	45
9=	Retirement	45

Psychiatrists Dr Thomas Holmes and Dr Richard Rahe devised what they called the 'Social Readjustment Rating Scale' to place a value on the likelihood of illness occurring as a result of stress caused by various 'life events'. Even agreeable occasions such as weddings, promotion at work and Christmas have been evaluated for their stress value on this scale. The cumulative effect of several incidents increases the risk factor – if an individual's points total over 300 in a given year, he is reckoned to have a 79 per cent chance of major illness.

THE 10 COMMONEST HOSPITAL CASUALTY COMPLAINTS

1 Cuts

2 Bruises

3 Dog bites

4 Sprained ankles

5 Eye injuries

6 Head injuries

7 Minor burns

8 Fractures

9 Upper respiratory tract infections

10 Gastroenteritis

The proportion of casualties varies considerably according to such factors as the time of the year – people suffer from more chest infections in the winter, and trip and injure themselves more frequently during icy weather, for example. The nature of the local community is also significant: in certain areas patients are more likely to consult their general practitioners for minor complaints, whereas in others they turn to the hospital casualty department first for treatment of anything from toothache to a nosebleed.

LEFT Capsules of the illegal drug Ecstasy. Laboratory-manufactured 'designer drugs' are among the most abused.

THE 10 LARGEST HUMAN ORGANS

Organ		Average weight gm	oz
1 Liver		1,560	55.0
2 Brain	male	1,408	49.7
	female	1,263	44.6
3 Lungs	right	580	20.5
	left	510	18.0
	total	1,090	38.5
4 Heart	male	315	11.1
	female	265	9.3
5 Kidneys	left	150	5.3
	right	140	4.9
	total	290	10.2
6 Spleen		170	6.0
7 Pancreas		98	3.5
8 Thyroid		35	1.2
9 Prostate	male only	20	0.7
10 Adrenals	left	6	0.2
	right	6	0.2
	total	12	0.4

Based on average immediate post-mortem weights, as recorded by St Bartholemew's Hospital, London, and other sources during the past 10 years. Various cases of organs far in excess of the average have been recorded, including male brains over 2,000 gm/70.6 oz.

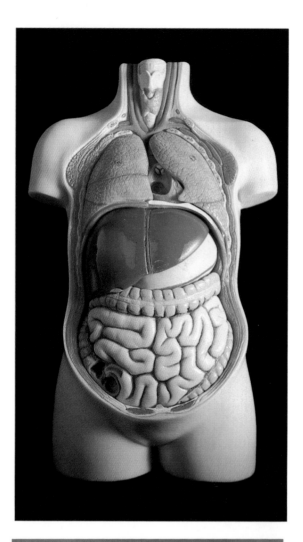

THE 10 MOST COMMONLY PERFORMED SURGICAL OPERATIONS

1 Appendectomy (removal of appendix)

2 Inguinal (groin) hernia repair

3 Tonsil and adenoid removal

4 Cholecystectomy (removal of gall bladder)

5 Hysterectomy (removal of womb)

6 Cataract removal (eye operation)

7 Prostatectomy (removal of prostate gland)

8 Hip replacement

9 Cystoscopy (bladder operation)

10 Myringotomy (eardrum operation)

BELOW The brain, the second largest organ in the human body.

TOP RIGHT A model of the torso showing the major organs.

THE 10 COUNTRIES WITH THE HIGHEST FEMALE LIFE EXPECTANCY

	Country	Life expectancy (years)
1	Japan	82.1
2	Switzerland	81.0
3	Sweden	80.2
4	France	80.0
5=	Canada	79.9
5=	Norway	79.9
7=	Netherlands	79.8
7=	Spain	79.8
9	Australia	79.6
10	Iceland	79.0
	USA	78.3
	UK	78.1

The lowest female life expectancy is that in Burkina Faso (formerly Upper Volta): 31 years.

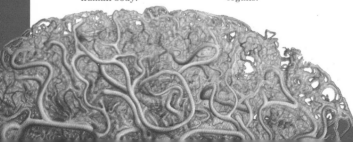

Human Body Quiz

1 What is the common name for the patella?
2 The name of which common illness comes from the Italian word meaning 'the influence of the stars'?
3 Where on the human body would you find arches, loops and whorls?
4 What medical invention is credited to Dr René Laënnec?
5 Why is Legionnaire's disease so called?
6 What would you have if you had a circumorbital haematoma?
7 Where are the bones known as the hammer, anvil and stirrup?
8 Does the bacterium salmonella gets its name from the man who discovered it, salmon infected with it or from the Spanish word for 'stomach ache'?
9 Why are Siamese twins so called?
10 What was involved in the ancient operation known as trepanning?

Japanese women enjoy the longest life expectancy in the world.

THE 10 COUNTRIES WITH THE HIGHEST MALE LIFE EXPECTANCY

	Country	Life expectancy (years)
1	Japan	75.9
2	Iceland	74.9
3	Greece	74.1
4=	Sweden	74.0
4=	Switzerland	74.0
6	Israel	73.4
7	Spain	73.2
8=	Canada	73.1
8=	Netherlands	73.1
10	Australia	73.0
	UK	72.4
	USA	71.5

The lowest male life expectancy is in Gabon: 25 years.

THE 10 LONGEST BONES IN THE HUMAN BODY

Bone	Average length cm	in
1 Femur (thighbone – upper leg)	50.50	19.88
2 Tibia (shinbone – inner lower leg)	43.03	16.94
3 Fibula (outer lower leg)	40.50	15.94
4 Humerus (upper arm)	36.46	14.35
5 Ulna (inner lower arm)	28.20	11.10
6 Radius (outer lower arm)	26.42	10.40
7 7th rib	24.00	9.45
8 8th rib	23.00	9.06
9 Innominate bone (hipbone – half pelvis)	18.50	7.28
10 Sternum (breastbone)	17.00	6.69

These are average dimensions of the bones of an adult male measured from their extremities (ribs are curved, and the pelvis measurement is taken diagonally). The same bones in the female skeleton are usually 6 to 13 per cent smaller, with the exception of the sternum which is virtually identical.

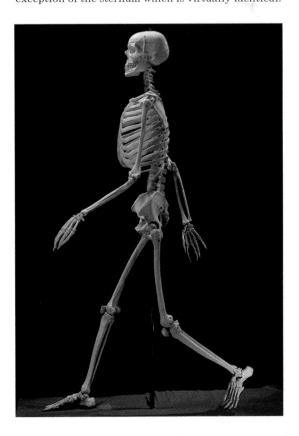

Vitamin E capsules: in Great Britain vitamins have recently fallen from first to second position in the Top 10 of non-prescription drugs.

THE 10 MOST POPULAR NON-PRESCRIPTION MEDICINES IN GREAT BRITAIN

Medicine	Sales (£)
1 Analgesics (painkillers such as aspirin)	129,000,000
2 Vitamins	80,000,000
3 Sore throat remedies	67,000,000
4 Cough remedies	53,000,000
5 Cold remedies	46,000,000
6 Indigestion remedies	36,000,000
7 Skin treatments (other than acne products)	29,000,000
8 Acne skin products	22,000,000
9 Laxatives	16,000,000
10 Stomach upset remedies	15,000,000

In 1989 we spent a total of £605,000,000 on non-prescription or 'over-the-counter' home remedies – more than £10 for every person in the country. The previous year, after a BBC television 'QED' programme suggested that vitamins contributed to increased intelligence among children, sales of vitamins generally went up by 12 per cent and those of children's vitamins soared by 25 per cent, making this the No. 1 item on the list. Sales declined again from their £144,000,000 record, and analgesics are once again the country's favourite home remedy.

HEALTH SPENDING: THE 10 LEADING COUNTRIES

Country	Average annual health spending per person (US$)
1 USA	2,051
2 Canada	1,483
3 Iceland	1,241
4 Sweden	1,233
5 Switzerland	1,225
6 Norway	1,149
7 France	1,105
8 West Germany	1,093
9 Luxembourg	1,050
10 Netherlands	1,041
UK	758

The USA not only spends the most per head on health care, but also the most as a percentage of gross domestic product (11.2 per cent, compared with the UK's 6.1 per cent). Among European countries, Turkey spends the least – just $148 per capita.

THE 10 MOST EFFECTIVE KEEP-FIT ACTIVITIES

1 Swimming

2 Cycling

3 Rowing

4 Gymnastics

5 Judo

6 Dancing

7 Football

8 Jogging

9 Walking (briskly!)

10 Squash

These are the sports and activities recommended by the Sports Council as the best means of acquiring all-round fitness, building stamina and strength and increasing suppleness.

RIGHT Cycling rates second after swimming in the Top 10 of most effective all-round fitness activities.

Human Activities & Achievements

THE TOP 10 NOBEL PRIZE WINNING COUNTRIES

	Country	Phy	Che	Phy/Med	Lit	Pce	Eco	Total
1	USA	53	35	65	9	17	15	194
2	UK	20	23	22	8	9	5	87
3	Germany	19	27	12	7	4	—	69
4	France	9	7	7	12	9	1	45
5	Sweden	4	4	7	7	5	2	29
6	Switzerland	2	4	5	2	3	—	16
7	USSR	7	1	2	3	1	1	15
8	Italy	3	1	3	5	1	—	13
9 =	Denmark	3	—	5	3	1	—	12
9 =	Netherlands	6	2	2	—	1	1	12

Key: Phy – Physics; Che – Chemistry; Phy/Med – Physiology or Medicine;
Lit – Literature; Pce – Peace; Eco – Economic Sciences. Germany includes the united
country before 1948 and West Germany since.

At his death in 1896, the Swedish scientist Alfred Nobel left his fortune of some £1,750,000, amassed through his invention of dynamite, to establish a trust fund. From this, annual prizes have been awarded since 1901 to those who have achieved the greatest common good in the fields of Physics, Chemistry, Physiology or Medicine, Literature, Peace and, since 1969, Economic Sciences. All the award ceremonies take place in Stockholm, Sweden, with the exception of the Peace Prize, which is awarded in Oslo, Norway. The list includes all winners up to 1989, when the prizes were each worth over £290,000. The 1990 prizes are worth over £400,000. Two other countries – Belgium and Austria – have each produced nine Nobel Prize laureates, and some 29 other countries between one and eight winners. However, it should be noted that the prizes are won by individuals, and not the countries from which they come, and that, in addition to these winners, various stateless institutions such as the Red Cross have won the Peace Prize a total of 16 times.

THE WORLD'S 10 LONGEST-REIGNING MONARCHS

	Monarch	Country	Reign	Age at accession	Reign years
1	Louis XIV	France	1643–1715	5	72
2	John II	Liechtenstein	1858–1929	18	71
3	Franz-Josef	Austria-Hungary	1848–1916	18	67
4	Victoria	Great Britain	1837–1901	18	63
5	Hirohito	Japan	1926–89	25	62
6	George III	Great Britain	1760–1820	22	59
7	Louis XV	France	1715–74	5	59
8	Pedro II	Brazil	1831–89	6	58
9	Wilhelmina	Netherlands	1890–1948	10	58
10	Henry III	England	1216–72	9	56

ABOVE Franz-Josef, Emperor of Austria, King of Hungary and third longest-ruling monarch of all time.

Some authorities have claimed a 73-year reign for Alfonso I of Portugal, but his father, Henry of Burgundy, who conquered Portugal, ruled as Count, and it was this title that Alfonso inherited on 30 April 1112, at the age of two. His mother, Theresa of Castile, ruled until he took power in 1128, but he did not assume the title of king until 25 July 1139, during the Battle of Ourique at which he vanquished the Moors. He thus ruled as king for 46 years until his death on 6 December 1185. Even more extravagant claims are sometimes made for long-reigning monarchs in the ancient world, such as the alleged 94 years of Phiops II, a 6th Dynasty Egyptian pharaoh, but since it is uncertain when he was either born or died, he has not been included.

RIGHT HRH The Prince of Wales, first in line to the British throne.

THE TOP 10 IN LINE TO THE BRITISH THRONE

1 HRH The Prince of Wales
(Prince Charles Philip Arthur George)
b. 14 November 1948
then his elder son:

2 HRH Prince William of Wales
(Prince William Arthur Philip Louis)
b. 21 June 1982
then his younger brother:

3 HRH Prince Henry of Wales
(Prince Henry Charles Albert David)
b. 15 September 1984
then his uncle:

4 HRH The Duke of York
(Prince Andrew Albert Christian Edward)
b. 19 February 1960
then his elder daughter:

5 HRH Princess Beatrice of York
(Princess Beatrice Elizabeth Mary)
b. 8 August 1988
then her younger sister:

6 HRH Princess Eugenie of York
(Princess Eugenie Victoria Helena)
b. 23 March 1990
then her uncle:

7 HRH Prince Edward
(Prince Edward Antony Richard Louis)
b. 10 March 1964
then his sister:

8 HRH The Princess Royal
(Princess Anne Elizabeth Alice Louise)
b. 15 August 1950
then her son:

9 Master Peter Mark Andrew Phillips
b. 15 November 1977
then his sister:

10 Miss Zara Anne Elizabeth Phillips
b. 15 May 1981

The birth in 1988 of Princess Beatrice altered the order of succession, ousting David Albert Charles Armstrong-Jones, Viscount Linley (b. 3 November 1961), from the No. 10 position, while the birth in 1990 of her sister, Princess Eugenie, evicted HRH Princess Margaret, Countess of Snowdon (Princess Margaret Rose, b. 21 August 1930) from the Top 10.

BRITAIN'S 10 SHORTEST-REIGNING MONARCHS

	Monarch	Reign	Duration
1	Jane	1553	14 days
2	Edward V	1483	75 days
3	Edward VIII	1936	325 days
4	Richard III	1483–85	2 years
5	James II	1685–88	3 years
6	Mary I	1553–58	5 years
7	Mary II	1689–94	5 years
8	Edward VI	1547–53	6 years
9	William IV	1830–37	7 years
10	Edward VII	1901–10	9 years

Royalty Quiz

1 Which of Henry VIII's wives survived him?
2 Who played King Arthur in the film *Monty Python and the Holy Grail*?
3 Which American film actor was seventh cousin twice removed to Princess Diana?
4 Which English king reputedly died of 'a surfeit of lampreys'?
5 What are the Queen Mother's middle names?
6 Who was the last British monarch to be buried abroad?
7 Before her marriage, which member of the Royal Family was known as Mrs Troubridge?
8 Which two English kings since King Harold met their deaths as a result of arrow wounds?
9 Where is it popularly believed that Queen Boadicea is buried?
10 Which English queen had 17 children, none of whom lived long enough to see her on the throne?

THE 10 LONGEST-REIGNING BRITISH MONARCHS

	Monarch	Reign	Age at access.	Age at death	Reign years
1	Victoria	1837–1901	18	81	63
2	George III	1760–1820	22	81	59
3	Henry III	1216–72	9	64	56
4	Edward III	1327–77	14	64	50
5	Elizabeth I	1558–1603	25	69	44
6	Elizabeth II	1952–	25	–	38
7	Henry VI	1422–61 (deposed; d.1471)	8 months	49	38
8	Henry VIII	1509–47	17	55	37
9	Charles II	1649–85	19	54	36
10	Henry I	1100–35	31/32*	66/67	35

Henry I's birthdate is unknown, so his age at accession and death are uncertain.

This list excludes the reigns of monarchs before 1066, so omits such rulers as Ethelred II who reigned for 37 years. Queen Elizabeth II overtook Henry VI's 38 years and 185 days reign in August 1990. If she is still on the throne on 11 September 2015, she will have beaten Queen Victoria's record by one day. She will then be 89 years old.

THE 10 LONGEST-LIVED BRITISH MONARCHS

	Monarch	Born	Reign	Age at death
1	Victoria	1819	1837–1901	81
2	George III	1738	1760–1820	81
3	Edward VIII	1894	1936 (abdicated; d.1972)	77
4	George II	1683	1727–60	76
5	William IV	1765	1830–37	71
6	George V	1865	1910–36	70
7	Elizabeth I	1533	1558–1603	69
8	Edward VII	1841	1901–10	68
9	Edward I	1239	1272–1307	68
10	James II	1633	1685–88	67

Queen Victoria and George III are close rivals for the title of longest-lived British monarch, and George's dates might suggest that he lived slightly longer than Victoria. However, during his lifetime, in 1752, the Gregorian Calendar was adopted in Great Britain, as a result of which 11 days were lost. Taking this into account, Queen Victoria lived for 81 years 243 days and George III for 81 years 239 days. The difference between the lifetimes of Edward VII and Edward I is also very slight, with Edward VII the winner by just six months; in fact, there is just a two-month difference between the length of the reigns of Edward I and James II, who ranks 10th.

BOTTOM LEFT King Henry VI ascended the throne at the age of eight months.

ABOVE Victoria and son, Edward VII (with Princess Alexandra), respectively first and eighth longest-lived British monarchs.

THE 10 YOUNGEST BRITISH MONARCHS

	Monarch	Reign	Age at accession years	months
1	Henry VI	1422–61	0	8
2	Henry III	1216–72	9	1
3	Edward VI	1547–53	9	3
4	Richard II	1377–99	10	5
5	Edward V	1483	12	5
6	Edward III	1327–77	14	2
7	Jane	1553	15	8
8	Henry VIII	1509–47	17	10
9	Victoria	1837–1901	18	1
10	Charles II	1649–85	18	8

Henry VI was born on 6 December 1421 and became King of England on 1 September 1422, the day after the death of his father, Henry V. At the age of 10 months (following the death of his grandfather, Charles VI, on 21 October 1422), he also became King of France. Before the Norman Conquest, Edward the Martyr became king in 975 when aged about 12 and Ethelred II ('the Unready') in 978 aged about 10.

THE 10 BEST-PAID MEMBERS OF THE ROYAL FAMILY

		£ 1989–90	1990–91
1	The Queen	4,658,000	5,090,000
2	The Queen Mother	404,000	439,500
3	The Duke of Edinburgh	225,300	245,000
4	The Duke of York	155,400	169,000
5	The Duke of Kent	148,500	161,500
6 =	Princess Alexandra	141,600	154,000
6 =	The Princess Royal	140,400	154,000
8	Princess Margaret	136,700	148,500
9	The Duke of Gloucester	110,000	119,500
10	Princess Alice, Duchess of Gloucester	55,400	60,500

The Civil List is not technically the Royal Family's 'pay' but the allowance made by the Government for their staff and costs incurred in the course of performing their public duties. The amount is announced annually at the time of the Budget. Of the total Civil List allocation of £6,762,000 for 1990–91 (£5,795,200 in 1989–90), The Queen refunds £435,000 (£400,100 in 1989–90). Prince Edward is No. 11 on the list, receiving £20,000. The Prince of Wales receives nothing from the Civil List, his income deriving largely from the Duchy of Cornwall.

THE 10 OLDEST MONARCHS TO ASCEND THE BRITISH THRONE

	Monarch	Reign	Age at accession
1	William IV	1830–37	64
2	Edward VII	1901–10	59
3	George IV	1820–30	57
4	George I	1714–27	54
5	James II	1685–88	51
6	George V	1910–36	44
7	George II	1727–60	43
8	George VI	1936–52	40
9	William I	1066–87	39
10	William III	1689–1702	38

WHO GOES FIRST? THE TOP 10 IN ORDER OF PRECEDENCE IN ENGLAND

1	Her Majesty The Queen
2	HRH The Prince Philip, The Duke of Edinburgh
3	HRH The Prince of Wales
4	The Queen's younger sons
5	The Queen's grandsons
6	The Queen's cousins
7	The Archbishop of Canterbury
8	The Lord High Chancellor
9	The Archbishop of York
10	The Prime Minister

The Order of Precedence is based on ancient customs and laws and determines the order of priority on occasions such as formal public processions and state ceremonies. After the Top 10, the order continues with an extensive list establishing precise precedence for dukes, earls and other members of the peerage and their children, bishops, judges and those who have received such honours as the OBE. Questions of precedence are decided in England by the Earl Marshal of England.

In Scotland the order of precedence is quite different, with The Lord High Commissioner to the General Assembly in third position, and the Lords Lieutenant of Counties taking precedence over the Lord Chancellor.

In the USA there is also an established order of precedence, with a sovereign or president coming first, followed by the President of the USA, Vice-President, ambassadors, the Chief Justice, and so on, with such oddities as the Postmaster General taking precedence over the Secretary of the Navy.

TOP RIGHT A not-so-close second: although No. 2 in the Civil List, The Queen Mother's payment is equal to less than 9 per cent of The Queen's.

THE TOP 10 POLITICAL PARTIES IN THE UK

Party	Seats won	Total votes
1 Conservative	376	13,760,583
2 Labour	229	10,029,807
3 Liberal/SDP Alliance	22	7,341,633
4 Scottish Nationalist Party	3	416,473
5 Official Unionist	9	276,230
6 Social Democratic and Labour Party	3	154,087
7 Plaid Cymru	3	123,599
8 Green Party	0	89,753
9 Democratic Unionist	3	85,642
10 Provisional Sinn Fein	1	83,389

Based on votes cast at the 1987 General Election.

The Liberal and SDP votes are amalgamated as the two parties fought the election as an alliance and did not stand against each other in any constituency. The votes cast for respective candidates were Liberal 4,173,450, SDP 3,168,183. After the election, a majority of the SDP merged with the Liberal Party to form the Social and Liberal Democrats, with a minority of Members of Parliament continuing as a separate party using the SDP name.

Although the Green Party's total vote was greater than those of both the Democratic Unionist Party and Provisional Sinn Fein, it was dispersed through a number of constituencies and hence the party failed to win a single seat, while the other two parties' electorate was confined to a small number of constituencies in Northern Ireland, where the Ulster Popular Unionist Party won Down with a total vote of 18,420.

Labour's 10,029,807 votes, though equivalent to nearly 73 per cent of those gained by the Conservatives, placed them in opposition with 147 fewer seats.

At the 1987 General Election the Conservative Party's 13,760,583 votes won it victory and 376 seats in the House of Commons.

THE FIRST 10 COUNTRIES TO GIVE WOMEN THE VOTE

	Country	Year
1	New Zealand	1893
2	Australia (South Australia: 1894; Western Australia: 1898; Australia was united in 1901)	1902
3	Finland (then a Grand Duchy under the Russian Crown)	1906
4	Norway (restricted franchise; all women over 25 in 1913)	1907
5	Denmark and Iceland (a Danish dependency until 1918)	1915
6=	Netherlands	1917
6=	USSR	1917
8=	Austria	1918
8=	Canada	1918
8=	Germany	1918
8=	Great Britain and Ireland (Ireland part of the United Kingdom until 1921; women over 30 only – lowered to 21 in 1928)	1918
8=	Poland	1918

Although not a country, the Isle of Man was the first place to give women the vote, in 1880. Until 1920 the only other European countries to enfranchise women were Sweden in 1919 and Czechoslovakia in 1920. Certain states of the USA gave women the vote at earlier dates (Wyoming in 1869, Colorado in 1894, Utah in 1895 and Idaho in 1896), but it was not granted nationally until 1920. A number of countries, such as France and Italy, did not give women the vote until 1945. Switzerland did not allow women to vote in elections to the Federal Council until 1971, and Liechtenstein was one of the last to relent, in 1984. In Saudi Arabia women are not allowed to vote at all – but neither can men.

THE 10 EUROPEAN PARLIAMENTS WITH MOST WOMEN MEMBERS

	Country	Women members	Total members	% women
1	Sweden	133	349	38.1
2	Norway	60	165	36.4
3	Finland	63	200	31.5
4	Denmark	52	179	29.1
5	Netherlands	32	150	21.3
6	Iceland	13	63	20.6
7	West Germany	80	519	15.4
8	Luxembourg	9	60	15.0
9	Switzerland	33	246	13.4
10	Italy	81	630	12.9

Based on the most recent general election results for all democratic European countries. With just 41 women MPs out of 650, the UK is in 16th place (only 6.4 per cent – although this is the highest ever proportion), beating Greece (4.3 per cent) and France (4.0 per cent – the worst ratio in Europe).

ABOVE After a long struggle, women's suffrage was achieved in Great Britain in 1918.

RIGHT Sirimavo Bandaranaike, the world's first female head of government.

THE WORLD'S FIRST 10 FEMALE PRIME MINISTERS AND PRESIDENTS

	Name	Country	Period in office
1	Sirimavo Bandaranaike (PM)	Ceylon (Sri Lanka)	1960–64 1970–77
2	Indira Gandhi (PM)	India	1966–84
3	Golda Meir (PM)	Israel	1969–74
4	Maria Estela Peron (President)	Argentina	1974–75
5	Elisabeth Domitien (PM)	Central African Republic	1975
6	Margaret Thatcher (PM)	UK	May 1979–
7	Dr Maria Lurdes Pintasilgo (PM)	Portugal	Aug–Nov 1979
8	Vigdís Finnbogadóttir (President)	Iceland	June 1980–
9	Mary Eugenia Charles (PM)	Dominica	Jul 1980–
10	Gro Harlem Brundtland (PM)	Norway	Feb–Oct 1981 May 1986–

Mrs Bandaranaike of Sri Lanka (then called Ceylon) became the world's first female prime minister on 21 July 1960. Mrs Thatcher became Britain's first on 4 May 1979 (re-elected 1983 and 1987). The first 10 have been followed by Corazón Aquino, who became President of the Philippines in 1986, by Benazir Bhutto, Prime Minister of Pakistan (1988–), Violeta Chamorro, President of Nicaragua (1990–) and Ertha Pascal-Trouillot, President of Haiti (1990–).

THE FIRST 10 PRESIDENTS OF THE USA

George Washington, first of 41 Presidents of the USA.

Foot first: Michael Foot is currently the UK's senior Member of Parliament.

President (dates)	Period in office
1 George Washington (1732–99)	1789–97
2 John Adams (1735–1826)	1797–1801
3 Thomas Jefferson (1743–1826)	1801–09
4 James Madison (1751–1836)	1809–17
5 James Monroe (1758–1831)	1817–25
6 John Quincy Adams (1767–1848)	1825–29
7 Andrew Jackson (1767–1845)	1829–37
8 Martin Van Buren (1782–1862)	1837–41
9 William Henry Harrison (1773–1841)	1841
10 John Tyler (1790–1862)	1841–45

THE 10 OLDEST MEMBERS OF PARLIAMENT

Name	Party*	Date of birth
1 Michael Foot	L	23 Jul 1913
2 Sir Bernard Braine	C	24 Jun 1914
3 Sir Julian Ridsdale	C	8 Jun 1915
4 Edward Heath	C	9 Jul 1916
5 Sydney Bidwell	L	14 Jan 1917
6 Sir John Stokes	C	23 Jul 1917
7 Denis Healey	L	30 Aug 1917
8 Sir William Clark	C	18 Oct 1917
9 Sir Trevor Skeet	C	28 Jan 1918
10 Martin Flannery	L	2 Mar 1918

*C – Conservative; L – Labour.

The span between the youngest and oldest MPs is nearly 50 years, and all the 10 most senior MPs have been drawing their old age pensions for between 7 and 12 years.

THE 10 YOUNGEST MEMBERS OF PARLIAMENT

Name	Party*	Date of birth
1 Matthew Taylor	SLD	1 Jan 1963
2 William Hague	C	26 Mar 1961
3 Charles Kennedy	SLD	25 Nov 1959
4 Timothy Devlin	C	13 Jun 1959
5 Patrick McLoughlin	C	30 Nov 1957
6 Keith Vaz	L	26 Nov 1956
7 Calum MacDonald	L	7 May 1956
8 Andrew Mitchell	C	23 Mar 1956
9 Phillip Oppenheim	C	20 Mar 1956
10 Colin Moynihan	C	13 Sep 1955

*C – Conservative; L – Labour; SLD – Social and Liberal Democrat.

Matthew Taylor, youngest Member of Parliament.

Juliette Gordon Low (centre), founder in 1912 of the United States Girl Guides (later Girl Scouts).

THE 10 COUNTRIES WITH THE HIGHEST GIRL GUIDE AND GIRL SCOUT MEMBERSHIP

Country	Membership
1 USA	2,917,622
2 Philippines	1,596,856
3 UK	750,438
4 India	442,129
5 Canada	268,928
6 South Korea	144,654
7 Indonesia	98,656
8 Japan	97,419
9 Australia	93,935
10 Pakistan	93,605

The Girl Guide Movement was started in 1910 by Sir Robert Baden-Powell and his sister, Agnes (1858–1945). Today the World Association of Girl Guides and Girl Scouts has 112 national member organizations with a total membership of more than 7,750,000.

THE 10 COUNTRIES WITH THE HIGHEST SCOUT MEMBERSHIP

Country	Membership
1 USA	3,884,400
2 Philippines	2,060,930
3 Indonesia	2,057,974
4 India	1,224,630
5 UK	681,257
6 Bangladesh	312,237
7 Canada	304,138
8 Pakistan	298,338
9 Japan	284,954
10 South Korea	278,765

The Scouting Movement was started in 1908 by Sir Robert Baden-Powell (1857–1941), a former general in the British army. There are now more than 16,000,000 Scouts in 150 countries and territories. Thailand, previously in 6th place with 330,190 members (1989: 241,351), has fallen out of the Top 10, while Pakistan has moved into 8th position.

THE 10 LARGEST TRADE UNIONS IN GREAT BRITAIN

Union	Members
1 Transport & General Workers' Union (TGWU)	1,312,000
2 General, Municipal Boilermakers and Allied Trades Union (GMW)	864,000
3 Amalgamated Engineering Union (AEU)	794,000
4 National & Local Government Officers Association (NALGO)	754,701
5 Manufacturing, Science & Finance (MSF)	653,000
6 National Union of Public Employees (NUPE)	635,000
7 Union of Shop, Distributive & Allied Workers (USDAW)	396,724
8 Electrical, Electronic, Tele-communications & Plumbing Union (EETPU)	365,883
9 Royal College of Nursing (RCN)	285,000
10 Union of Construction, Allied Trades & Technicians (UCATT)	250,042

Total trade union membership is around 9,000,000, but there are fewer than half the number of unions affiliated to the Trades Union Congress (TUC) that there were 30 years ago, when there were still unions serving such bygone trades as glass bevelling and felt hat making – though some still retain splendid descriptive names evoking highly specialized industries, among them the Card Setting Machine Tenters' Society and The Amalgamated Association of Beamers, Twisters and Drawers (Hand and Machine). Many of the smaller unions have been disbanded in recent years – the Spring Trapmakers' Society, for example, was dissolved in 1988 – although in marked contrast to the unions in the Top 10 there are some tiny survivors, such as the Military and Orchestral Musical Instrument Makers' Trade Society (35 members), the Society of Shuttlemakers (31) and the Sheffield Wool Shearers' Union (17).

HUMAN ACTIVITIES & ACHIEVEMENTS

THE 10 LARGEST TRADE (LABOR) UNIONS IN THE USA

	Union	Members
1	National Education Association	1,900,000
2	International Brotherhood of Teamsters, Chauffeurs, Warehousemen and Helpers of America	1,600,000
3	Food and Commercial Workers' International Union	1,235,000
4	American Federation of State, County and Municipal Employees	1,200,000
5	International Union of Automobile, Aerospace and Agricultural Implement Workers of America	1,102,675
6	International Union of Service Employees	925,000
7	International Brotherhood of Electrical Workers	845,000
8	International Association of Machinists and Aerospace Workers	767,000
9=	Communications Workers of America	700,000
9=	American Federation of Teachers	700,000

THE TOP 10 WOMEN'S ORGANIZATIONS IN THE UK

	Organization	Approx. membership
1	Trades Union Congress Women's Committee	2,800,000
2	Conservative Women's National Committee	500,000
3	National Federation of Women's Institutes	330,000
4	Transport and General Workers Union Women's Committee	220,000
5	Mothers' Union	180,000
6	Townswomen's Guilds	125,000
7	National Childbirth Trust	54,000
8	Young Women's Christian Association	20,000
9	National Women's Register	17,500
10	Soroptimist International of Great Britain and Ireland	17,000

THE TOP 10 ENVIRONMENTAL ORGANIZATIONS IN THE UK

	Organization	Membership
1	National Trust	1,864,951
2	Royal Society for the Protection of Birds	680,000*
3	Greenpeace	326,000
4	Civic Trust	304,000
5	Royal Society for Nature Conservation	250,000**
6	English Heritage	221,000
7	World Wide Fund for Nature†	200,000
8	National Trust for Scotland	195,000
9	Friends of the Earth	180,000
10	Ramblers Association	74,000‡

*Includes 107,000 members of the Young Ornithologists Club.
**Includes junior body, WATCH, with 50,000 members.
†Formerly the World Wildlife Fund.
‡Includes membership in the Republic of Ireland.

Greenpeace in action. It ranks as one of the UK's largest environmental organizations.

THE TOP 10 PROFESSIONS ON COMPUTER DATING AGENCIES' REGISTERS

WOMEN

Profession	% of those registered
1 Teachers	13.37
2 Secretaries	7.93
3 Nurses	7.37
4 Women at home	3.75
5 Civil servants	3.40
6 Clerks	3.15
7 Students	2.93
8 Social workers	1.46
9 Receptionists	1.44
10 Sales staff	1.18

MEN

1 Teachers	4.88
2 Civil servants	4.38
3 Engineers	4.18
4 Company directors	4.14
5 Accountants	3.57
6 Students	2.69
7 Self-employed	2.64
8 Computer programmers	2.43
9 Managers	1.61
10 Farmers	1.16

THE TOP 10 MONTHS FOR MARRIAGES IN ENGLAND AND WALES

Month	Marriages
1 August	50,278
2 September	44,303
3 July	41,165
4 June	37,973
5 May	36,780
6 October	31,550
7 April	27,039
8 March	19,707
9 November	17,373
10 February	17,101

The figures are for 1987, when there were a total of 351,761 marriages in England and Wales (1988 total: 348,500). As Saturday is the most popular day for weddings, the number of Saturdays in the month can have a dramatic effect on the totals (in 1987 January, May, August, and October all had five Saturdays). The least popular months are December (16,454) and January (12,038).

Based on figures supplied by Dateline, Britain's largest and oldest-established computer dating agency.

LEFT Contrary to popular belief, spring weddings are less popular than those in the summer months.

THE 10 COMMONEST SURNAMES IN GREAT BRITAIN

1 Smith
2 Jones
3 Williams
4 Brown
5 Taylor
6 Davies/Davis
7 Evans
8 Thomas
9 Roberts
10 Johnson

THE 10 COMMONEST SURNAMES IN THE USA

1 Smith
2 Johnson
3 Williams/Williamson
4 Brown
5 Jones
6 Miller
7 Davis
8 Martin/Martinez/Martinson
9 Anderson
10 Wilson

THE TOP 10 GIRLS' AND BOYS' NAMES ANNOUNCED IN THE BIRTHS COLUMN OF THE TIMES

FIRST NAME ONLY

	Girls' names	No.		Boys' names	No.
1	Charlotte	94	1	James	180
2	Emily	87	2	Thomas	149
3	Sophie	77	3	Alexander	119
4	Emma	71	4	William	118
5	Alice	64	5	Edward	102
6	Olivia	55	6	Charles	86
7	Alexandra	54	7	Oliver	75
8 =	Elizabeth	49	8	George	64
8 =	Katherine	49	9 =	Robert	55
8 =	Lucy	49	9 =	Henry	55

ALL NAMES (INCLUDING MIDDLE NAMES)

		No.			No.
1	Elizabeth	254	1	James	392
2	Charlotte	148	2	William	272
3	Alice	124	3	Alexander	233
4	Emily	111	4	Edward	203
5	Victoria	101	5	Thomas	192
6 =	Emma	95	6	Charles	190
6 =	Sophie	95	7	John	154
8	Alexandra	91	8	George	146
9	Sarah	78	9	David	138
10	Lucy	74	10	Robert	117

THE TOP 10 GIRLS' AND BOYS' NAMES IN ENGLAND AND WALES

Girls		Boys
Rebecca	1	Daniel
Sarah	2	Christopher
Emma	3	Michael
Laura	4	James
Rachel	5	Matthew
Samantha	6	Andrew
Charlotte	7	Adam
Kirsty	8	Thomas
Nicola	9	David
Amy	10	Richard

Since 1947, various people have monitored the Births column of The Times and listed the frequency of given names, a task now carried out by the paper's own Social Editor. In 1989 a total of 5,425 births were recorded: 2,645 girls and 2,780 boys. James has been the most popular boy's name since 1964, while the order of the other names has fluctuated a good deal, George and Olivia, for example, both entering the first name list for the first time in 1989.

A survey of first names registered in England and Wales reveals that only three girls' names – Charlotte, Emma and Sarah – and three boys' names – James, Thomas and David – also make an appearance in the Top 10 Times names lists. Other popular names on the Times lists are placed much lower in the national Top 10, with 'traditional' names such as Alice, Olivia, Charles and Henry, which are perennial favourites among Times readers, not even appearing in the England and Wales Top 50. Kylie is moving up the British list but has some way to go to make the Top 10 – as it did in Australia.

Town & Country

THE 10 LARGEST CITIES IN THE USA

	City	State	Population
1	New York	New York	7,262,700
2	Los Angeles	California	3,259,340
3	Chicago	Illinois	3,009,530
4	Houston	Texas	1,728,910
5	Philadelphia	Pennsylvania	1,642,900
6	Detroit	Michigan	1,086,220
7	San Diego	California	1,015,190
8	Dallas	Texas	1,003,520
9	San Antonio	Texas	914,350
10	Phoenix	Arizona	894,070

These are estimates for central city areas only, not for the total metropolitan areas that surround them, which may be several times as large.

The Manhattan skyline: New York City was the USA's largest metropolis 100 years ago and remains so today.

THE 10 LARGEST CITIES IN THE USA IN 1900

	City	Population
1	New York	3,437,202
2	Chicago	1,698,575
3	Philadelphia	1,293,697
4	St Louis	575,238
5	Boston	560,892
6	Baltimore	508,957
7	Cleveland	381,768
8	Buffalo	352,387
9	San Francisco	342,782
10	Cincinnati	325,902

Only the first three cities are in the present Top 10, the rest having been overtaken by seven others that had relatively small populations at the turn of the century: Detroit (285,704 in 1900), Los Angeles (102,479), San Antonio (53,321), Houston (44,633), Dallas (42,638), San Diego (17,700) and Phoenix (5,444).

THE 10 LARGEST CITIES IN THE WORLD

City	Country	Population 1985	Estimate for AD 2000 [position]
1 Tokyo/Yokohama	Japan	25,434,000	29,971,000 [1]
2 Mexico City	Mexico	16,901,000	27,872,000 [2]
3 São Paulo	Brazil	14,911,000	25,354,000 [3]
4 New York	USA	14,598,000	14,648,000 [6]
5 Seoul	South Korea	13,665,000	21,976,000 [4]
6 Osaka/Kobe/Kyoto	Japan	13,562,000	14,333,000 [7]
7 Buenos Aires	Argentina	10,750,000	12,911,000 [11]
8 Calcutta	India	10,462,000	14,088,000 [10]
9 Bombay	India	10,137,000	15,357,000 [5]
10 Rio de Janeiro	Brazil	10,116,000	14,169,000 [9]
13 London	*UK*	*9,442,000*	*8,574,000 [23]*

THE 10 LARGEST NON-CAPITAL CITIES IN THE WORLD

City	Country	Population	(Capital/population)
1 Shanghai	China	12,620,000	(Peking 9,957,000)
2 Calcutta	India	9,166,000	(Delhi 6,220,000)
3 São Paulo	Brazil	8,490,763	(Brasília 1,576,657)
4 Bombay	India	8,202,000	(Delhi 6,220,000)
5 New York	USA	7,262,700	(Washington DC 626,000)
6 Karachi*	Pakistan	6,500,000	(Islamabad 350,000)
7 Tien-tsing (Tianjin)	China	5,460,000	(Peking 9,957,000)
8 Rio de Janeiro*	Brazil	5,094,396	(Brasília 1,576,657)
9 Alexandria	Egypt	5,000,000	(Cairo 14,000,000)
10 Leningrad*	USSR	4,948,000	(Moscow 8,815,000)

*Former capital.

Based on comparison of population within administrative boundaries – hence not comparable with list of 10 Largest Cities in the World.

Calculating the populations of the world's cities is fraught with difficulties, not least that of determining whether the city is defined by its administrative boundaries or by its continuously built-up areas or conurbations. Since different countries adopt different schemes, and some have populations concentrated in city centres while others are spread out in suburbs sprawling over hundreds of square miles, it has been impossible to compare them meaningfully. In order to resolve this problem, the US Bureau of the Census has adopted the method of defining cities as population clusters or 'urban agglomerations' with densities of more than 5,000 inhabitants per square mile, and – though it should be stressed that these totals will differ considerably from those based on other methods – this list is based on their figures for 1985, with projections to the year 2000. London was once the most populous city in the world, reaching its peak (though calculated on a different basis) of almost 9,000,000 in 1939. It has been in decline ever since, and fell behind Tokyo in 1957. By 2000 its continuing fall will relegate it to 23rd place in the world league, while Tehran, 19th in the 1985 assessment, will have risen to occupy 8th position with its population virtually doubling from 7,354,000 to 14,251,000.

ABOVE LEFT Tokyo, the world's most populous city.

THE 10 LARGEST CITIES IN THE UK IN 1801

City	Population
1 London	864,845
2 Manchester	94,876
3 Edinburgh	82,560
4 Liverpool	79,722
5 Glasgow	77,385
6 Birmingham	73,670
7 Portsmouth	43,461
8 Plymouth	43,194
9 Newcastle-upon-Tyne	36,963
10 Norwich	36,832

THE 10 LARGEST CITIES IN THE UK IN 1851

City	Population
1 London	2,362,236
2 Manchester	404,465
3 Liverpool	375,955
4 Glasgow	340,653
5 Birmingham	232,841
6 Edinburgh	193,929
7 Leeds	172,270
8 Bristol	137,328
9 Sheffield	135,310
10 Plymouth	102,380

In 1801 Britain's first Census indicated a total population of 10,942,646 for England, Wales and Scotland and serving members of the Army and Navy. Ireland was not included.

The total population of England, Wales and Scotland (and the Army and Navy, which were separately enumerated) as shown by the 1851 Census was 20,936,468 and that of Ireland 6,515,794.

LEFT At the time of the 1851 Great Exhibition, London's population was the world's highest.

THE 10 LARGEST CITIES IN THE UK

City	Area		Population density per sq km	Total population
	sq km	sq miles		
1 Greater London	1,579	609.7	4,291	6,775,400
2 Birmingham	264	102.0	3,803	1,004,100
3 Glasgow	198	76.3	3,662	725,100
4 Leeds	562	217.0	1,265	710,900
5 Sheffield	368	141.9	1,452	534,300
6 Liverpool	113	43.6	4,274	483,000
7 Bradford	370	142.9	1,252	463,100
8 Manchester	116	44.9	3,891	451,400
9 Edinburgh	261	100.6	1,679	438,232
10 Bristol	110	42.3	3,559	391,500

BELOW Capital city: its declining population places London top in the UK but third in Europe.

THE 10 LARGEST CITIES IN THE UK IN 1901

City	Population
1 London	4,613,812
2 Glasgow	786,897
3 Liverpool	716,810
4 Manchester	553,486
5 Birmingham	533,039
6 Leeds	443,559
7 Sheffield	425,528
8 Dublin	375,350
9 Belfast	349,180
10 Bristol	338,895

THE 10 LARGEST CITIES IN THE UK IN 1951

City	Population
1 London	8,346,137
2 Birmingham	1,112,340
3 Glasgow	1,093,337
4 Liverpool	789,532
5 Manchester	703,175
6 Sheffield	512,834
7 Leeds	504,954
8 Edinburgh	466,770
9 Bradford	462,500
10 Belfast	443,143

Dublin is included as the whole of Ireland was part of the UK until the Partition of 1921. If only the cities of the current UK are included, however, Belfast and Bristol move up to 8th and 9th positions and Edinburgh becomes the new No. 10 with a population of 327,441 at the time of the 1901 Census.

THE 10 LARGEST CITIES IN THE WORLD 100 YEARS AGO

City	Population
1 London	4,231,431
2 Paris	2,423,946
3 Peking	1,648,814
4 Canton (Kwangchow)	1,600,000
5 Berlin	1,579,244
6 Tokyo	1,552,457
7 New York	1,515,301
8 Vienna	1,364,548
9 Chicago	1,099,850
10 Philadelphia	1,046,964

In 1890, Nanking in China was the only other city in the world with a population of more than 1,000,000, with another Chinese city, Tien-tsing, close behind. Several other cities, including Constantinople (called Istanbul since 1930), St Petersburg (Leningrad since 1924) and Moscow, all had populations in excess of 750,000. However, it is remarkable to consider that as a result of the rapid growth of American cities in the second half of the nineteenth century, Brooklyn, with a population in 1890 of 806,343, was marginally larger than Bombay (804,470). Today, Bombay's population of over 10,000,000 makes it more than four times as large as Brooklyn, while Calcutta (840,130 in 1890) is even larger.

ABOVE Moscow is Europe's most populous city.

BOTTOM LEFT Paris was the world's second largest city at the turn of the century.

THE 10 LARGEST CITIES IN EUROPE

City	Population
1 Moscow*	8,815,000
2 Paris*	8,706,963
3 London*	6,775,400
4 Leningrad	4,948,000
5 Istanbul	4,870,747
6 Madrid*	4,731,224
7 Barcelona	4,597,429
8 Berlin	3,126,072†
9 Athens*	3,027,331
10 Rome*	2,821,420

*Capital city.
†West Berlin 1,879,200
 East Berlin 1,246,872.

The problem of defining a city's boundaries means that population figures generally relate to 'urban agglomerations', which often include suburbs sprawling over very large areas. In addition to the Top 10, Valencia, Kiev and Budapest all have populations in excess of 2,000,000, and many other European cities have populations of more than 1,000,000.

THE 10 MOST HIGHLY POPULATED COUNTRIES 100 YEARS AGO

	Country	Population
1	China	360,250,000
2	India	286,696,960
3	Russia	108,843,192
4	USA	62,981,000
5	Germany	49,421,803
6	Austria	41,345,329
7	Japan	40,072,020
8	France	38,343,192
9	UK	37,888,153
10	Turkey	32,978,100

In the 1890s many national boundaries were quite different from their present form: for example, India encompassed what are now Pakistan and Bangladesh, Poland was part of Russia and Austria and Turkey were extensive empires that included all their territories in their censuses. The 1891 Census of the UK indicated that the population of England and Wales was 29,001,018, Scotland, 4,033,103 and Ireland (then part of the UK) 4,706,162, with the populations of the Channel Islands, Isle of Man, etc, accounting for a further 147,870. The estimated total population of the entire British Empire at this time was 340,220,000, making it second only to China's.

THE 10 COUNTRIES WITH THE HIGHEST ESTIMATED POPULATION IN THE YEAR 2000

	Country	Population
1	China	1,255,656,000
2	India	961,531,000
3	USSR	314,818,000
4	USA	268,079,000
5	Indonesia	204,486,000
6	Brazil	179,487,000
7	Nigeria	161,930,000
8	Bangladesh	145,800,000
9	Pakistan	142,554,000
10	Japan	127,683,000
	UK	56,235,000

The estimates for the population of the Top 10 countries all assume increases, while that of the UK predicts a decrease as a result of the trend towards smaller families.

THE 10 COUNTRIES WITH THE HIGHEST POPULATION

	Country	Population
1	China	1,104,000,000
2	India	796,600,000
3	USSR	283,680,000
4	USA	246,330,000
5	Indonesia	174,950,000
6	Brazil	144,430,000
7	Japan	122,610,000
8	Pakistan	105,410,000
9	Nigeria	104,960,000
10	Bangladesh	104,530,000
16	UK	57,080,000

These figures, based on latest United Nations estimates, show that the population of China is more than 19 times that of the UK and represents some 22 per cent of the total population of the world (more than 5,000,000,000), proving the commonly stated statistic that 'one person in five is Chinese'.

A family planning poster in China. Despite efforts to reverse the trend, it is estimated that the country's population will top $1\frac{1}{4}$ billion by the end of the century.

THE 10 MOST HIGHLY POPULATED COUNTRIES IN EUROPE

	Country	Population
1	USSR (in Europe)	218,607,000
2	West Germany	61,200,000
3	Italy	57,440,000
4	UK	57,080,000
5	France	55,870,000
6	Spain	39,050,000
7	Poland	37,860,000
8	Yugoslavia	23,560,000
9	Romania	23,050,000
10	East Germany	16,670,000

BELOW A May Day parade in Moscow. European USSR is the continent's most highly populated country.

RIGHT A crowded beach in Hong Kong, one of the most densely populated territories in the world.

THE 10 MOST DENSELY POPULATED COUNTRIES AND COLONIES IN THE WORLD

	Country/colony	Area sq km	Area sq miles	Population	Population per sq mile
1	Macau	16.06	6.2	450,000	72,581
2	Monaco	1.81	0.7	27,063	38,661
3	Hong Kong	1,037.29	400.5	5,680,000	14,182
4	Gibraltar	6.47	2.5	30,077	12,031
5	Singapore	619.01	239.0	2,650,000	11,088
6	Vatican City	0.44	0.17	1,000	5,882
7	Bermuda	53.35	20.6	60,000	2,913
8	Malta	313.39	121.0	350,000	2,893
9	Bangladesh	143,998.15	55,598.0	104,530,000	1,880
10	Bahrein	675.99	261.0	480,000	1,839
	UK	244,046.79	94,227.0	57,080,000	606
	USA	9,372,614.90	3,618,787.0	246,330,000	68
	World total	135,597,770.00	52,509,600.0	5,054,798,000	*average 96*

Among the *least* densely populated countries in the world are the Falkland Islands, an area of 12,168 sq km/4,698 sq miles with a population of 1,916, or 0.41 of a person per sq mile, and Greenland (2,175,590 sq km/840,000 sq miles) with a population of 54,000, equivalent to 0.06 of a person per sq mile.

THE 10 LEAST POPULATED COUNTRIES IN EUROPE

	Country	Population
1	Vatican City	1,000
2	San Marino	22,361
3	Monaco	27,063
4	Liechtenstein	28,181
5	Gibraltar	30,077
6	Andorra	40,000
7	Iceland	247,024
8	Malta and Gozo	345,636
9	Luxembourg	372,000
10	Cyprus	691,700

LEFT Long Beach, California: the appeal of the 'Golden State' makes it the most highly populated in the USA.

ABOVE Monaco has the third lowest population in Europe, but the second highest density in the world.

THE 10 COUNTRIES WITH THE LOWEST POPULATION

	Country	Population
1	Vatican City	1,000
2	Falkland Islands	1,916
3	Nauru	8,042
4	Tuvalu	8,229
5	Wallis and Fortuna	13,100
6	Cook Islands	17,185
7	San Marino	22,361
8	Monaco	27,063
9	Liechtenstein	28,181
10	Gibraltar	30,077

THE 10 MOST HIGHLY POPULATED STATES IN THE USA

	State	Population 1900	1988
1	California	1,485,053	28,314,000
2	New York	7,268,894	17,909,000
3	Texas	3,048,710	16,841,000
4	Florida	528,542	12,335,000
5	Pennsylvania	6,302,115	12,001,000
6	Illinois	4,821,550	11,614,000
7	Ohio	4,157,545	10,855,000
8	Michigan	2,420,982	9,240,000
9	New Jersey	1,883,669	7,721,000
10	North Carolina	1,893,810	6,489,000

The total population of the United States in 1900 was 76,212,168 – less than 31 per cent of its present population of 246,330,000 – a 63 times expansion in the 200 years since 1790, when it was just 3,929,214. Some states continue to grow faster than others: between 1987 and 1988, for example, the population of Florida overtook that of Pennsylvania. When the data has been processed, the 21st US Census which took place on 21 April 1990 will reveal more details of recent population changes and enable further historical comparisons to be made.

THE 10 COUNTRIES WHERE SHEEP MOST OUTNUMBER PEOPLE

Country	Sheep	Human population	Sheep per person (approx.)
1 Falkland Islands	695,000	1,916	363
2 New Zealand	64,970,000	3,290,000	20
3 Australia	164,000,000	16,530,000	10
4 Uruguay	26,049,000	3,060,000	9
5 Mongolia	13,234,000	2,090,000	6
6 Namibia	6,400,000	1,760,000	4
7 Iceland	770,000	250,000	3
8 Mauritania	4,100,000	1,920,000	2
9 Somalia	13,500,000	7,110,000	1.9
10 Libya	5,750,000	4,230,000	1.4

The estimated total world sheep population (among livestock, second only to that of cattle) is 1,172,828,000 – an average of one sheep for every four people.

An insomniac's paradise: counting some of the 363 sheep per person in the Falkland Islands.

THE 10 LONGEST PLACE NAMES IN THE WORLD

1   Krung Thep Mahanakhon Bovorn Ratanakosin Mahintharayutthaya Mahadilok pop Noparatratchathani Burirom Udomratchanivetmahasathan Amornpiman Avatarnsathit Sakkathattiyavisnukarmprasit (167 letters)

     When the poetic name of Bangkok, capital of Thailand, is used, it is usually abbreviated to 'Krung Thep' (city of angels).

2   Taumatawhakatangihangakoauauotamateaturi-pukakapikimaungahoronukupokaiwhenuaki-tanatahu (85 letters)

     This is the longer version (the other has only 83 letters) of the Maori name of a hill in New Zealand. It translates as 'The place where Tamatea, the man with the big knees, who slid, climbed and swallowed mountains, known as land-eater, played on the flute to his loved one'.

3   Gorsafawddachaidraigddanheddogleddollônpen-rhynareurdraethceredigion (67 letters)

     A name contrived by the Fairbourne Steam Railway, Gwynedd, North Wales, for publicity purposes and in order to out-do No. 4.

4   Llanfairpwllgwyngyllgogerychwyrndrobwll-llantysiliogogogoch (58 letters)

     This is the place in Gwynedd famed especially for the length of its railway tickets. It means 'St Mary's Church by the pool of the white hazel trees, near the rapid whirlpool, by the red cave of the church of St Tysilio'. Its official name comprises only the first 20 letters.

5   El Pueblo de Nuestra Señora la Reina de los Angeles de la Porciuncula (57 letters)

     The site of a Franciscan mission and the full Spanish name of Los Angeles; it means 'the town of Our Lady the Queen of the Angels of the Little Portion'. Nowadays it is customarily known by its initial letters, 'LA', making it also one of the shortest-named cities in the world.

6   Chargoggagoggmanchauggagoggchaubunagunga-maugg (45 letters)

     America's longest place name, a lake near Webster, Massachusetts. Its Indian name, loosely translated, means 'You fish on your side, I'll fish on mine, and no one fishes in the middle'. It is pronounced 'Char-gogg-a-gogg (pause) man-chaugg-a-gogg (pause) chau-bun-a-gung-a-maugg'.

7 = Lower North Branch Little Southwest Miramichi (40 letters)

     Canada's longest place name – a short river in New Brunswick.

7 = Villa Real de la Santa Fe de San Francisco de Asis (40 letters)

     The full Spanish name of Santa Fe, New Mexico, translates as, 'Royal city of the holy faith of St Francis of Assisi'.

9   Te Whakatakanga-o-te-ngarehu-o-te-ahi-a-Tamatea (38 letters)

     The Maori name of Hammer Springs, New Zealand; like the second name in this list, it refers to a legend of Tamatea, explaining how the springs were warmed by 'the falling of the cinders of the fire of Tamatea'.

10   Loch Airidh Mhic Fhionnlaidh Dhuibh (31 letters)

     This is the name of a loch on the island of Lewis, Scotland.

THE 10 COUNTRIES WITH THE LONGEST OFFICIAL NAMES

	Official name	Common English name	Number of letters
1	al-Jamāhīrīyah al-'Arabīya al-Lībīyah ash-Sha'biyah al-Ishtirākīyah	Libya	56
2	al-Jumhūrīyah al-Jazā'irīyah ad-Dīmuqrāṭīyah ash-Sha'biyah	Algeria	49
3=	United Kingdom of Great Britain and Northern Ireland	United Kingdom	45
3=	Socijalistička Federativna Republika Jugoslavija	Yugoslavia	45
5=	Soyuz Sovetskikh Sotsialisticheskikh Respublik	USSR	43
5=	Sri Lankā Prajathanthrika Samajavadi Janarajaya	Sri Lanka	43
7	Jumhūrīyat al-Yaman ad-Dimuqrātīyah ash-Sha'bīyah	People's Democratic Republic of Yemen	42
8=	Republika Popullore Socialiste e Shqipërisë	Albania	39
8=	YeĒtiyop'iya Hezbawi Dimokrasīyawī Republēk	Ethiopia	39
10	Jamhuuriyadda Dimuqraadiga Soomaaliya	Somalia	35

Since many official names have to be translated from languages that do not use the Roman alphabet, their length may vary according to the method used. Fortunately, most have a short version, otherwise considerable problems could arise – not least that of fitting their names onto stamps . . .

THE 10 COMMONEST PLACE NAMES IN THE USA

	Name	Number of occurrences
1	Fairview	104
2	Midway	90
3	Centerville	72
4	Oak Grove	68
5	Riverside	67
6	Five Points	65
7	Mount Pleasant	56
8=	Oakland	54
8=	Pleasant Hill	54
10	Georgetown	49

THE 10 COMMONEST PLACE NAMES IN GREAT BRITAIN

	Name	Number of occurrences
1	Newton	150
2	Blackhill/Black Hill	141
3	Mountpleasant/Mount Pleasant	130
4	Castlehill/Castle Hill	127
5	Woodside/Wood Side	116
6	Newtown/New Town	111
7	Greenhill/Green Hill	108
8	Woodend/Wood End	106
9	Burnside	105
10	Beacon Hill	94

Research undertaken specially for *The Top 10 of Everything* by Adrian Room (the author of *A Concise Dictionary of Modern Place-names in Great Britain and Ireland*) reveals the place names most frequently encountered in Great Britain. These include the names of towns and villages, as well as woods, hills and other named locations, but exclude combinations of these names with others (Newton Abbot and Newton-le-Willows, for example, are not counted with the Newtons). A further study of the 250,000 names appearing on the Ordnance Survey 1:50,000 scale 'Landranger' maps shows that certain names of farms and houses appear even more frequently than the general names in this list:

	Name	Number of occurrences
1	Manor Farm	590
2	Park Farm	357
3	Hill Farm	355
4	Home Farm	341
5	Manor House	288
6=	Grange Farm	265
6=	Lodge Farm	265
8	The Grange	202
9	Hall Farm	182
10	Glebe Farm	171

THE 10 LONGEST PLACE NAMES IN THE UK

1   Gorsafawddachaidraigddanheddogleddollônpen-rhynareurdraethceredigion (67 letters) (see p. 75, World List, No. 3)

2   Llanfairpwllgwyngyllgogerychwyrndrobwll-llantysiliogogogoch (58) (see World List, No. 4)

3   Sutton-under-Whitestonecliffe, North Yorkshire (27)

4   Llanfihangel-yng-Ngwynfa, Powys (22)

5 = Llanfihangel-y-Creuddyn, Dyfed (21)

5 = Llanfihangel-y-traethau, Gwynedd (21)

7   Cottonshopeburnfoot, Northumberland (19)

8 = Blakehopeburnhaugh, Northumberland (18)

8 = Coignafeuinternich, Inverness-shire (18)

10 = Claddochknockline and Claddochbaleshare, North Uist, Outer Hebrides (both 17)

These are all single and hyphenated names. The longest multiple name in England is North Leverton with Habblesthorpe, Nottinghamshire (30 letters), followed by Skidbrooke cum Saltfeet Haven, Lincolnshire (26) and Preston upon the Weald Moors, Shropshire (24). In Wales it is Lower Llanfihangel-y-Creuddyn, Dyfed (26) followed by Llansantffraid Cwmdeuddwr, Powys (24), and in Scotland Huntingtower and Ruthvenfield (27) – although there is also a loch on the island of Lewis called Loch Airidh Mhic Fhionnlaidh Dhuibh (31) (see World List, No. 10).

If the parameters are extended to encompass Ireland, the single word Muckanaghederdauhaulia (22) is scooped into the net. Runners-up include Doddiscombsleigh, Moretonhampstead, Woolfardisworthy (pronounced 'Woolsery'), Combe-in-Teignhead and Stoke-in-Teignhead, all of which are in Devon and have 16 letters.

The longest parish name in the UK was for many years Saint Andrew, Holborn above the Bars, with Saint George the Martyr (54) in London, until the formation on 5 April 1971 of Saint Mary le More and All Hallows with Saint Leonard and Saint Peter, Wallingford (68).

THE 10 COMMONEST STREET NAMES IN THE USA

1 Second Street

2 Park Street

3 Third Street

4 Fourth Street

5 Fifth Street

6 First Street

7 Sixth Street

8 Seventh Street

9 Washington Street

10 Maple Street

The list continues with Oak, Eighth, Elm, Lincoln, Ninth, Pine, Walnut, Tenth and Cedar.

THE 10 SMALLEST COUNTRIES IN THE WORLD

Country	Population	Area sq km	sq miles
1 Vatican City	1,000	0.44	0.17
2 Monaco	27,063	1.81	0.7
3 Gibraltar	30,077	6.47	2.5
4 Macau	450,000	16.06	6.2
5 Nauru	8,042	21.23	8.2
6 Tuvalu	8,229	25.90	10.0
7 Bermuda	60,000	53.35	20.6
8 San Marino	22,361	59.57	23.0
9 Liechtenstein	28,181	157.99	61.0
10 Antigua	80,000	279.72	108.0

Vatican City has 1,000 residents in an area of 43.7 hectares/ 108 acres, ranking it as both the least populated and the smallest country in the world.

THE 10 COUNTRIES WITH THE GREATEST AREAS OF INLAND WATER

Country	% of total area	Water area sq km	sq miles
1 Canada	7.60	754,093	291,157
2 India	9.56	314,399	121,390
3 China	2.82	270,550	104,460
4 USA	2.20	206,010	79,541
5 USSR	0.58	130,199	50,270
6 Ethiopia	9.89	120,900	46,680
7 Colombia	8.80	100,209	38,691
8 Indonesia	4.88	92,999	35,907
9 Australia	0.90	68,920	26,610
10 Tanzania	6.25	59,049	22,799

Large areas of some countries are occupied by major rivers and lakes. Lake Victoria, for example, raises the water area of Uganda to 15.40 per cent of the total. In Europe, three Scandinavian countries have considerable areas of water: Sweden – 38,340 sq km/14,803 sq miles (8.52%), Finland – 33,623 sq km/12,942 sq miles (9.91%) and Norway – 17,071 sq km/6,591 sq miles (5.27%). The Netherlands has a total water area of 3,411 sq km/1,317 sq miles (9.13%), while that of the UK is not far behind at 3,279 sq km/1,266 sq miles (1.34%) – more than twice Switzerland's 1,520 sq km/587 sq miles (3.68%). Ireland's inland water covers 1,391 sq km/537 sq miles (1.98%).

THE 10 COUNTRIES WITH THE LONGEST COASTLINES

Country	Coastline length km	miles
1 Canada	90,908	56,488
2 Indonesia	54,718	34,000
3 USSR	46,671	29,000
4 Greenland	44,087	27,394
5 Australia	25,760	16,007
6 Philippines	22,540	14,006
7 USA	19,924	12,380
8 Norway	16,093	10,000
9 New Zealand	15,134	9,404
10 China	14,500	9,010
12 UK	12,429	7,723

The coastline of Canada is more than twice as long as the circumference of Earth (40,076 km/24,901.8 miles at the Equator); even the coastline of Great Britain is approximately equivalent to the distance from London to Honolulu. No. 11, incidentally, is Greece (13,676 km/8,498 miles).

THE 10 LONGEST FRONTIERS IN THE WORLD

Country	Frontiers km	miles
1 China	24,000	14,913
2 USSR	20,619	12,812
3 Brazil	13,076	8,125
4 India	12,700	7,891
5 USA	12,002	7,458
6 Zaire	9,902	6,153
7 Argentina	9,414	5,850
8 Canada	9,010	5,599
9 Mongolia	8,000	4,971
10 Sudan	7,805	4,850

This list represents the *total* length of frontiers, compiled by adding together the lengths of individual borders. The 12,002 km/7,458 miles of the USA's frontiers include those shared with Canada (6,416 km/3,987 miles – the longest *continuous* frontier in the world), with Alaska (2,475 km/1,538 miles) and with Mexico (3,111 km/1,933 miles).

THE 10 LARGEST COUNTRIES IN THE WORLD

Country	Area sq km	sq miles
1 USSR	22,402,000	8,649,461
2 Canada	9,970,537	3,849,646
3 China	9,596,961	3,705,408
4 USA	9,372,614	3,618,787
5 Brazil	8,511,965	3,286,488
6 Australia	7,686,848	2,967,909
7 India	3,287,590	1,269,346
8 Argentina	2,766,889	1,068,302
9 Sudan	2,505,813	967,500
10 Algeria	2,381,741	919,595
75 UK	244,046	94,227
World total	136,597,770	52,509,600

The 10 largest countries comprise some 57.7 per cent of the total Earth's surface. The USSR alone occupies approximately 16.5 per cent and has an area 92 times greater than the UK.

LEFT Canada has not only the world's longest coastline but also the largest area of inland water.

THE 10 LARGEST NATIONAL PARKS IN THE USA

National Park	Established	Area sq km	sq miles
1 Wrangell-St Elias, Alaska	Dec 1980	33,716	13,018
2 Gates of the Arctic, Alaska	Dec 1980	30,448	11,756
3 Denali (formerly Mt McKinley), Alaska	Feb 1917	19,088	7,370
4 Katmai, Alaska	Dec 1980	15,037	5,806
5 Glacier Bay, Alaska	Dec 1980	13,054	5,040
6 Lake Clark, Alaska	Dec 1980	10,671	4,120
7 Yellowstone, Wyoming/Montana/Idaho	Mar 1872	8,982	3,468
8 Kobuk Valley, Alaska	Dec 1980	7,084	2,735
9 Everglades, Florida	May 1934	5,662	2,186
10 Grand Canyon, Arizona	Feb 1919	4,931	1,904

Yellowstone National Park was established on 1 March 1872 as the first national park in the world with its role 'as a public park or pleasuring ground for the benefit and enjoyment of the people'. There are now some 1,200 national parks in more than 100 countries. There are 49 National Parks in the USA, with a total area of over 191,183 sq km/ 73,816 sq miles (more than double their area before 1980, when large tracts of Alaska were added). With the addition of various National Monuments, National Historic Parks, National Preserves and other specially designated areas under the aegis of the National Park Service, the total area is 322,138 sq km/124,378 sq miles, visited by almost 300,000,000 people a year.

THE FIRST 10 STATES OF THE USA

State	Entered Union
1 Delaware	7 December 1787
2 Pennsylvania	12 December 1787
3 New Jersey	18 December 1787
4 Georgia	2 January 1788
5 Connecticut	9 January 1788
6 Massachusetts	6 February 1788
7 Maryland	28 April 1788
8 South Carolina	23 May 1788
9 New Hampshire	21 June 1788
10 Virginia	26 June 1788

THE 10 LARGEST STATES IN THE USA

State	Area sq km	sq miles
1 Alaska	1,478,425	570,823
2 Texas	678,924	262,134
3 California	404,973	156,361
4 Montana	377,069	145,587
5 New Mexico	314,456	121,412
6 Arizona	293,749	113,417
7 Nevada	284,611	109,889
8 Colorado	268,753	103,766
9 Wyoming	251,288	97,023
10 Oregon	249,115	96,184

Alaska, the largest state, has the second smallest population (524,000; Wyoming is the smallest with 479,000), equivalent to one person per square mile. The smallest US state is Rhode Island (2,717 sq km/1,049 sq miles); the District of Columbia covers 174 sq km/67 sq miles.

By comparison, the UK (244,046 sq km/94,227 sq miles) is smaller than the 10th largest state, and the area of England (103,440 sq km/50,363 sq miles) slightly smaller than that of Alabama (131,333 sq km/ 50,708 sq miles).

Its hot springs and geysers are among the many attractions of Yellowstone, the USA's oldest national park.

TOP RIGHT Liberty beckons to the world's outcasts.

RIGHT Immigrants arrive in New York, c 1900.

THE TOP 10 COUNTRIES OF ORIGIN OF IMMIGRANTS TO THE USA, 1820–1988

Country	Number
1 Germany	7,058,000
2 Italy	5,346,000
3 Great Britain	5,095,000
4 Ireland	4,707,000
5 Austria/Hungary	4,331,000
6 Canada	4,249,000
7 Russia	3,426,000
8 Mexico	2,805,000
9 West Indies	1,284,000
10 Sweden	1,130,000*

Figures combined with Norway during 1820–68.

'Give me your tired, your poor/Your huddled masses yearning to breathe free...' So started Emma Lazarus's poem, 'The New Colossus', which is inscribed on the Statue of Liberty. For many years the United States was the magnet that attracted vast numbers of immigrants: in 1903–15, for example, an average of 982,655 arrived every year. From 1820, when detailed records were first kept, until 1988, the total numbered 54,367,607. In 1988, the last year for which complete statistics are available, the US Immigration and Naturalization Service admitted 643,025 immigrants.

'Where On Earth?' Quiz

Where do the following people come from:

1 A Haligonian?
2 A Cisestrian?
3 A Hoosier?
4 A Moonraker?
5 An Angeleno?
6 A Chilango?
7 An Exonian?
8 An Aquisextain?
9 A Lett?
10 A Carioca?

THE 10 LARGEST NATIONAL PARKS IN GREAT BRITAIN

	National Park	Estab.	Area sq km	sq miles
1	Lake District	May 1951	2,292	885
2	Snowdonia	Oct 1951	2,170	838
3	Yorkshire Dales	Oct 1954	1,761	680
4	North York Moors	Nov 1952	1,432	553
5	Peak District	Apr 1951	1,404	542
6	Brecon Beacons	Apr 1957	1,344	519
7	Northumberland	Apr 1956	1,031	398
8	Dartmoor	Oct 1951	945	365
9	Exmoor	Oct 1954	686	265
10	Pembrokeshire Coast	Feb 1952	583	225

Following the National Parks and Access to the Countryside Act of 1949, the National Parks were established in the 1950s to conserve and protect some of the most picturesque landscapes of England and Wales from unsuitable development, at the same time allowing the public free access to them. In addition to the 10 National Parks, the Norfolk and Suffolk Broads (288 sq km/111 sq miles) became a National Park in all but name on 1 April 1989. The possibility of the New Forest and parts of Scotland being designated National Parks is also under consideration.

THE 10 LEAST POPULATED COUNTIES OF BRITAIN

	County	Population
1	Orkney	19,455
2	Western Isles	21,413
3	Shetland	22,939
4	Borders	102,592
5	Powys	113,300
6	Isle of Wight	126,900
7	Dumfries and Galloway	147,036
8	Highland	201,866
9	Gwynedd	236,300
10	Central	272,077

This Top (or Bottom) 10 is dominated by the sparsely populated counties of Scotland and Wales. An England-only version of the list would start with the Isle of Wight, followed by Northumberland, Shropshire, Somerset, Cornwall, Warwickshire, Cumbria, Gloucestershire, Bedfordshire and Wiltshire, all of which have populations of under 552,000.

THE 10 LARGEST COUNTIES AND REGIONS IN THE UK

	County/region	sq km	sq miles
1	Western Isles	77,174	29,797
2	Highland	25,392	9,804
3	Strathclyde	13,856	5,350
4	Grampian	8,705	3,361
5	North Yorkshire	8,309	3,208
6	Tayside	7,503	2,897
7	Cumbria	6,809	2,629
8	Devon	6,711	2,591
9	Dumfries and Galloway	6,369	2,459
10	Lincolnshire	5,916	2,284

Dyfed is the 11th largest county at 5,765 sq km/2,226 sq miles.

THE 10 MOST HIGHLY POPULATED COUNTIES OF BRITAIN

County	Population
1 Greater London	6,775,400
2 West Midlands	2,642,300
3 Greater Manchester	2,580,100
4 Strathclyde	2,332,500
5 West Yorkshire	2,052,400
6 Hampshire	1,537,000
7 Essex	1,521,800
8 Kent	1,510,500
9 Merseyside	1,456,800
10 Lancashire	1,381,300

LEFT The Lake District National Park comprises one-third of the area of the county of Cumbria.

TOP Orkney, least populated of Britain's counties.

ABOVE Commuters adding to London's population.

Buildings & Structures

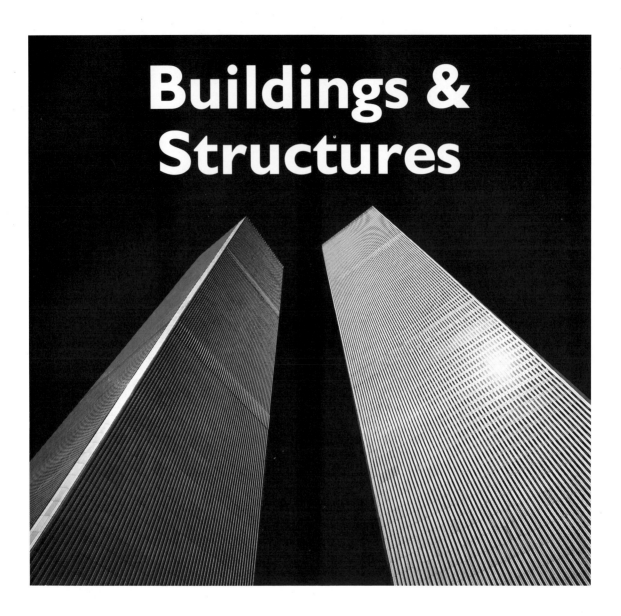

1 Employment
(relocating to a new area to take a new job or a different job within the same company).

2 Change in family requirements
(increase in family size or divorce).

3 Retirement.

4 Economics
(moving to a smaller property to reduce mortgage and other costs, to a larger property as a result of increased income, inheritance, etc, or because the property needs extensive repairs and the owners cannot afford to undertake them).

5 Schooling.

6 Environment
(health, development of industrial or housing estates, new roads, etc, near the existing property, or unpleasant neighbours).

7 Death of a partner or family member.

8 Commuting
(relocating closer to a motorway, airport or railway station to reduce journey time or expense).

9 Burglary
(one in three people move after a burglary).

10 Status.

Based on a survey by the Association of Relocation Agents.

THE TOP 10 AREAS FOR NEW HOUSE BUILDING IN GREAT BRITAIN

	County/region	No. of 'starts'
1	Greater London	13,810
2	Strathclyde	6,910
3	Greater Manchester	6,840
4	Hampshire and Isle of Wight	6,310
5	Essex	5,560
6	West Yorkshire	4,470
7	West Midlands	4,240
8	Kent	4,100
9	Devon	4,040
10	Lancashire	3,970

THE 10 TALLEST HABITABLE* BUILDINGS IN THE UK

	Building	Year completed	Height m	ft
1	National Westminster Tower, London EC2	1979	183	600
2	Post Office Tower, London W1	1966	177	580
3	Blackpool Tower	1894	158	519
4	Shakespeare Tower Cromwell Tower Lauderdale Tower Barbican, London EC2	1971 1973 1974	128 128 128	419 419 419
5	Euston Centre, Euston Road, London NW1	1969	124	408
6	Cooperative Insurance Society Building, Miller Street, Manchester	1962	122	399
7	Centrepoint, New Oxford Street, London WC1	1966	121	398
8	Britannic House, Moor Lane, London EC2	1967	120	395
9=	Commercial Union, Undershaft, London EC3	1969	118	387
9=	Millbank Tower, Millbank, London SW1	1963	118	387

*Excludes radio masts, chimneys and church spires.

Figures prepared by the National House-Building Council show that in 1989 a total of 185,800 private houses were completed and 163,400 started in Great Britain – 27 per cent fewer than in 1988, but more than the yearly average for the past 10 years. The regions with the lowest number of starts were Orkney, the Western Isles and Shetland with 13, 4 and 3 respectively.

LEFT Making a move: the average family in the UK relocates every seven years.

Although the National Westminster Tower is Britain's tallest office building, it does not even rank in the Top 100 in the league table of the world's tallest. The Barbican towers are the tallest blocks of flats in the UK. Canary Wharf, currently under construction in London, is planned to attain 243.8 m/800 ft, while a private company recently unveiled its plans to build a 610 m/2,000 ft tower in Dudley, West Midlands.

Completed in 1979, the NatWest Tower remains the tallest habitable building in the UK.

THE 10 TALLEST CHURCHES IN THE WORLD

	Church	Year completed	Height m	ft
1	Chicago Methodist Temple	1924	173	568
2	Ulm Cathedral	1890	161	528
3	Cologne Cathedral	1880	156.4	513
4	Rouen Cathedral	1876	148	485
5	St Nicholas, Hamburg	1847	145	475
6	Notre Dame, Strasbourg	1439	142	465
7	St Peter's, Rome	1612	140	458
8	St Stephen's Cathedral, Vienna	1433	136	446
9	St Joseph's Oratory, Montreal	1922	126	412
10	Antwerp Cathedral	1525	124	406
	Salisbury Cathedral	*1375*	*123*	*404*

THE 10 LARGEST CEMETERIES IN LONDON

	Cemetery	Founded	Area (acres)
1	St Pancras and Islington, N2	1854	182
2	City of London, E12	1856	130*
3	Kensal Green, NW19	1832	77
4=	Battersea New, Morden	1891	70
4=	Streatham Park, SW16	1909	70
6	Lee, SE6	1873	65
7	Camberwell New, SE23	1927	61
8	Great Northern, N11	1861	60
9	Merton and Sutton, Morden	1947	57.5**
10	Tottenham, N17	1856	56

Plus 46 in reserve.
**22 in use.*

Despite the appalling overcrowding of inner-city church graveyards, public cemeteries such as Père-Lachaise, Paris, which opened in 1804, were much longer in becoming established in England. In 1832 Kensal Green became the first to open in London, and was gradually followed by some 100 more serving London's needs. Today, though many are neglected and overgrown, they are worth visiting for their often remarkable last resting places of both the famous and unknown – some, such as Highgate Cemetery, even organize guided tours. Among the interesting tombs in the 10 largest are those of Henry Croft, the original 'Pearly King', and Ford Madox-Brown, the Pre-Raphaelite painter, both at St Pancras and Islington, the comedian Will Hay at Streatham Park, and world light-heavyweight boxing champion Freddie Mills at Camberwell New Cemetery. Kensal Green contains many tombs of eminent people, including King George III's son Augustus and daughter Sophia, the engineer Isambard Kingdom Brunel, Blondin the tightrope walker, and Major Walter Wingfield, the inventor of lawn tennis. 'James' Barry, who was buried there in 1865, was actually a woman who posed as a man all her adult life and became the first qualified female doctor in Britain.

OPPOSITE Cologne Cathedral, the third tallest in the world.

LEFT Kensal Green, London's first public cemetery.

THE WORLD'S 10 TALLEST BUILDINGS BEFORE THE AGE OF SKYSCRAPERS

Building	Location	Year completed	Height m	ft
1 Eiffel Tower	Paris, France	1889	300	984
2 Washington Memorial	Washington DC, USA	1885	169	555
3 Ulm Cathedral	Ulm, Germany	1890	161	528
4 Lincoln Cathedral	Lincoln, England	c1307 (destroyed 1548)	160	525
5 Cologne Cathedral	Cologne, Germany	1880	156.4	513
6 Notre-Dame	Rouen, France	1530	156	512
7 St Pierre Church	Beauvais, France	1568 (collapsed 1573)	153	502
8 St Paul's Cathedral	London, England	1315 (destroyed 1561)	149	489
9 Great Pyramid	Giza, Egypt	c2580BC	146.5	480.9
10 St Nicholas Church	Hamburg, Germany	1846–47	145	475

The first tall office buildings of 10 storeys or more were constructed in Chicago and New York in the 1880s, with the Eiffel Tower following at the end of the decade. It was not until 1913 that the first true 'skyscraper' – a secular building exceeding the height of the great medieval cathedrals – was built: the Woolworth Building, New York. At 241 m/792 ft it remained the tallest habitable building in the world until 1930, when the Chrysler Building (*see* The World's 10 Tallest Habitable Buildings, p. 89) overtook both it *and* the Eiffel Tower. A year later the Empire State Building topped them all, and remained the world's tallest for 40 years.

The height of the Washington Memorial is less than it was when it was erected, as it has steadily sunk into the ground. Lincoln Cathedral was the tallest building in the world for over 200 years, but fell in a storm. St Pierre at Beauvais collapsed in 1573. 'Old St Paul's' was destroyed by lightning on 4 June 1561; the present St Paul's Cathedral is only 112 m/366 ft high. The Great Pyramid stood as the world's tallest building for nearly 4,000 years, and was numbered among the Seven Wonders of the World. The loss of its topstone reduced its height to 137 m/449 ft.

Some 60 years on, the
Chrysler Building remains
in the Top 10 of the world's
tallest buildings.

THE WORLD'S 10 TALLEST HABITABLE BUILDINGS

Building	Location	Year completed	Storeys	Height m	ft
1 Sears Tower	Chicago, USA	1974	110	443	1,454
2 World Trade Center (twin towers)	New York City, USA	1972	110	417	1,388
3 Empire State Building	New York City, USA	1931	102	381	1,250
4 Bank of China	Hong Kong	1989	72	368	1,209
5 Standard Oil Building	Chicago, USA	1971	80	346	1,136
6 John Hancock Center	Chicago, USA	1967	100	344	1,127
7 Chrysler Building	New York City, USA	1930	77	319	1,046
8 Library Tower	Los Angeles, USA	1989	73	310	1,017
9 Texas Commerce Plaza	Houston, USA	1981	75	305	1,002
10 Allied Bank Plaza	Houston, USA	1983	71	302	992

LEFT Opened in 1889, the
Eiffel Tower held its record
as the world's tallest
structure until the
completion of the Chrysler
Building in 1930.

Heights are of buildings less their TV and radio antennae and uninhabited extensions. Moscow State University, for example, is disqualified as its 303 m/994 ft overall height includes a tall spire. The completion in 1989 of the Los Angeles Library Tower has evicted the Columbia Seafirst Center, Seattle, Washington, from 10th position. The 445 m/1,460 ft Central Place skyscraper, under construction in Brisbane, Australia, was planned to become the world's tallest inhabited building, but local objections have halted its construction. Trump City Tower, under construction in New York and scheduled for completion in 1999, is intended to top them all at 559 m/1,835 ft.

Culture & Learning

THE 10 BEST-ATTENDED POST-WAR ART EXHIBITIONS IN THE UK

Subject	Location*	Date	Total attendance
1 Treasures of Tutankhamun	BM	1972	1,694,117
2 Britain Can Make It	V&A	1947	1,500,000
3 Chinese	RA	1974	771,466
4 Post-Impressionism	RA	1980	648,281
5 Pompeii	RA	1977	633,347
6 Great Japan	RA	1982	523,005
7 The Vikings	BM	1980	465,000
8 Genius of Venice	RA	1983	452,885
9 Turner	RA	1975	424,629
10 Renoir	HG	1985	365,000

Although the Treasures of Tutankhamun exhibition remains the best attended art exhibition of all time, many exhibitions during the nineteenth century attracted enormous numbers of visitors, among them the 1881 Spanish Art Treasures exhibition at the Victoria & Albert Museum, which was seen by 1,220,000 people, and the display of the wedding presents of the Prince and Princess of Wales (also at the V&A) in 1863, which was on for just 17 days but was visited by 262,000. The more general exhibitions, in which art shows were only a part of the extravaganza, were often visited by staggering numbers; more than 6,000,000 saw the 1851 Great Exhibition, while 8,500,000 attended the 1951 Festival of Britain.

*BM – British Museum; HG – Hayward Gallery; RA – Royal Academy; V&A – Victoria & Albert Museum.

CULTURE & LEARNING

THE 10 MOST EXPENSIVE PAINTINGS BY TWENTIETH-CENTURY ARTISTS

	Price (£)
1 Pablo Picasso (1881–1973), *Les Noces de Pierette* Binoche et Godeau, Paris, 30 November 1989 (FF315,000,000)	33,083,023
2 Pablo Picasso, *Self Portrait: Yo Picasso* Sotheby's, New York, 9 May 1989 ($47,850,000)	28,825,301
3 Pablo Picasso, *Au Lapin Agile* Sotheby's, New York, 15 November 1989 ($40,700,000)	25,710,675
4 Pablo Picasso, *Acrobate et Jeune Arlequin* Christie's, London, 28 November 1988	20,900,000
5 Pablo Picasso, *Le Miroir* Sotheby's, New York, 15 November 1989 ($26,400,000)	16,677,195
6 Pablo Picasso, *Maternité* Christie's, New York, 14 June 1988 ($24,750,000)	13,026,315*
7 Wassily Kandinsky, *Fugue* Sotheby's, New York, 15 May 1990 ($20,900,000)	12,440,476*
8 Willem de Kooning (b.1904), *Interchange* Sotheby's, New York, 8 November 1989 ($20,680,000)	13,039,092*
9 Pablo Picasso, *Mère et Enfant* Sotheby's, New York, 15 November 1989 ($18,700,000)	11,813,013
10 Jasper Johns (b.1930), *False Start* Sotheby's, New York, 10 November 1988 ($17,050,000)	9,406,896

*Ranked by price at location of auction; as a result of exchange rate variations between sales, converting into sterling alters the order.

Willem de Kooning's *Interchange* currently holds the world record for a painting by a living artist. It is a measure of the enormous escalation in prices during the late 1980s that a painting by Georges Braque (1882–1963) *Femme Lisant*, sold at Sotheby's, London, on 2 December 1986 for £6,600,000, and which was at the time the most expensive twentieth-century painting, now only just finds a place in the Top 20.

Picasso dominates the Top 10 most expensive twentieth-century paintings. His *Acrobate et Jeune Arlequin*, which made £20,900,000 at auction, ranks fourth.

THE 10 MOST EXPENSIVE PAINTINGS EVER SOLD AT AUCTION

Price (£)

1 Vincent Van Gogh, *Portrait of Dr Gachet* 49,107,142
Christie's, New York, 15 May 1990
($82,500,000)

Purchased by Hibeto Kobayashi, a Tokyo dealer, bidding on behalf of an unnamed Japanese corporation.

2 Pierre-Auguste Renoir, 46,488,095
Au Moulin de la Galette
Sotheby's, New York, 16 May 1990
($78,100,000)

Bought by Japanese paper manufacturer, Ryouei Saito.

3 Vincent Van Gogh, *Irises* 30,187,623
Sotheby's, New York, 11 November 1987
($53,900,000)

After much speculation, its mystery purchaser was eventually confirmed as Australian businessman Alan Bond. However, as he was unable to pay for it in full, its former status as the world's most expensive work of art has been disputed and regarded by some as 'artificial'. Early in 1990 it was revealed that it had been sold privately to the J. Paul Getty Museum, Malibu, for an undisclosed sum, with speculation ranging from $60,000,000 to as little as $35,000,000.

4 Pablo Picasso, *Les Noces de Pierette* 33,083,023
Binoche et Godeau, Paris, 30 November 1989 (FF315,000,000/$51,895,000)

Is this the third or fourth most expensive painting ever sold at auction? The answer depends on whether the 315,000,000 French francs paid for it is converted into pounds or US dollars. As a result of exchange rate fluctuations, converted into sterling it breaks the record set by *Irises*. However, if the price is converted into dollars, it falls short by over $2,000,000. Another consideration is that the price includes a 5 per cent buyer's premium, whereas the prices of paintings sold in New York and London are inflated by a 10 per cent premium. If this is deducted, *Les Noces de Pierette* becomes the more expensive by $424,000. Whatever its place in the league table, it is the most expensive twentieth-century work of art. It was sold by Swedish financier Fredrik Roos and bought by Tomonori Tsurumaki, a Japanese property developer, bidding from Tokyo by telephone. He plans to exhibit it in an art gallery due to open in 1991 at 'Autopolis', a motor racing circuit he is building near Mount Aso, some 700 miles south of Tokyo.

5 Pablo Picasso, *Self Portrait: Yo Picasso* 28,825,301
Sotheby's, New York, 9 May 1989
($47,850,000)

The purchaser has remained anonymous but unconfirmed reports have identified him as Stavros Niarchos, the Greek shipping magnate.

6 Pablo Picasso, *Au Lapin Agile* 25,710,675
Sotheby's, New York, 15 November 1989
($40,700,000)

The painting depicts Picasso as a harlequin at the bar of the café Lapin Agile. The owner of the café acquired the picture in exchange for food and drink at a time when Picasso was hard up. In 1989 it was bought by the Walter Annenberg Foundation.

7 Vincent Van Gogh, *Sunflowers* 24,750,000
Christie's, London, 30 March 1987

At the time, the most expensive picture ever sold, it was bought by the Yasuda Fire and Marine Insurance Company of Tokyo.

8 Jacopo da Carucci (Pontormo), 22,370,511
Portrait of Duke Cosimo I de Medici
Christie's, New York, 31 May 1989
($35,200,000)

The world record price for an Old Master – and the only one in the Top 10 – it was bought by the J. Paul Getty Museum, Malibu. The previous record for an Old Master was held by Andrea Mantegna's *Adoration of the Magi*, sold at Christie's, London, on 18 April 1985 for £8,100,000.

9 Pablo Picasso, 20,900,000
Acrobate et Jeune Arlequin
Christie's, London, 28 November 1988

Until the sale of *Yo Picasso*, this held the world record for a twentieth-century painting. It was bought by Mitsukoshi, a Japanese department store.

10 Edouard Manet,   16,708,860
La rue Mosnier aux drapeaux
Christie's, New York, 14 November 1989
($26,400,000)

Until the sale of Renoir's *Au Moulin de la Galette,* this held the world record price for a French Impressionist painting. Few top quality Impressionist works have been auctioned during the art boom period of the late 1980s, with the result that Van Gogh (a Post-Impressionist) and Picasso have tended to dominate the scene. When the same painting was previously sold in 1958, it held the then record price for a Manet of £113,000.

All prices include buyer's premium; $/£ conversion at rate then prevailing.

Art Quiz

1 Claude Monet's garden with its water-lily pond features in many of his paintings. Where is it?

2 Because people had difficulty pronouncing the name of painter Domenikos Theotocopoulos, he was called after his country. What was this nickname?

3 What painting was stolen from the Louvre in 1911 and recovered two years later?

4 Which famous outlaw has Australian artist Sidney Nolan portrayed in many of his paintings?

5 Which American artist is best known for his painting of his mother?

6 Of what style of painting were Salvador Dali and René Magritte leading exponents?

7 Whose painting of *Mr and Mrs Clark and Percy* hangs in the Tate Gallery, London?

8 Who invented the type of sculpture known as a 'mobile'?

9 Who painted *The Laughing Cavalier*?

10 What happened to the Portland Vase on 24 February 1845?

ABOVE Van Gogh's *Sunflowers*, once the most expensive painting in the world.

OPPOSITE Van Gogh's *Portrait of Dr Gachet* is the most expensive painting or work of art ever sold.

THE 10 MOST EXPENSIVE PAINTINGS BY VINCENT VAN GOGH

	Price (£)
1 *Portrait of Dr Gachet* Christie's, New York, 15 May 1990 ($82,500,000)	49,107,142
2 *Irises* Sotheby's, New York, 11 November 1987 ($53,900,000)	30,187,623
3 *Sunflowers* Christie's, London, 30 March 1987	24,750,000
4 *Self Portrait* Christie's, New York, 15 May 1990 ($26,400,000)	15,714,285
5 *Le Vieil If* Christie's, New York, 14 November 1989 ($20,350,000)	12,798,742
6 *Le Pont de Trinquetaille* Christie's, London, 29 June 1987	12,650,000
7 *Paysage au Soleil Levant* Sotheby's, New York, 24 April 1985 ($9,900,000)	8,140,000
8 *Portrait of Adeline Ravoux* Christie's, New York, 11 May 1988 ($13,750,000)	7,325,519
9 *Carriera près de Saint-Rémy* *(Entrance to a quarry)* Sotheby's, New York, 15 November 1989 ($11,550,000)	7,296,272
10 *Romans Parisiens (Les Livres Jaunes)* Christie's, London, 27 June 1988	7,150,000

THE 10 MOST EXPENSIVE PAINTINGS BY IMPRESSIONISTS AND POST-IMPRESSIONISTS*

		Price (£)
1	Pierre-Auguste Renoir, *Au Moulin de la Galette* Sotheby's, New York, 16 May 1990 ($78,100,000)	46,488,095
2	Edouard Manet, *La rue Mosnier aux drapeaux* Christie's, New York, 14 November 1989 ($26,400,000)	16,708,860
3	Claude Monet, *Dans La Prairie (Camille in the Meadow)* Sotheby's, London, 28 June 1988	14,300,000**
4	Paul Gauguin, *Mata Mua (In Olden Times)* Sotheby's, New York, 9 May 1989 ($24,200,000)	14,578,313**
5	Paul Cézanne, *Pommes et Serviette* Christie's, London, 27 November 1989	11,000,000
6	Pierre-Auguste Renoir, *La Promenade* Sotheby's, London, 4 April 1989	10,340,000
7	Edouard Manet, *Le Banc (Le Jardin de Versailles)* Christie's, New York, 15 May 1990 ($16,500,000)	9,821,429
8	Edouard Manet, *La Promenade* Sotheby's, New York, 15 November 1989 ($14,850,000)	9,380,922
9 =	Claude Monet, *Le Parlement, coucher de soleil* Christie's, New York, 10 May 1989 ($14,300,000)	8,614,753**
9 =	Pierre-Auguste Renoir, *La Liseuse* Christie's, New York, 14 November 1989 ($14,300,000)	9,033,480**

*Excluding Vincent Van Gogh.
**Ranked by price at location of auction; as a result of exchange rate variations between sales, converting into sterling alters the order.

The USA's first university, named after John Harvard who came originally from England.

THE 10 OLDEST UNIVERSITIES AND COLLEGES IN THE USA

	University/college	Location	Founded
1	Harvard University	Cambridge, Massachusetts	1636
2	College of William and Mary	Williamsburg, Virginia	1693
3	Yale University	New Haven, Connecticut	1701
4	University of Pennsylvania	Philadelphia, Pennsylvania	1740
5	Moravian College	Bethlehem, Pennsylvania	1742
6	Princeton University	Princeton, New Jersey	1746
7	Washington and Lee University	Lexington, Virginia	1749*
8	Columbia University	New York, New York	1754
9	Brown University	Providence, Rhode Island	1764
10	University of Delaware	Newark, Delaware	1765**

*Founded as Augusta Academy 1749, name changed to Liberty Hall Academy 1782, Washington Academy 1798, Washington

College 1813, present name 1871.
**Founded as Newark Academy 1765, chartered 1769, name changed 1833.

THE 10 MOST POPULAR OPEN UNIVERSITY COURSES

1 Fundamentals of Computing

2 Culture and Belief in Europe

3 The Enlightenment

4 Social Problems and Social Welfare

5 The Digital Computer

6 Mathematical Models and Methods

7 The Nineteenth-century Novel and its Legacy

8 Programming and Programming Languages

9 Introduction to Information Technology: Social and Technological Issues

10 Personality, Development and Learning

The Open University was established in 1969 and has grown to become the UK's largest single teaching institution. Over 100,000 students a year register for a wide variety of 'distance-teaching' courses, using radio and television broadcasts in place of the lecture hall, so that students are able to work at home. Approximately the same number use study packs to follow non-degree courses. The largest single group of Open University students are those studying for a Bachelor of Arts (BA) degree (72,000 in 1990). Some 9 per cent of all first degrees in the UK are now OU degrees.

THE 10 LARGEST UNIVERSITIES IN THE UK

	University	Full-time students
1	London	52,776 internal + 24,856 external
2	Manchester	16,372
3	Leeds	11,161
4	Glasgow	11,015
5	Ulster	10,550
6	Edinburgh	10,477
7	Cambridge	10,081
8	Oxford	10,005
9	Birmingham	9,851
10	Liverpool	8,360

LEFT Renoir's *Au Moulin de la Galette*, sold in 1990.

RIGHT Oxford ranks as the UK's eighth largest university.

THE 10 LARGEST LIBRARIES IN THE WORLD

	Library	Location	Founded	Books
1	Library of Congress	Washington, DC, USA	1800	22,000,000
2	British Library	London, UK	1753*	18,000,000
3	State V.I. Lenin Library of the USSR	Moscow, USSR	1862	11,750,000
4	Harvard University Library	Cambridge, MA, USA	1638	11,496,906
5	New York Public Library	New York, NY, USA	1848	9,496,024
6	Biblioteca Academiei Republicii Socialiste Romania	Bucharest, Romania	1867	9,100,000
7	Bibliothèque Nationale	Paris, France	1480	9,000,000
8	Yale University Library	New Haven, CT, USA	1701	8,538,156
9	State M.E. Saltykov-Shchedrin State Public Library	Leningrad, USSR	1795	8,000,000
10	University of Illinois	Urbana, IL, USA	1867	7,377,051

Founded as part of the British Museum, 1753; became an independent body, 1973.

Rivalries between Iron Curtain libraries and the West seem to have been responsible for the hugely inflated figures claimed for the State M.E. Saltykov-Shchedrin (21,500,000) and State V.I. Lenin Libraries (28,216,000). As these appear to include individual copies of newspapers and periodicals, they cannot be compared with the holdings of bound books in Western libraries. It is also known that a very large number of books were recently destroyed in a disastrous fire at the Saltykov-Shchedrin. The figures for books in such vast collections as those of the British Library represent only the tip of a cultural iceberg which encompasses millions of additional items, including manuscripts, microfilms, maps, prints and records. The Library of Congress has perhaps 60,000,000 and the New York Public Library 20,000,000 catalogued items other than books.

BELOW One of the reading halls of the State V.I. Lenin Library, Moscow.

The courtyard of the Bodleian, the second largest UK library.

THE 10 LARGEST LIBRARIES IN THE UK

	Library	Location	Founded	Books
1	British Library	London	1753	18,000,000
2=	Bodleian Library	Oxford	1602	5,000,000
2=	National Library of Scotland	Edinburgh	1682	5,000,000
4	University of Cambridge	Cambridge	c1400	4,200,000
5	Hampshire County Library	Winchester	1925	3,500,000
6	Lancashire County Library	Preston	1924	3,452,895
7	John Rylands Library*	Manchester	1851	3,350,000
8	Kent County Library	Maidstone	1921	3,300,000
9	Birmingham Public Library	Birmingham	1861	2,562,000
10	National Library of Wales	Aberystwyth	1907	2,500,000

In 1972 the John Rylands Library (founded 1900) was amalgamated with Manchester University Library (1851).

In addition to the books held by these libraries, many have substantial holdings of manuscripts, periodicals and other printed material: the Bodleian Library, for example, has almost 1,000,000 maps.

RIGHT The Library of Congress, the largest library in the world.

THE 10 LARGEST LIBRARIES IN THE USA

	Library	Location	Founded	Books
1	Library of Congress	Washington, DC	1800	22,000,000
2	Harvard University Library	Cambridge, MA	1638	11,496,906
3	New York Public Library	New York, NY	1848	9,496,024
4	Yale University Library	New Haven, CT	1701	8,538,156
5	University of Illinois	Urbana, IL	1867	7,377,051
6	University of California	Berkeley, CA	1868	7,190,821
7	University of Michigan	Ann Arbor, MI	1817	6,133,171
8	University of Texas	Austin, TX	1883	5,888,776
9	University of California	Los Angeles, CA	1919	5,812,163
10	Columbia University	New York, NY	1754	5,740,832

THE 10 MOST WIDELY SPOKEN LANGUAGES IN THE WORLD

	Language	Where spoken*	Number of speakers
1	Mandarin Chinese	North and east-central China	825,000,000
2	English	British Isles, North America, Australia, New Zealand and former British colonies	431,000,000
3	Hindi	India	325,000,000
4	Spanish	Spain, Spanish America	320,000,000
5	Russian	USSR	289,000,000
6	Arabic	Middle East and North Africa	187,000,000
7	Bengali	India	178,000,000
8	Portuguese	Portugal, Brazil and former Portuguese colonies	169,000,000
9	Malay-Indonesian	Malaya, Indonesia	135,000,000
10	Japanese	Japan	124,000,000

*Adopted as national language.

A Chinese democracy poster. Mandarin, with 825,000,000 speakers, is the most spoken language in the world.

THE 10 LONGEST WORDS IN THE ENGLISH LANGUAGE

1 Acetylseryltyrosylserylisoleucylthreonylserylpro-
lylserylglutaminylphenylalanylvalylphenylalanyl-
leucylserylserylvalyltryptophylalanylaspartylpro-
lylisoleucylglutamylleucylleucyllasparaginylvalyl-
cysteinylthreonylserylserylleucylglycllasparagi-
nylglutaminylphenylalanylglutaminylthreonylglu-
taminylglutaminylalanylarginylthreonylthreonyl-
glutaminylvalylglutaminylglutaminylphenylala-
nylserylglutaminylvalyltryptophyllysylprolyl-
phenylalanylprolylglutaminylserylthreonylvalyl-
arginylphenylalanylprolylglycylaspartylval-
yltyrosyllsyslvalyltyrosylarginyltyrosylasparaginyl-
alanylvalylleucylaspartylprolylleucylisoleucylthreo-
nylalanylleucylleucylglycylthreonylphenylalanylas-
partylthreonylarginylasparaginylarginylisoleucyliso-
leucylglutamylvalylglutamylasparaginylglutaminyl-
glutaminylserylprolylthreonylthreonylalanylglutamyl-
threonylleucylaspartylalanylthreonylarginylarginyl-
valylaspartylaspartylalanylthreonylvalylalanyl-
isoleucylarginylserylalanylasparaginylisoleu-
cylasparaginylleucylvallasparaginylglutamylleucyl-
valylarginylglycylthreonylglycylleucyltyrosylaspar-
aginylglutaminylasparaginylthreonylphenylalanyl-
glutamylserylmethionylserylglycylleucylvalyl-
tryptophylthreonylserylalanylprolylalanylserine
(1,185 letters)

The word for the Tobacco Mosaic Virus, Dahl-emense Strain, qualifies as the longest word in English because it has actually been used in print (in the American Chemical Society's *Chemical Abstracts*) whereas certain even longer words for chemical compounds, which have been cited in such sources as the *Guinness Book of Records*, are bogus in the sense that they have never been used by scientists or appeared in print. Long words for chemical compounds may be regarded by purists as cheating, since such words as trinitrophenylmethyl-nitramine (29 letters) – a type of explosive – can be created by linking together the scientific names of their components. Other words that are also discounted are those that have been invented with the sole intention of being long words, such as James Joyce's 100-letter examples in *Finnegans Wake*.

2 Aopadotenachoselachogaleokranioleipsanodrim-
hipotrimmatosilphioparaomelitokatakechymeno-
kichlepikossyphophattoperisteralektryo-
noptekephalliokigklopeleiolagoiosiraiobaphetra-
ganopterygon (182 letters)

The English transliteration of a 170-letter Greek word that appears in *The Ecclesiazusae* (a comedy on government by women) by the Greek playwright, Aristophanes (c448–380BC). It is used as a description of a 17-ingredient dish.

3 Aequeosalinocalcalinosetaceoaluminosocupreo-
vitriolic (52 letters)

Invented by a medical writer, Dr Edward Strother (1675–1737), to describe the spa waters at Bath.

4 Asseocarnisanguineoviscericartilaginonervo-
medullary (51 letters)

Coined by writer and East India Company official Thomas Love Peacock (1785–1866), and used in his satire *Headlong Hall* (1816) as a description of the structure of the human body.

5 Pneumonoultramicroscopicsilicovolcanoconiosis (45 letters)

It first appeared in print (though ending in '-koniosis') in F. Scully's *Bedside Manna* [sic] (1936), then found its way into *Webster's Dictionary* and is now in the *Oxford English Dictionary* – but with the note that it occurs 'chiefly as an instance of a very long word'. It is said to mean a lung disease caused by breathing fine dust.

6 Hepaticocholangiocholecystenterostomies (39 letters)

A surgical operation to create channels of communication between gall bladders and hepatic ducts or intestines.

7 Pseudoantidisestablishmentarianism (34 letters)

A word meaning 'false opposition to the withdrawal of state support from a Church', derived from that perennial favourite long word, antidisestablishmentarianism (a mere 28 letters). Another composite made from it (though usually hyphenated) is ultra-antidisestablishmentarianism, which means 'extreme opposition to the withdrawal of state support from a Church' (33 letters).

8 Supercalifragilisticexpialidocious (34 letters)

An invented word, but perhaps now eligible since it has appeared in the *Oxford English Dictionary*. It was popularized by the song of this title in the film *Mary Poppins* (1964) where it is used to mean 'wonderful', but it was originally written in 1949 in an unpublished song by Parker and Young who spelt it 'supercalafajalistickespialadojus' (32 letters). In 1965–66, Parker and Young unsuccessfully sued the makers of *Mary Poppins*, claiming infringement of copyright. In summarizing the case, the US Court decided against repeating this mouthful, stating that 'All variants of this tongue twister will hereinafter be referred to collectively as "the word".'

9 Encephalomyeloradiculoneuritis (30 letters)

A syndrome caused by a virus associated with encephalitis.

10 Hippopotomonstrosesquipedalian (30 letters)

Appropriately, the word that means 'pertaining to an extremely long word'.

If the rules are changed and No. 1 is disqualified as a compound chemical name, and No. 2 because it is a transliteration from Greek, the next two longest words, both with respectable literary pedigrees, are:

Floccinaucinihilipilification (29 letters)

Alternatively spelt 'Flocci-nauci-nihili-pilification' or, by Sir Walter Scott in his *Journal* (18 March 1829) 'Floccipaucinihilipilification', it means the action of estimating as worthless. Until 'supercalifragilisticexpialidocious', 'flocci-naucinihilipilification' was the longest word in the *Oxford English Dictionary*.

Honorificabilitudinitatibus (27 letters)

Invented by Shakespeare to mean 'with honourableness', it appears in *Love's Labour's Lost* (Act V, Scene I).

THE 10 MOST STUDIED LANGUAGES

English is the most studied language in the UK, and high on the curriculum of such countries as the USSR.

1	English
2	French
3	Russian
4	Spanish
5	German
6	Italian
7	Japanese
8	Chinese
9	Arabic
10 =	Greek
10 =	Turkish

Based on total number of hours studied per language by students at the Polytechnic of Central London, the largest provider of language teaching in the state sector in the whole of Europe, which offers courses in 28 different languages.

THE 10 COMMONEST WORDS IN WRITTEN ENGLISH

1	the
2	of
3	and
4	a
5	to
6	in
7	is
8	you
9	that
10	it

THE OXFORD ENGLISH DICTIONARY

Although conceived earlier, work on the *Oxford English Dictionary* started in earnest in 1879 under the editorship of James Murray. The first part covering A–Ant was published in 1884 and others followed at intervals. Murray died in 1915, but the work continued until 1928 when the first edition was complete. In 12 volumes, it defined 414,825 words and phrases, with about 2,000,000 quotations providing information on the first recorded use, continuing usage and later variations in the use of each word. Supplements were added over the ensuing years until it was decided to computerize all the material, work on which commenced in 1984. The original *Dictionary, Supplements* and new entries were incorporated onto a gigantic database occupying 540 megabytes of storage. Over 120 keyboard operators keyed in more than 350,000,000 characters, their work checked by over 50 proof-readers. The complete second edition, costing about £10,000,000 to produce, was published in 1989. Its 20 volumes, currently priced at £1,650, contain 21,728 pages with about 60,000,000 words of text defining some 557,889 words (over 34 per cent more than the first edition), together with 2,435,671 quotations. Work is now in hand for putting the entire dictionary onto CD-ROM (a single compact disc).

THE 10 EARLIEST DATED WORDS IN THE OXFORD ENGLISH DICTIONARY

	Word	Source	Date
1 =	Town	Laws of Ethelbert	601–4
1 =	Priest	Laws of Ethelbert	601–4
3	Earl	Laws of Ethelbert	616
4	This	Bewcastle Column	c670
5	Streale	Ruthwell Cross	c680
6	Ward	Caedmon, *Hymn*	680
7	Thing	Laws of Hlothaer and Eadric	685–6
8	Theft	Laws of Ine	688–95
9	Worth	Laws of Ine	695
10	Then	Laws of King Wihtraed	695–6

The 10 earliest citations in the *OED* come from seventh-century Anglo-Saxon documents and stone inscriptions. All have survived as commonly used English words, with the exception of 'streale', which is another name for an arrow. A few other English words can be definitely dated to before 700, among them 'church' which, like 'then', appears in a law of King Wihtraed.

THE 10 WORDS WITH MOST MEANINGS IN THE OXFORD ENGLISH DICTIONARY

	Word	Meanings
1	Set	464
2	Run	396
3	Go	368
4	Take	343
5	Stand	334
6	Get	289
7	Turn	288
8	Put	268
9	Fall	264
10	Strike	250

A sampling of the 464 entries for 'set' in the *Oxford English Dictionary*.

THE 10 LONGEST WORDS IN THE OXFORD ENGLISH DICTIONARY

	Word	Letters
1	Pneumonoultramicroscopicsilicovol- canoconiosis	45
2	Supercalifragilisticexpialidocious	34
3	Pseudopseudohypoparathyroidism	30
4=	Floccinaucinihilipilification	29
4=	Triethylsulphonemethylmethane	29
6=	Antidisestablishmentarianism	28
6=	Octamethylcyclotetrasiloxane	28
6=	Tetrachlorodibenzoparadioxin	28
9	Hepaticocholangiogastronomy	27
10=	Radioimmunoelectrophoresis	26
10=	Radioimmunoelectrophoretic	26

Words that are hyphenated, including such compound words as 'transformational-generative' and 'tristhio-dimethyl-benzaldehyde', have not been included. Only one unhyphenated word did not quite make it into the Top 10, the 25-letter 'psychophysicotherapeutics'. After this, there is a surprisingly large number of words containing 20–24 letters – few of which are ever used by anyone except scientists and crossword compilers.

John Wyclif, fifth most-quoted in the *Oxford English Dictionary*.

Words Quiz

1 What is the origin of the word 'scuba' as in scuba diving?
2 What do the words nincompoop, puzzle and slang have in common?
3 What is the tag on the end of a shoelace called?
4 Is a pogonologist an expert on apes, beards or cheese?
5 What is the name given to a flock of larks?
6 What is the origin of the word 'spoof'?
7 What do the words propriety and typewriter have in common?
8 Does the word 'braille' (the writing system for the blind) come from a French word meaning 'little dots', the Flemish for blind or the name of its inventor?
9 What name did the sixteenth-century scientist Paracelsus invent for an imaginary creature who guards a hoard of treasure?
10 What is the origin of the words muscle and mussel?

THE 10 LETTERS OF THE ALPHABET WITH MOST ENTRIES IN THE OXFORD ENGLISH DICTIONARY

	Letter	Entries
1	S	34,556
2	C	26,239
3	P	24,980
4	M	17,495
5	A	15,880
6	T	15,497
7	R	15,483
8	B	14,633
9	D	14,519
10	U	12,943

THE 10 LETTERS OF THE ALPHABET WITH FEWEST ENTRIES IN THE OXFORD ENGLISH DICTIONARY

	Letter	Entries
1	X	152
2	Z	733
3	Q	1,824
4	Y	2,298
5	J	2,326
6	K	3,491
7	V	5,430
8	N	5,933
9	O	7,737
10	W	8,804

THE 10 MOST-QUOTED AUTHORS IN THE OXFORD ENGLISH DICTIONARY

Geoffrey Chaucer is fourth most-quoted author in the *Oxford English Dictionary* with 11,013 references.

Author	Dates	Approximate number of references*
1 William Shakespeare	1564–1616	29,142
2 Sir Walter Scott	1771–1832	15,732
3 John Milton	1608–74	12,000
4 Geoffrey Chaucer	c1343–1400	11,013
5 John Wyclif	c1330–84	10,776
6 William Caxton	c1422–91	9,553
7 John Dryden	1631–1700	8,777
8 Charles Dickens	1812–70	8,189
9 Philemon Holland	1552–1637	7,947
10 Alfred, Lord Tennyson	1809–92	6,680

These figures may not be absolutely precise because of variations in the way in which sources are quoted, where there is more than one example from the same author, etc.

THE 10 MOST-QUOTED SOURCES IN THE OXFORD ENGLISH DICTIONARY

Source	Approximate number of references*
1 *The Times*	19,098
2 *Cursor Mundi*	11,035**
3 *Encyclopaedia Britannica*	10,102
4 *Daily News*	9,650
5 *Nature*	9,150
6 *Transactions of the Philological Society*	8,972
7 *Chronicle*	8,550
8 *Westminster Gazette*	7,478
9 *History of England*	7,180
10 *Listener*	7,139

These figures may not be absolutely precise because of variations in the way in which source books and journals are quoted, where there is more than one example from the same source, etc.

**Cursor Mundi *is a long fourteenth-century Northumbrian poem which is extensively cited for early uses of English words.*

References to Daily News, Chronicle *and* History of England *may include several different works with similar titles.*

ABOVE LEFT William Shakespeare heads the list with 29,142 quotations in the *Oxford English Dictionary*.
LEFT Its 10,102 references place *Encyclopaedia Britannica* as third most-quoted work in the *Oxford English Dictionary*.

THE 10 MOST EXPENSIVE BOOKS AND MANUSCRIPTS EVER SOLD AT AUCTION

	Price (£)
1 The Gospels of Henry the Lion, c1173–75 Sotheby's, London, 6 December 1983	7,400,000
The most expensive manuscript, book or work of art other than a painting ever sold.	
2 The Gutenberg Bible, 1455 Christie's, New York, 22 October 1987	2,934,131
One of the first books ever printed, by Johann Gutenberg and Johann Fust in 1455, it holds the record for the most expensive printed book.	
3 Autograph manuscript of nine symphonies by Wolfgang Amadeus Mozart, c1773–74 Sotheby's, London, 22 May 1987	2,350,000
The record for a music manuscript and for any post-medieval manuscript.	
4 John James Audubon's *The Birds of America*, 1827–38 Sotheby's, New York, 6 June 1989	2,292,993
The record for any natural history book.	
5 The Bible in Hebrew, a manuscript written in Iraq, Syria or Babylon in the 9th or 10th century Sotheby's, London, 5 December 1989	1,850,000
The record for any Hebrew manuscript.	
6 The Monypenny Breviary, illuminated manuscript, c1490–95 Sotheby's, London, 19 June 1989	1,700,000
7 The Hours and Psalter of Elizabeth de Bohun, Countess of Northampton, c1340–45 Sotheby's, London, 21 June 1988	1,400,000
The record for any English manuscript.	
8 The Gospels of St Hubert, c860–80 Sotheby's, London, 26 November 1985	1,300,000
The record for any French manuscript.	
9 Life of Thomas Becket, attributed to Matthew Paris, c1230–40 Sotheby's, London, 24 June 1986	1,250,000
The record for any 13th-century manuscript.	
10 The Hours of Albrecht of Brandenburg, c1522–23 Sotheby's, London, 21 June 1988	1,100,000
The record for any Flemish manuscript.	

Franz Kafka's manuscript of *The Trial*, sold at Sotheby's, London, on 17 November 1988 for £1,000,000, holds the record for any modern literary manuscript.

The 1455 *Gutenberg Bible*, with printed text and hand-drawn illuminations, is the most expensive printed book ever sold at auction.

THE FIRST 10 POETS LAUREATE

Poet (dates)	Period of office
1 John Dryden (1631–1700)	1670–88
2 Thomas Shadwell (c1642–92)	1689–92
3 Nahum Tate (1652–1715)	1692–1715
4 Nicholas Rowe (1674–1718)	1715–18
5 Rev Laurence Eusden (1688–1730)	1718–30
6 Colley Cibber (1671–1757)	1730–57
7 William Whitehead (1715–85)	1757–85
8 Rev Thomas Warton (1728–90)	1785–90
9 Henry James Pye (1745–1813)	1790–1813
10 Robert Southey (1774–1843)	1813–43

The role of 'royal versifier' dates back to Geoffrey Chaucer in the fourteenth century, and perhaps even earlier. He was followed by other court-appointed poets including Ben Jonson (c1572–1637) who served from 1619–37 and Sir William D'Avenant (1606–68) from 1638–68, but none was actually called 'Poet Laureate' until Dryden.

The principal function of the poet laureate is to write odes to celebrate royal birthdays, marriages and important state occasions. They are under no obligation to do so, and many of them have done it so badly that they have been ridiculed for their poor 'instant' verses.

Poets laureate, who are appointed by the Prime Minister, remain in office until their deaths (although Dryden and Tate were dismissed). The successors of the first 10, some memorable, others completely forgotten, included in the nineteenth century William Wordsworth and Alfred, Lord Tennyson, and in the twentieth John Masefield, Cecil Day Lewis and Sir John Betjeman, who was followed in 1984 by the present incumbent, Ted Hughes.

They receive a salary of £70 per annum – unchanged since the seventeenth century. Charles I added to this a gift of a 'tierce [equivalent to 42 gallons] of canary wine', which was presented annually until 1800 when it was replaced by a £27 honorarium. When Sir John Betjeman became poet laureate, this sum was converted back to wine to this value – which today is a good deal less than 42 gallons.

John Dryden, regarded as the first Poet Laureate.

THE TOP 10 LITERARY PRIZES AND AWARDS IN THE UK

	Prize/award	Category	Total value (£)
1	Eric Gregory Award	For poets under 30	30,000
2	NCR Book Award for non-fiction	Best non-fiction book: First prize £25,000 + three prizes of £1,500	29,500
3	Whitbread Book of the Year	Books by residents of UK or Ireland: First prize £20,000 + five other prizes of £1,500	27,500
4	Betty Trask Awards	First novel of a traditional or romantic nature: Total value	25,000
5=	Booker Prize	Best novel in English	20,000
5=	Sunday Express Book of the Year	Fiction	20,000
7=	Commonwealth Writers' Prize	A work of fiction by a Commonwealth citizen: First prize £10,000 + £1,000 to runner-up and four regional prizes of £1,000 each	15,000
7=	Wolfson Literary Awards for History and Biography	Historical works: Two prizes total	15,000
7=	Radio Times Drama Award	Work for Radio or TV: Two prizes of £7,500	15,000
10=	Ian St James Prize	Unpublished short stories	11,000
10=	Thomas Cook Travel Book Awards	Best travel book: First prize £7,500 + £2,500 for best guide book and £1,000 for best illustrated book	11,000

Although the Booker Prize attracts the most publicity, there are many other valuable literary prizes awarded in the UK. Those that are not exclusively British, and writing bursaries awarded to enable writers to survive while working on their books, are not included. In addition, there are many other awards of £10,000 or less – some for as little as £100 or just a certificate or gift, such as the bronze eggs given to winners of the Mother Goose Award or the diamond dagger received by Crime Writers' Association Award winners. The qualifications for entry for some prizes are very specialized, such as the Sagittarius Prize for a first novel by an author aged over 60 or the Pro Dogs Open Creative Writing Competition for the best short story or poem about a dog. Irish citizens are in a more privileged position than UK residents, as they alone are eligible for the biggest literary award in the British Isles – the IR£50,000 Guinness Peat Aviation Book Award.

THE 10 BESTSELLING BOOKS OF ALL TIME

It is extremely difficult to establish precise sales even of contemporary books, and virtually impossible to do so with books published long ago. The publication of variant editions, translations and pirated copies all affect the global picture, and few publishers or authors are willing to expose their royalty statements to public scrutiny. As a result, this Top 10 list offers no more than the 'best guess' at the great bestsellers of the past, and it may well be that there are other books with a valid claim to a place on it.

There are problems of definition: what, for example, is the status of a book that is revised and re-issued annually, and what precisely is a 'book'? A UNESCO conference in 1950 decided it was 'a non-periodical literary publication containing 49 or more pages, not counting the covers' (which is baffling in itself, since all publications have to contain an even number of pages, while, according to this criterion, a 32-page children's book would not be regarded as a book at all!). If *Old Moore's Almanac* is classed as a book rather than a periodical or a pamphlet, it would appear high on the list. Having been published annually since 1697, its total sales to date are believed to be well over 100,000,000. Numerous translations of books by Marx, Lenin and Stalin have probably sold more than 20,000,000 copies, and among runners-up that are known to have sold in excess of 10,000,000 copies are a number of bestselling American publications including the *Better Homes and Gardens Cook Book* (first published in 1930), *Webster's New World Dictionary of the American Language*, *Betty Crocker's Cookbook* (1950), Mario Puzo's *The Godfather* (1969), William Blatty's *The Exorcist* (1971), Harper Lee's *To Kill a Mockingbird* (1960), *The Pocket Atlas* (1917), and Grace Metalious's *Peyton Place* (1956).

Nearly 107,000,000 copies of the Jehovah's Witness tract, *The Truth That Leads to Eternal Life*, first published in 1968, are believed to have been distributed, usually in return for a donation to the sect, but as they were not sold through bookshops, it does not technically rank as a 'bestseller'.

1 *The Bible*
3,000,000,000

No one really knows how many copies of the Bible have been printed, sold or distributed. The Bible Society's attempt to calculate the number printed between 1816 and 1975 produced the figure of 2,458,000,000. It is now thought to be closer to 3,000,000,000 in over 300 languages. Whatever the precise figure, it is by far the bestselling book of all time.

2 *Quotations from the Works of Mao Tse-tung*
800,000,000

Chairman Mao's 'Little Red Book' could scarcely fail to become a bestseller: between the years 1966 and 1971, it was compulsory for every Chinese adult to own a copy. It was both sold and distributed to the people of China – though what proportion voluntarily bought it must remain open to question.

3 *American Spelling Book* by Noah Webster
100,000,000

First published in 1783, this reference book by American man of letters Noah Webster (1758–1843) – of *Webster's Dictionary* fame – remained a bestseller throughout the nineteenth century.

4 *The Guinness Book of Records*
61,000,000 +

First published in 1955, the *Guinness Book of Records* stands out as the greatest contemporary publishing achievement. In the UK there have now been 31 annual editions, as well as numerous foreign language editions.

5 *The McGuffey Readers* by William Holmes McGuffey
60,000,000

Published in numerous editions from 1853, some authorities have put the total sales of these educational textbooks, originally compiled by American anthologist William Holmes McGuffey (1800–73), as high as 122,000,000. It has also been claimed that 60,000,000 copies of the 1879 edition were printed, but as this is some 10,000,000 more than the entire population of the USA at the time, the publishers must have been extremely optimistic about its success.

6 *A Message to Garcia* by Elbert Hubbard
40–50,000,000

Now forgotten, Hubbard's polemic on the subject of labour relations was published in 1899 and within a few years had achieved these phenomenal sales largely because many American employers purchased bulk supplies to distribute to their employees. The literary career of Elbert Hubbard (1856–1915) was cut short in 1915 when he went down with the *Lusitania*, but even in death he was a record-breaker: his posthumous *My Philosophy* (1916) was published in the largest-ever 'limited edition' of 9,983 copies!

7 *The Commonsense Book of Baby and Child Care* by Benjamin Spock
39,200,000

Dr Spock's 1946 manual became the bible of infant care for subsequent generations of parents.

8 *World Almanac*
36,000,000 +

Having been published annually since 1868 (with a break from 1876 to 1886), this wide-ranging reference book has remained a bestseller ever since.

9 *Valley of the Dolls* by Jacqueline Susann
28,712,000 +

This racy tale of sex, violence and drugs by Jacqueline Susann (1921–74), first published in 1966, is perhaps surprisingly the world's bestselling novel.

10 *In His Steps: 'What Would Jesus Do?'* by Rev Charles Monroe Sheldon
28,500,000

Though virtually unknown today, Charles Sheldon (1857–1946) achieved fame and fortune with this 1896 religious treatise.

Though now discredited, Chairman Mao's 'Little Red Book' became the world's bestseller after the Bible.

THE 10 BESTSELLING BOOKS OF THE 1980s IN THE UK

	Title	Author	Pub.	Estimated sales
1	*The Secret Diary of Adrian Mole, Aged 13¾*	Sue Townsend	1982/83	3,200,000
2	*Kane and Abel*	Jeffrey Archer	1981	3,000,000
3	*F-Plan Diet*	Audrey Eyton	1982	2,300,000
4	*The Restaurant at the End of the Universe*	Douglas Adams	1980	2,200,000
5	*The House Plant Expert*	Dr David Hessayon	1980	2,100,000
6	*A Woman of Substance*	Barbara Taylor Bradford	1981	2,000,000
7	*Lace*	Shirley Conran	1983	1,800,000
8 =	*The Prodigal Daughter*	Jeffrey Archer	1983	1,700,000
8 =	*The Tree and Shrub Expert*	Dr David Hessayon	1983	1,700,000
10	*Hollywood Wives*	Jackie Collins	1984	1,600,000

Barbara Taylor Bradford, whose *A Woman of Substance* was one of the bestselling books of the 1980s.

This list is based on UK sales figures estimated by Bookwatch, the book trade monitoring organization, and are not official publishers' figures, which are virtually impossible to obtain. All are for paperback sales, with the exception of *The Secret Diary of Adrian Mole, Aged 13¾*, which combines hardback (published 1982) and paperback (1983) sales (in general, hardback sales even of 'bestselling' novels are relatively small compared with those of paperback editions). In addition to these sales, many more copies of the hardback editions would have been sold through book clubs, and further income generated from the sale of extracts in newspapers and magazines, foreign editions, and in some instances TV, radio and film rights and 'merchandising', covering everything from T-shirts to videos.

Appearances are cumulative (as at 11 March 1990), but not necessarily consecutive. Two dates indicate hardback and paperback appearances, which are combined in the totals.

THE 10 BOOKS LONGEST IN THE UK TOP 10 DURING THE 1980s

	Title	Author	Pub.	Total weeks in Top 10
1	*The Secret Diary of Adrian Mole, Aged 13¾*	Sue Townsend	1982/83	139
2	*Delia Smith's Complete Cookery Course*	Delia Smith	1982	98*
3	*The Complete Yes Minister*	Jonathan Lynn and Anthony Jay	1984	85
4	*The Growing Pains of Adrian Mole*	Sue Townsend	1984/85	83
5	*Rosemary Conley's Hip and Thigh Diet*	Rosemary Conley	1988	82
6	*A Brief History of Time*	Stephen Hawking	1988	81
7	*Chronicle of the 20th Century*	Derrik Mercer (ed.)	1988	65
8	*F-Plan Diet*	Audrey Eyton	1982	58
9	*Rosemary Conley's Complete Hip and Thigh Diet*	Rosemary Conley	1989	57
10	*The Official Sloane Ranger Handbook*	Ann Barr and Peter York	1982	53

Enlarged version has appeared 17 times, and parts of the course have appeared separately as paperbacks.

THE 10 BOOKS WITH MOST APPEARANCES AT NO.1 IN THE UK

This Top 10 list is based on the total number of appearances at No.1 since the *Sunday Times* bestseller lists were first published in April 1974.

*Collins edition; the Reader's Digest version also had two appearances at No.1.
**Hardback edition.
†Paperback edition.

	Title	Author	Pub.	Appearances at No.1
1	The Country Diary of an Edwardian Lady	Edith Holden	1977	66
2	Life on Earth	David Attenborough	1979	40*
3	The Growing Pains of Adrian Mole	Sue Townsend	1984	39**
4	Watership Down	Richard Adams	1974	30
5 =	The Silmarillion	J. R. R. Tolkien	1977	26
5 =	The Secret Diary of Adrian Mole, Aged 13¾	Sue Townsend	1983	26†
7	A Brief History of Time	Stephen Hawking	1988	23
8	Chronicle of the 20th Century	Derrik Mercer (ed.)	1988	22
9 =	The Ascent of Man	Jacob Bronowski	1974	19
9 =	The Human Factor	Graham Greene	1978	19

Publicity-shy Michael Palin and his 1989 bestseller.

THE 10 BESTSELLING HARDBACK BOOKS OF 1989 IN THE UK

	Title	Author	Estimated sales*
1	The Guinness Book of Records	Donald McFarlan (ed.)	250,000
2	Chronicle of the 20th Century	Derrik Mercer (ed.)	230,000
3	Around the World in 80 Days	Michael Palin	180,000
4	A Brief History of Time	Stephen Hawking	165,000
5	The Satanic Verses	Salman Rushdie	100,000
6	Hugh Johnson's Pocket Wine Book 1989	Hugh Johnson	90,000
7	The Russia House	John Le Carré	80,000
8	The Negotiator	Frederick Forsyth	67,000
9	Miller's Antique Price Guide 1990	Judith and Martin Miller	60,000
10	A Time to Die	Wilbur Smith	55,000

*Excluding book club sales.

THE TOP 10 PAPERBACK BOOKS OF 1989 IN THE UK

	Title	Author	Estimated sales
1	*Rivals*	Jilly Cooper	600,000
2	*To Be the Best*	Barbara Taylor Bradford	580,000
3	*A Twist in the Tale*	Jeffrey Archer	550,000
4	*Rosemary Conley's Hip and Thigh Diet*	Rosemary Conley	500,000
5	*Rock Star*	Jackie Collins	450,000
6	*The BBC Diet*	Barry Lynch	350,000
7	*Callanetics*	Callan Pinckney	320,000
8	*The Shell Seekers*	Rosamunde Pilcher	315,000
9	*Stark*	Ben Elton	310,000
10	*Haunted*	James Herbert	300,000

Seen here with Christopher Robin, A. A. Milne's Winnie the Pooh remains a best-seller after over 60 years.

Patrick Branwell Brontë's portrait of his sister Emily Brontë, c1833. Her novel *Wuthering Heights* is the bestselling Penguin Classic.

THE 10 BESTSELLING PENGUIN CLASSICS

	Author	Book
1	Emily Brontë	*Wuthering Heights*
2	Charles Dickens	*Hard Times*
3	Jane Austen	*Pride and Prejudice*
4	Charlotte Brontë	*Jane Eyre*
5	Charles Dickens	*Great Expectations*
6	Thomas Hardy	*Tess of the D'Urbervilles*
7	Thomas Hardy	*The Mayor of Casterbridge*
8	Thomas Hardy	*Far from the Madding Crowd*
9	Jane Austen	*Emma*
10	Jane Austen	*Mansfield Park*

The Penguin Classics series was started in 1944 by E. V. Rieu, whose own translation of Homer's *Odyssey*, the first title published, has sold over 1,000,000 copies. The Top 10 of the now huge list of books in print is dominated by nineteenth-century novels – to some extent reflecting their use as 'set books' in English literature courses – but the same authors, with others such as Joseph Conrad and E. M. Forster, also predominate in the Top 50, with only a few earlier writers making an appearance, among them Geoffrey Chaucer, Jonathan Swift, John Bunyan and Daniel Defoe.

THE 10 BESTSELLING CHILDREN'S HARDBACKS OF 1989*

Title	Author
1 Rhyme Stew	Roald Dahl
2 Batman: Funhouse of Fear	Constance Lynch
3 Matilda	Roald Dahl
4 The Jolly Postman	Janet and Allan Ahlberg
5 Budgie the Little Helicopter	HRH The Duchess of York
6 The Snowman	Raymond Briggs
7 The Very Hungry Caterpillar	Eric Carle
8 The Tale of Peter Rabbit	Beatrix Potter
9 Winnie the Pooh	A.A. Milne
10 Peace at Last	Jill Murphy

*Based on number of appearances in Bookwatch's weekly lists.

THE 10 BESTSELLING CHILDREN'S PAPERBACKS OF 1989*

Title	Author
1 Matilda	Roald Dahl
2 The Lion, the Witch and the Wardrobe	C.S. Lewis
3 The Witches	Roald Dahl
4 Please Mrs Butler	Allan Ahlberg
5 Charlie and the Chocolate Factory	Roald Dahl
6 A Bad Spell for the Worst Witch	Jill Murphy
7 Hodgeheg	Dick King-Smith
8 Gargling with Jelly	Brian Patten
9 Five Minutes Peace	Jill Murphy
10 Woof!	Allan Ahlberg

Newspaper	Average daily sale (Jul to Dec 1989)
1 *The Sun*	4,016,787
2 *Daily Mirror/ Daily Record* (Scotland)	3,862,916
3 *Daily Mail*	1,723,385
4 *Daily Express*	1,574,978
5 *Daily Telegraph*	1,102,609
6 *Daily Star*	891,405
7 *Today*	589,235
8 *The Guardian*	430,962
9 *The Times*	428,162
10 *The Independent*	411,953

BELOW The *London Standard*, the UK's bestselling regional newspaper.

ABOVE An early riser buys his daily papers.

The 11th bestselling daily newspaper in Great Britain is the *Financial Times*, with total average worldwide daily sales during this period of 287,885 copies (including 90,517 copies of editions published in Frankfurt and New York). The total sales of all the 'quality' daily newspapers (*Daily Telegraph, Guardian, The Times, Independent* and *Financial Times*) are more than 1,000,000 less than the *Daily Mirror*.

THE TOP 10 UK REGIONAL NEWSPAPERS

	Newspaper	Average sales per issue (Jul to Dec 1989)
1	*London Standard*	467,582
2	*Manchester Evening News*	265,553
3	*Wolverhampton Express & Star*	238,557
4	*Birmingham Evening Mail*	216,527
5	*Liverpool Echo**	200,516
6	*Glasgow Evening Times*	172,455
7	*Birmingham Sunday Mercury*	149,607
8	*Newcastle Evening Chronicle*	139,642
9	*Leicester Mercury*	139,357
10	*Yorkshire Evening Post* (Leeds)	138,887

*Monday to Friday (Saturday = 180,418).

TOP Britain's second bestselling Sunday paper, the *Sunday Mirror*, and celebrity readership.

THE TOP 10 BRITISH NATIONAL SUNDAY NEWSPAPERS

	Newspaper	Average sales per issue (Jul to Dec 1989)
1	*News of the World*	5,185,742
2	*Sunday Mirror*	2,925,540
3	*The People*	2,641,973
4	*Mail on Sunday*	1,892,158
5	*Sunday Express*	1,854,492
6	*Sunday Times*	1,248,027
7	*Observer*	639,294
8	*Sunday Telegraph*	632,923
9	*Sunday Sport*	472,489*
10	*Sunday Correspondent*	309,857**

*Average for Jul to Nov (Dec not yet available).
**Average for Oct to Dec (first published 17 September 1989).

All the national Sunday newspapers lost circulation during this period as compared with the same period in 1988.

THE TOP 10 CONSUMERS OF NEWSPRINT

Country	Consumption per inhabitant		
	kg	lb	oz
1 USA	54.043	119	2
2 Denmark	44.928	99	1
3 New Zealand	44.475	98	1
4 Switzerland	44.041	97	1
5 Finland	38.790	85	8
6 Australia	36.828	81	3
7 Canada	34.920	77	0
8 Austria	33.022	72	13
9 Netherlands	31.979	70	8
10 UK	30.031	66	3

National consumption of newsprint – the cheap wood-pulp paper used for printing newspapers – provides a measure of the extent of newspaper sales in the Top 10 countries.

THE TOP 10 DAILY NEWSPAPER PUBLISHERS

Country	No. of daily newspapers	Average daily circulation
1 USSR*	2,495	148,569,000
2 Japan	124	68,653,000
3 USA	1,657	62,502,000
4 China	73	37,860,000
5 UK	105	23,913,000
6 India	1,978	21,857,000
7 West Germany	318	20,987,000
8 France	92	10,670,000
9 Mexico	308	10,356,000
10 East Germany	39	9,467,000

*Including Byelorussian SSR and Ukrainian SSR.

This list ranks the Top 10 countries according to average total daily circulation. However, if the table is arranged by total sales of daily newspapers per 1,000 inhabitants, the result is somewhat different:

Country	Sales per 1,000 inhabitants
1 East Germany	570
2 Japan	566
3 Finland	543
4 Sweden	534
5 Norway	530
6 Switzerland	500
7 Liechtenstein	486
8 Iceland	469
9 USSR*	442
10 UK	421

*Excluding Byelorussian SSR and Ukrainian SSR.

One curious anomaly is that of the Vatican City's one newspaper, *l'Osservatore Romano*, of which an average of 70,000 copies are printed. Since the population of the Vatican is only about 1,000, it implies a daily sale of 70,000 per 1,000, or 70 copies per head! In fact, of course, most of them are sent outside the Holy See.

Printers at the *Moscow Evening News*, just one of the USSR's world record 2,495 daily papers.

THE 10 BESTSELLING BRITISH COMICS OF ALL TIME

1 *Beano* (1938–)

2 *Comic Cuts* (1890–1953)

3 *Dandy* (1937–)

4 *Eagle* (1950–69; revived 1982)

5 *Film Fun* (1920–62)

6 *Illustrated Chips* (1890–1953)

7 *Mickey Mouse Weekly* (1936–57)

8 *Radio Fun* (1938–61)

9 *Rainbow* (1914–56)

10 *School Friend* (1950–65)

Accurate circulation figures for British comics are hard to come by, but information supplied by the Association of Comics Enthusiasts indicates that all 10 comics listed (in alphabetical order) achieved very high circulation figures – *Eagle, Film Fun, Rainbow* and *School Friend* all hitting 1,000,000 at peak.

THE 10 MOST VALUABLE AMERICAN COMICS

Comic	Value	
	$	£
1= *Action Comics* No. 1 Published in June 1938, the first issue of *Action Comics* contained the original appearance of Superman.	32,500	19,345
1= *Detective Comics* No. 27 Issued in May 1939, it is prized as the first comic to feature Batman.	32,500	19,345
3 *Marvel Comics* No. 1 The Human Torch and other heroes were first introduced in the issue dated November 1939.	27,500	16,369
4 *Superman* No. 1 The first comic devoted to Superman, it reprinted the original *Action Comics* story and was published in summer 1939.	26,000	15,476
5 *Whiz Comics* No. 1 Published in February 1940 – and confusingly numbered '2' – it was the first comic to feature Captain Marvel.	18,200	10,833
6 *Batman* No. 1 Published in spring 1940.	14,500	8,631
7 *Detective Comics* No. 1 Published in March 1937, it was the first in a long running series.	11,400	6,786
8 *All American Comics* No. 16 The Green Lantern made his debut in this issue, dated July 1940.	10,000	5,952
9 *More Fun Comics* No. 52 Its February 1940 publication was notable for the first appearance of The Spectre.	9,600	5,714
10 *Captain America* No. 1 Published in March 1941, this was the original comic in which Captain America appeared.	9,000	5,357

Based on information supplied by the Association of Comics Enthusiasts.

All the most expensive comic books in the Top 10 come from the so-called 'Golden Age' (1938–1945) and to command these very high prices would have to be in Very Fine or Near Mint condition. A complete run of a comic such as *Action Comics* that includes the highly-prized first issue may be valued at almost $200,000.

Comic culture: *Dandy* and *Beano* are two of the bestselling British comics of all time – and they remain firm favourites today.

THE TOP 10 D.C. THOMSON COMICS AND CHILDREN'S MAGAZINES

Comic	First issue
1 Beano	30 July 1938
2 Dandy	4 December 1937
3 Jackie	11 January 1964
4 Bunty	14 January 1958
5 Hi	4 December 1988
6 Blue Jeans	22 January 1977
7 Mandy	21 January 1967
8 Beezer	21 January 1956
9 Judy	16 January 1960
10 Topper	7 February 1953

D.C. Thomson & Co of Dundee began publishing comics in the 1920s. Their boys' adventure papers, *Rover* (1922–61), *Wizard* (1922–63) and *Hotspur* (1933–59), presented footballers and other working-class heroes with whom their audiences could identify more readily than the public school chaps featured in rival publications such as *The Boy's Own Paper* (1879–1967) and *Magnet* (1908–40), but by the early 1960s changing fashions and the rise of popular culture based on television and pop music ousted this style of publication. D.C. Thomson's old-established humour favourites are still going strong, however, and their two pre-war comics are still their bestsellers: *Dandy*, first published in 1937 and featuring Desperate Dan and Korky the Cat, and *Beano*, dating from 1938, which introduced its best-known character, Dennis the Menace, in 1951.

THE 10 BESTSELLING BRITISH CHILDREN'S COMICS AND MAGAZINES

1 Beano

2 Dandy

3 Look In

4 2000 AD

5 Hi

6 Thomas the Tank Engine and Friends

7 The Real Ghostbusters

8 My Little Pony

9 Roy of the Rovers

10 Disney Magazine

THE TOP 10 MAGAZINES IN THE UK

Magazine	Average sale per issue
1 Radio Times	2,961,137
2 TV Times	2,825,292
3 Reader's Digest	1,609,713
4 Woman's Weekly	1,196,797
5 Woman's Own	931,295
6 Woman	886,888
7 Best	885,657
8 Prima	853,329
9 Smash Hits	786,886
10 Viz	680,593

Music

THE 10 BESTSELLING ELVIS PRESLEY SINGLES IN THE UK

	Song	Year
1	It's Now Or Never	1960
2	Jailhouse Rock	1958
3	Are You Lonesome Tonight?	1961
4	Wooden Heart	1961
5	Return To Sender	1962
6	Can't Help Falling In Love	1962
7	The Wonder Of You	1970
8	Surrender	1961
9	Way Down	1977
10	All Shook Up	1957

Elvis Presley attained his peak sales in the UK not in his 1950s heyday, but shortly after he left the army (5 March 1960). 'It's Now Or Never' was his only million-seller in the UK, although all the singles in the Top 10 registered sales in excess of 600,000 and between them accounted for a total of 46 weeks at the top of the UK singles chart.

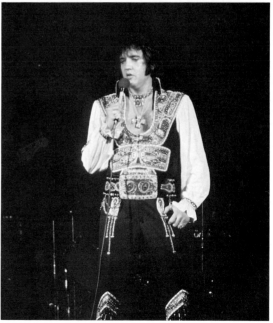

Elvis Presley's Top 10 UK chart hits spanned a period of almost 20 years.

THE 10 BESTSELLING CLIFF RICHARD SINGLES WORLDWIDE

	Song	Year
1	We Don't Talk Anymore	1979
2	The Young Ones	1962
3	Devil Woman	1976
4	Congratulations	1968
5	The Next Time/Bachelor Boy	1962
6	Living Doll	1959
7	Summer Holiday	1963
8	Please Don't Tease	1960
9	Travellin' Light/Dynamite	1959
10	Living Doll (re-released, with 'accompaniment' by stars of BBC TV series, 'The Young Ones')	1986

Cliff Richard (born 14 October 1940, Lucknow, India, real name Harry Roger Webb) had his first chart hit in 1958 with 'Move It'. Since then, he has habitually achieved several hits virtually every year, the five most successful of which have sold in excess of 2,000,000 records with 'We Don't Talk Anymore' clocking up sales of 2,500,000.

The Beatles, hitmakers extraordinaires in the UK and globally.

THE TOP 10 BEATLES SINGLES IN THE UK

1	She Loves You
2	I Want To Hold Your Hand
3	Can't Buy Me Love
4	I Feel Fine
5	We Can Work It Out
6	Help!
7	Hey Jude
8	A Hard Day's Night
9	From Me To You
10	Hello Goodbye

UK sales of Beatles singles range from almost 2,000,000 for 'She Loves You' to less than 700,000 for 'Hello Goodbye'. The UK-only list differs in some respects from the global list published in the last edition of *The Top 10 of Everything*, which itself may be subject to revision, with 'I Want To Hold Your Hand' now considered to be The Beatles' bestselling single worldwide.

LEFT Cliff Richard has achieved Top 10 hits for over 30 years.

RIGHT Mick Jagger and Keith Richards, still rolling after two decades of hit singles.

THE TOP 10 ROLLING STONES SINGLES IN THE UK

	Song	Year
1	Honky Tonk Women	1969
2	The Last Time	1965
3	It's All Over Now	1964
4	(I Can't Get No) Satisfaction	1965
5	Get Off Of My Cloud	1965
6	Paint It Black	1966
7	Jumpin' Jack Flash	1968
8	Miss You	1978
9	Little Red Rooster	1964
10	Brown Sugar	1971

All these were No. 1 hits except 'Miss You' (highest position 3) and 'Brown Sugar' (2).

THE 10 ALL-TIME BESTSELLING MOTOWN SINGLES IN THE UK

	Song	Artist	Release
1	I Just Called To Say I Love You	Stevie Wonder	1984
2	I Heard It Through The Grapevine	Marvin Gaye	1969
3	Hello	Lionel Richie	1984
4	Three Times A Lady	The Commodores	1978
5	Reach Out, I'll Be There	The Four Tops	1966
6	One Day In Your Life	Michael Jackson	1981
7	I'm Still Waiting	Diana Ross	1971
8	Baby Love	The Supremes	1964
9	I Want You Back	Jackson Five	1970
10	Tears Of A Clown	Smokey Robinson and the Miracles	1970

Stevie Wonder's song, 'I Just Called To Say I Love You', came from the film, *The Woman In Red*, and won an Academy Award for Best Song. The single sold almost 1,800,000 copies in the UK, making it one of the UK's all-time bestselling singles. Michael Jackson's 'One Day In Your Life' was recorded on the Motown label and not released until long after he had left, when it became his biggest-selling Motown single in the UK.

TOP Stevie Wonder heads the Motown Top 10.

THE TOP 10 ONE-HIT WONDERS

	Song	Artist	Year	Weeks at No. 1
1	Sugar Sugar	Archies	1969	8
2	When	Kalin Twins	1958	5
3	Eye Level	Simon Park Orchestra	1973	4
4=	Tell Laura I Love Her	Ricky Valance	1960	3
4=	Michelle	Overlanders	1966	3
4=	In The Year 2525	Zager and Evans	1969	3
4=	Wand'rin' Star	Lee Marvin	1970	3
4=	Woodstock	Matthews Southern Comfort	1970	3
4=	Grandad	Clive Dunn	1971	3
4=	Matchstalk Men And Matchstalk Cats And Dogs	Brian and Michael	1978	3
4=	One Day At A Time	Lena Martell	1979	3
4=	Theme From M*A*S*H	Mash	1980	3
4=	Shaddap You Face	Joe Dolce	1981	3
4=	Every Loser Wins	Nick Berry	1986	3
4=	First Time	Robin Beck	1988	3

These are the 10 (15, in fact!) singles that became No. 1 hits in the UK ranked according to how long they remained in that slot – and with the proviso that the artist never again had a record in the charts at any position. They represent fewer than half the one-hit wonders, since there are even more acts that achieved momentary fame by remaining at No.1 for just one or two weeks, among them B. Bumble and the Stingers: 'Nut Rocker' (1962), Crazy World of Arthur Brown: 'Fire' (1968), Jane Birkin and Serge Gainsbourg: 'Je T'Aime.. Moi Non Plus' (1969), Norman Greenbaum: 'Spirit In The Sky' (1970), Althia and Donna: 'Up Town Top Ranking' (1977), Anita Ward: 'Ring My Bell' (1979), St Winifred's School Choir: 'There's No One Quite Like Grandma' (1980) and Timelords: 'Doctorin' The Tardis' (1988). Of course, any member of the One-Hit Wonder Club who succeeds in having a *second* hit is immediately expelled from this august body.

OPPOSITE Mr Acker Bilk's 'Stranger On The Shore' remains the top instrumental single in the UK.

THE 10 MOST SUCCESSFUL FOREIGN-LANGUAGE SINGLES IN THE UK

	Song	Artist	Year	Language
1	Je T'Aime... Moi Non Plus	Jane Birkin and Serge Gainsbourg	1969	French
2	Rock Me Amadeus	Falco	1986	German
3	Begin The Beguine	Julio Iglesias	1981	Spanish
4	Chanson D'Amour	Manhattan Transfer	1977	French
5	La Bamba	Los Lobos	1987	Spanish
6	Come Prima/Volare	Marino Marini	1958	Italian
7	Joe Le Taxi	Vanessa Paradis	1988	French
8	Lambada	Kaoma	1989	Portuguese
9	Dominique	Singing Nun	1963	French
10	Voyage Voyage	Desireless	1987/88	French

Although foreign-language hits are fairly rare in the UK, as in most English-speaking markets, the Top 5 in this list all reached No. 1 in the UK singles chart, and the rest made the Top 10. Half of them are sung in French, by far the most familiar foreign language to infiltrate the UK market. There are also several other notable chart hits containing passages sung in French, such as the Overlanders' cover version of The Beatles' 'Michelle' (No. 1 in 1966) and Bill Wyman's 'Franglais' '(Si Si) Je Suis Un Rock Star' (No. 14 in 1981).

ABOVE Jane Birkin and Serge Gainsbourg gasped their way through 'Je T'Aime', the UK's most successful foreign language single.

'Tell Laura I Love Her' was Ricky Valance's only hit.

THE TOP 10 INSTRUMENTAL SINGLES OF ALL TIME IN THE UK

	Song	Year	Artist
1	Stranger On The Shore	1961	Mr Acker Bilk
2	Albatross	1968	Fleetwood Mac
3	Wonderful Land	1962	The Shadows
4	Amazing Grace	1972	Royal Scots Dragoon Guards
5	Floral Dance	1977	Brighouse and Rastrick Brass Band
6	Eye Level	1972–74	Simon Park Orchestra
7	Apache	1960	The Shadows
8	Birdie Song	1981	The Tweets
9	Fanfare For The Common Man	1977	Emerson, Lake and Palmer
10	The Good The Bad And The Ugly	1968	Hugo Montenegro

THE 10 BESTSELLING ORIGINAL SOUNDTRACK ALBUMS IN THE UK

1 Saturday Night Fever
2 Grease
3 The Sound Of Music
4 Fame
5 That'll Be The Day
6 A Star Is Born
7 South Pacific
8 West Side Story
9 Dirty Dancing
10 Blues Brothers

Although it never made No. 1, 'Stranger On The Shore' spent over a year in the UK charts. The Simon Park Orchestra, Brighouse and Rastrick Brass Band, Emerson, Lake and Palmer, and The Tweets never had another single in the charts, before or after. In 1973 'Eye Level' was the last instrumental No. 1 record.

THE 10 BESTSELLING EUROVISION WINNERS IN THE UK

	Song	Artist	Country represented	Year
1	Save Your Kisses For Me	Brotherhood Of Man	UK	1976
2	Puppet On A String	Sandie Shaw	UK	1967
3	Making Your Mind Up	Bucks Fizz	UK	1981
4	Waterloo	Abba	Sweden	1974
5	All Kinds Of Everything	Dana	Ireland	1970
6	What's Another Year	Johnny Logan	Ireland	1980
7	A Little Peace	Nicole	Germany	1982
8	Boom Bang-A-Bang	Lulu	UK	1969
9	Come What May	Vicky Leandros	Luxembourg	1972
10	Hold Me Now	Johnny Logan	Ireland	1987

A characteristically barefoot Sandie Shaw – Eurovision winner in 1967 with 'Puppet On A String'.

The top seven records all reached No. 1, as did 'Congratulations' by Cliff Richard, runner-up in the 1968 contest.

THE 10 ALL-TIME BESTSELLING SINGLES IN THE WORLD

	Song	Artist	Sales exceed
1	White Christmas	Bing Crosby	30,000,000
2	Rock Around The Clock	Bill Haley and his Comets	17,000,000
3	I Want To Hold Your Hand	The Beatles	12,000,000
4	It's Now Or Never	Elvis Presley	10,000,000
5 =	Hound Dog/ Don't Be Cruel	Elvis Presley	9,000,000
5 =	Diana	Paul Anka	9,000,000
7 =	Hey Jude	The Beatles	8,000,000
7 =	I'm A Believer	The Monkees	8,000,000
9 =	We Are The World	USA for Africa	7,000,000
9 =	Can't Buy Me Love	The Beatles	7,000,000

Global sales are notoriously difficult to calculate, particularly in countries outside the UK and USA and especially in the Far East. 'Worldwide' is thus usually taken to mean the known minimum 'western world' sales. Bing Crosby's 1942 record, 'White Christmas', is indisputably the all-time bestselling single, and the *song*, recorded by others and sold as sheet music, has also achieved such enormous sales that it would additionally appear in the No. 1 position in any list of bestselling songs.

THE 10 SINGLES THAT STAYED LONGEST IN THE UK CHARTS

	Song	Artist	First chart entry	Weeks in charts
1	My Way	Frank Sinatra	1969	122
2	Amazing Grace	Judy Collins	1970	67
3	Rock Around The Clock	Bill Haley and his Comets	1955	57
4	Release Me	Engelbert Humperdinck	1967	56
5	Stranger On The Shore	Mr Acker Bilk	1961	55
6	Relax!	Frankie Goes To Hollywood	1983	52
7	Blue Monday	New Order	1983	49
8	I Love You Because	Jim Reeves	1964	47
9	Let's Twist Again	Chubby Checker	1961	44
10	White Lines (Don't Do It)	Grandmaster Flash and Melle Mel	1983	43

THE 10 UK CHART SINGLES WITH THE LONGEST TITLES

	Title	Artist	Highest chart position	Year	No. of letters
1	I'm In Love With The Girl On A Certain Manchester Megastore Checkout Desk	Freshies	54	1981	60
2	If I Said You Had A Beautiful Body Would You Hold It Against Me?	Bellamy Brothers	3	1979	50
3	Gilly Gilly Ossenfeffer Katzenallen Bogen By The Sea	Max Bygraves	7	1954	45
4=	There's A Guy Works Down The Chipshop Swears He's Elvis	Kirsty MacColl	14	1981	44
4=	Have You Seen Your Mother Baby, Standing In The Shadow?	Rolling Stones	5	1966	44
6	When The Girl In Your Arms Is The Girl In Your Heart	Cliff Richard	3	1961	41
7	I'm Gonna Sit Right Down And Write Myself A Letter	Billy Williams	22	1957	40
8=	Loving You's A Dirty Job But Someone's Got To Do It	Bonnie Tyler	73	1985	39
8=	Itsy Bitsy Teeny Weeny Yellow Polka Dot Bikini	Brian Hyland	8	1960	39
8=	You Don't Have To Be In The Army To Fight In The War	Mungo Jerry	13	1971	39
8=	Two Pints Of Lager And A Packet Of Crisps Please	Splodgenessabounds	7	1980	39

This list includes only titles that do not contain words or phrases in brackets. It also includes only chart hits, and thus does not contain such gems as Fairport Convention's 171-letter album track, 'Sir B. McKenzie's Daughter's Lament for the 77th Mounted Lancers' Retreat from the Straits of Loch Knombe in the Year of Our Lord 1717, on the Occasion of the Announcement of her Marriage to the Laird of Kinleakie'. The shortest title of a chart record is Shirley Bassey's 'I' – although '(Who Have Nothing)' is often added as part of the title.

BELOW The Bellamy Brothers held their record for the longest chart title for less than two years.

THE TOP 10 SINGLES OF ALL TIME IN THE UK

	Song	Artist	Release
1	Do They Know It's Christmas?	Band Aid	1984
2	Mull Of Kintyre	Wings	1977
3	Rivers Of Babylon/Brown Girl In The Ring	Boney M	1978
4	She Loves You	The Beatles	1963
5	You're The One That I Want	John Travolta and Olivia Newton-John	1978
6	Relax!	Frankie Goes To Hollywood	1983
7	Mary's Boy Child/Oh My Lord	Boney M	1978
8	I Just Called To Say I Love You	Stevie Wonder	1984
9	I Want To Hold Your Hand	The Beatles	1963
10	Tears	Ken Dodd	1965

OPPOSITE Bill Haley's 'Rock Around The Clock' is beaten into second place in the list of all-time bestselling hit singles in the world by Bing Crosby's 'White Christmas'.

Sales of singles have steadily declined over the years and now account for only about nine per cent of the record market. As a result, unless there are further exceptional records such as Band Aid's colossal hit (with sales in the UK of almost 4,000,000 and over 8,000,000 globally), it seems unlikely that this Top 10 will change much over the coming years.

THE TOP 10 ALBUMS OF ALL TIME IN THE UK

	Album	Artist
1	Brothers In Arms	Dire Straits
2	Bad	Michael Jackson
3	Thriller	Michael Jackson
4	Sgt Pepper's Lonely Hearts Club Band	The Beatles
5	Greatest Hits Vol 1	Abba
6	Bridge Over Troubled Water	Simon and Garfunkel
7	Dark Side Of The Moon	Pink Floyd
8	Rumours	Fleetwood Mac
9	Greatest Hits	Queen
10	Tubular Bells	Mike Oldfield

THE TOP 10 ALBUMS OF ALL TIME WORLDWIDE

	Album	Artist
1	Thriller	Michael Jackson
2	Saturday Night Fever Soundtrack	Various
3	Grease Soundtrack	Various
4	Sgt Pepper's Lonely Hearts Club Band	The Beatles
5	Bridge Over Troubled Water	Simon and Garfunkel
6	Born In The USA	Bruce Springsteen
7	The Sound Of Music Soundtrack	Various
8	Abbey Road	The Beatles
9	Rumours	Fleetwood Mac
10	Brothers In Arms	Dire Straits

THE 10 ALBUMS THAT STAYED LONGEST IN THE UK CHARTS

	Album	Artist	First year in chart
1	Rumours	Fleetwood Mac	1977
2	Bat Out Of Hell	Meatloaf	1978
3	The Sound Of Music	Original Cast	1965
4	Greatest Hits	Queen	1981
5	Bridge Over Troubled Water	Simon and Garfunkel	1970
6	Dark Side Of The Moon	Pink Floyd	1973
7	South Pacific	Original Cast	1958
8	Greatest Hits	Simon and Garfunkel	1972
9	Face Value	Phil Collins	1981
10	Tubular Bells	Mike Oldfield	1973

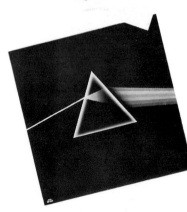

The 10 longest-staying records virtually took up residence in the album charts (the Top 50, 75 or 100, depending on the years during which the charts were compiled), remaining there for periods ranging from over five years for 'Tubular Bells' to the astonishing eight-and-a-half year occupation of Fleetwood Mac's 'Rumours'.

THE 10 ALL-TIME BESTSELLING POP CDs IN THE UK

	CD	Artist
1	Brothers In Arms	Dire Straits
2	Thriller	Michael Jackson
3	Bad	Michael Jackson
4	Greatest Hits	Queen
5	Tango In The Night	Fleetwood Mac
6	No Jacket Required	Phil Collins
7	Whitney	Whitney Houston
8	The Joshua Tree	U2
9	Graceland	Paul Simon
10	A New Flame	Simply Red

Compact discs have been the music marketing success story of the 1980s, overtaking vinyl's share of the album market by the end of the decade. Generally, albums appealing to the 20–30 age group tend to have the greater percentage of their sales on CD, but among the Top 10 there are close parallels with the list of bestselling albums of the 1980s.

THE TOP 10 ON CD JUKEBOXES

	CD	Artist
1	Dirty Dancing	Original soundtrack
2	Blues Brothers	Original soundtrack
3	Cream Of Clapton	Eric Clapton
4	Appetite For Destruction	Guns 'N' Roses
5	Rattle And Hum	U2
6	Bat Out Of Hell	Meatloaf
7	Greatest Hits	Fleetwood Mac
8	Best Of The Eagles	The Eagles
9	Raw And The Cooked	Fine Young Cannibals
10	Money For Nothing	Dire Straits

The Top 10 is based on the most-played compact discs on Arbiter Discmaster CD Jukeboxes. Approximately 2,000 have been installed in the UK and offer listeners the opportunity to select individual tracks from a range of popular CDs.

ABOVE RIGHT Black Box's 'Ride On Time' was voted top single of 1989 in the Capital FM poll.

CAPITAL FM LISTENERS' TOP 10 ALBUMS OF 1989

	Album	Artist
1	Like A Prayer	Madonna
2	A New Flame	Simply Red
3	But Seriously	Phil Collins
4	Club Classics	Soul II Soul
5	The Time	Bros
6	Don't Be Cruel	Bobby Brown
7	Hanging Tough	New Kids On The Block
8	Holding Back The River	Wet Wet Wet
9	Ten Good Reasons	Jason Donovan
10	Affection	Lisa Stansfield

CAPITAL FM LISTENERS' TOP 10 SINGLES OF 1989

	Song	Artist
1	Ride On Time	Black Box
2	Like A Prayer	Madonna
3	Back To Life	Soul II Soul
4	Too Much	Bros
5	All Around The World	Lisa Stansfield
6	You've Got It	New Kids On The Block
7	Another Day In Paradise	Phil Collins
8	Sister	Bros
9	Pump Up The Jam	Technotronic
10	Sowing The Seeds Of Love	Tears For Fears

Capital FM, an independent London radio station, conducted this, their largest ever listeners' poll, between Christmas 1989 and New Year 1990.

Some of the top singers from the Capital FM poll: **FAR LEFT** Madonna, **CENTRE** Michael Jackson, **LEFT** Pet Shop Boys.

CAPITAL FM LISTENERS' TOP 10 FEMALE SOLO ARTISTS OF 1989

1 Madonna
2 Kylie Minogue
3 Neneh Cherry
4 Lisa Stansfield
5 Tina Turner
6 Dusty Springfield
7 Whitney Houston
8 Gloria Estefan
9 Karyn White
10 Martika

CAPITAL FM LISTENERS' TOP 10 MALE SOLO ARTISTS OF 1989

1 Bobby Brown
2 Michael Jackson
3 Phil Collins
4 Prince
5 Jason Donovan
6 Cliff Richard
7 George Michael
8 Luther Vandross
9 Sydney Youngblood
10 Alexander O'Neal

CAPITAL FM LISTENERS' TOP 10 GROUPS OF 1989

1 Simply Red
2 Pet Shop Boys
3 Bros
4 Soul II Soul
5 Wet Wet Wet
6 Fine Young Cannibals
7 New Kids On The Block
8 Milli Vanilli
9 Big Fun
10 U2

CAPITAL FM LISTENERS' TOP 10 NEWCOMERS OF 1989

1 New Kids On The Block
2 Soul II Soul
3 Lisa Stansfield
4 Bobby Brown
5 Big Fun
6 Neneh Cherry
7 Jason Donovan
8 Martika
9 Sydney Youngblood
10 Sonia

ABOVE New Kids On The Block, Capital FM listeners' favourite newcomers and seventh favourite group.

RIGHT A 1947 Wurlitzer jukebox, promoted with the slogan 'Always the life of the party'.

The list is based on a survey by the USA Amusement and Music Operators' Association, and is of most-played records in the USA – the home of the jukebox. The first, a hand-operated Edison phonograph with coinbox and four listening tubes, was unveiled at the Palais Royal Saloon, San Francisco, on 23 November 1889. No choice of recordings was offered, the listener hearing whatever cylinder happened to be in the machine. The first in which records could be selected in advance, the 'Multiphone', patented in 1905 by John C. Dunton of Grand Rapids, Michigan, gave a choice of 24 recordings. The first all-electric model was made in 1927 by the Automatic Musical Instrument Co. The word jukebox first appeared in print in *Time* magazine of 27 November 1939, which noted that 'Glenn Miller attributes his crescendo to the "juke-box", which retails recorded music at 5¢ a shot in bars, restaurants and roadside dance joints'. Wurlitzer, the best-known manufacturer of jukeboxes, dominated the market in the post-war period, the Wurlitzer 1015 selling 56,000 models in 1946. In the 1950s the introduction of the 45-rpm single revolutionized the design of the jukebox, and models from this period are now highly prized by collectors for their decorative appearance and nostalgic associations.

THE TOP 10 JUKEBOX HITS OF ALL TIME

	Song	Artist	Year
1	Hound Dog/Don't Be Cruel	Elvis Presley	1956
2	Crazy	Patsy Cline	1961
3	Rock Around The Clock	Bill Haley and his Comets	1955
4	Dock Of The Bay	Otis Redding	1968
5	I Heard It Through The Grapevine	Marvin Gaye	1968
6	Mack The Knife	Bobby Darin	1959
7	Light My Fire	The Doors	1967
8	Blueberry Hill	Fats Domino	1956
9	Old Time Rock & Roll	Bob Seger	1979
10	My Girl	The Temptations	1965

THE 10 MOST EXPENSIVE ITEMS OF POP MEMORABILIA

1 John Lennon's 1965 Rolls-Royce Phantom V touring limousine, finished in psychedelic paintwork
Sotheby's, New York, 29 June 1985
$2,299,000/£1,768,462

2 Jimi Hendrix's Fender Stratocaster guitar
Sotheby's, London, 25 April 1990
£198,000

3 John Lennon's 1970 Mercedes-Benz 600 Pullman four-door limousine
Christie's, London, 27 April 1989
£137,500

4 Elvis Presley's 1963 Rolls-Royce Phantom V touring limousine
Sotheby's, London, 28 August 1986
£110,000

5 Elvis Presley's one-piece 'Shooting Star' stage outfit, 1972
Phillips, London, 24 August 1988
£28,600

6 An unreleased 8 mm film of The Beatles in America, 1965
Christie's, London, 29 August 1986
£24,000

7 Tape-recorded interview with John Lennon, 1968
Sotheby's, London, 5 August 1987
£23,650

8 Biographical booklet annotated by John Lennon
Sotheby's, London, 28 August 1986
£20,900

9= Original unpublished manuscript for a book by John Lennon
Sotheby's, London, 31 August 1984
£17,600

9= Elton John's Wurlitzer Model 750 jukebox, c1940
Sotheby's, London, 6 September 1988
£17,600

Pioneered particularly by Sotheby's in London, pop memorabilia has become big business, especially if it involves personal association with mega-stars such as The Beatles. In addition to the Top 10, high prices have also been paid for pianos that were once owned by Paul McCartney and John Lennon.

TOP RIGHT Elvis Presley's 'Shooting Star' stage outfit, designed by Bill Belew.

THE 10 BESTSELLING STOCK AITKEN WATERMAN PRODUCTIONS

	Song	Artist
1	Especially For You	Kylie Minogue and Jason Donovan
2	Never Gonna Give You Up	Rick Astley
3	I Should Be So Lucky	Kylie Minogue
4	Respectable	Mel and Kim
5	You Spin Me Round (Like A Record)	Dead Or Alive
6	Do They Know It's Christmas?	Band Aid II
7	Let It Be	Ferry Aid
8	Too Many Broken Hearts	Jason Donovan
9	Hand On Your Heart	Kylie Minogue
10	Loco-Motion	Kylie Minogue

For three years the UK charts have been dominated by (Mike) Stock (Matt) Aitken (Pete) Waterman-written/produced records. Stock Aitken Waterman have also produced records for stars including Cliff Richard and Donna Summer.

Kylie Minogue and Jason Donovan's 'Especially For You' is the No. 1 Stock Aitken Waterman production.

THE 10 FEMALE SINGERS WITH THE MOST US AND UK TOP 10 HITS*

	Singer	Hits
1 =	Connie Francis	28
1 =	Aretha Franklin (including one duet with George Michael)	28
1 =	Diana Ross (including three duets with Marvin Gaye, one with Lionel Richie and one with Julio Iglesias)	28
4	Olivia Newton-John (including two duets with John Travolta and one each with Andy Gibb, Cliff Richard and ELO)	26
5	Brenda Lee	24
6 =	Donna Summer (including one duet with Barbra Streisand)	23
6 =	Madonna	23
8	Petula Clark	21
9	Dionne Warwick (including one duet with The Detroit Spinners and one with 'Friends': Stevie Wonder, Gladys Knight and Elton John)	19
10	Dusty Springfield (including one duet with The Pet Shop Boys)	17

*To 28 February 1990.

This covers US and/or UK Top 10 hits, including the listed duets with other acts, but not those achieved as a member of a group – Diana Ross's successes with The Supremes are therefore not counted. The principal change to the Top 10 in the past year is that Madonna has moved up from 8 = position to 6 = by increasing her tally of hits from 19 to 23.

THE 10 MOST SUCCESSFUL ALL-GIRL GROUPS IN THE UK*

	Group	No. 1	Top 10	Top 20
1	The Supremes	1	13	17
2	Bananarama	—	9	13
3	The Three Degrees	1	5	7
4	Sister Sledge	1	4	7
5	The Nolans	—	3	7
6	The Bangles	1	3	5
7	Mel and Kim	—	4	4
8	The Pointer Sisters	—	2	5
9	The Beverley Sisters	—	2	4
10	The Crystals	—	2	3

*To 28 February 1990. Ranked according to total number of hits.

The Supremes also had three other Top 20 hits which have not been included because they were recorded in partnership with Motown male groups The Four Tops and The Temptations. However, Bananarama's charity revival of 'Help!', shared with comediennes Dawn French and Jennifer Saunders, has been included as all the participants are female.

Bananarama, the second most successful all-girl group after The Supremes.

THE 10 MOST SUCCESSFUL WOMEN IN THE UK ALBUM CHARTS

1	Madonna
2	Barbra Streisand
3	Diana Ross
4	Shirley Bassey
5	Kate Bush
6	Tina Turner
7	Whitney Houston
8 =	Elkie Brooks
8 =	Nana Mouskouri
10	Donna Summer

Based on total number of weeks their albums have stayed in the UK charts. Madonna comes out top because, although she has released only five albums, they have spent a total of over 420 weeks in the charts.

DISCS OF THE DECADE

THE TOP 10 ALBUMS OF THE 1980s IN THE UK

	Album	Artist
1	Brothers In Arms	Dire Straits
2	Bad	Michael Jackson
3	Thriller	Michael Jackson
4	Greatest Hits	Queen
5	Kylie	Kylie Minogue
6	Whitney	Whitney Houston
7	Tango In The Night	Fleetwood Mac
8	No Jacket Required	Phil Collins
9	The Joshua Tree	U2
10	True Blue	Madonna

The bestselling album of all time in the UK is 'Brothers In Arms', which has now sold 3,200,000 copies. Worldwide, 'Thriller' has now sold over 45,000,000 copies.

THE 10 MOST SUCCESSFUL GROUPS OF THE 1980s IN THE UK

1 The Police

2 Wham!

3 Dire Straits

4 U2

5 Queen

6 Simple Minds

7 Pet Shop Boys

8 Duran Duran

9 Adam and the Ants

10 Madness

TOP RIGHT Dire Straits' bestselling album is also the UK's bestselling CD.

This is based on estimated UK record sales (both singles and albums), taking account of both highest chart positions and chart longevity. The Police and Simple Minds shared the position of groups with most No. 1 albums during the 1980s (four each), while Pet Shop Boys was the group with the most No. 1 singles (four).

Many other groups were consistently successful during the decade, among them UB40, Culture Club and the Eurythmics, who are all close contenders for the No. 10 slot. The most successful female group was Bananarama, although they never had a single higher than No. 3 and did not quite make the Top 10 of Most Successful Groups.

THE TOP 10 REVIVALS OF THE 1980s IN THE UK

	Song	Artist	Original release
1	Imagine	John Lennon	1975
2	Reet Petite	Jackie Wilson	1957
3	Stand By Me	Ben E. King	1961
4	He Ain't Heavy He's My Brother	The Hollies	1969
5	When A Man Loves A Woman	Percy Sledge	1966
6	I Get The Sweetest Feeling	Jackie Wilson	1972
7	Wonderful World	Sam Cooke	1960
8	You To Me Are Everything	The Real Thing	1976
9	Lovely Day	Bill Withers	1978
10	Love Me Do	The Beatles	1962

The 1980s fashion for using old hits as the backing tracks on TV and cinema advertisements for products from lager to Levi Jeans was partly responsible for their resurrection. Sadly, three of the artists did not live long enough to see their records become hits the second time around: John Lennon (shot in New York by Mark Chapman, 8 December 1980), Jackie Wilson (died 21 January 1984 after spending eight years in a coma following a heart attack while on stage) and Sam Cooke (shot in a Hollywood motel, 11 December 1964).

THE TOP 10 SINGLES OF THE 1980s IN THE UK

	Song	Year	Artist
1	Do They Know It's Christmas?	1984	Band Aid
2	Relax	1984	Frankie Goes To Hollywood
3	I Just Called To Say I Love You	1984	Stevie Wonder
4	Two Tribes	1984	Frankie Goes To Hollywood
5	Don't You Want Me	1981	Human League
6	Last Christmas/Everything She Wants	1984	Wham!
7	Karma Chameleon	1983	Culture Club
8	Careless Whisper	1984	George Michael
9	The Power Of Love	1985	Jennifer Rush
10	Come On Eileen	1982	Dexy's Midnight Runners

ABOVE Frankie Goes To Hollywood had the second biggest hit of the 1980s.

BELOW John Lennon's 'Imagine' was the top 1980s revival.

Band Aid's 'Do They Know It's Christmas?' has sold over 3,600,000 copies in the UK (making it the bestselling single of all time in the UK), and over 8,000,000 worldwide. It contributed significantly to the £90,000,000 raised for the Ethiopian Famine Relief Fund from record sales and the proceeds of the 13 July 1985 Live Aid concerts.

Jennifer Rush's 'The Power Of Love' is the only single by a female solo singer to achieve sales of more than 1,000,000 in the UK.

THE 10 MOST SUCCESSFUL SOLO SINGERS OF THE 1980s IN THE UK

1	Madonna
2	Michael Jackson
3	Phil Collins
4	Cliff Richard
5	Shakin' Stevens
6	Paul McCartney
7	Kylie Minogue
8	Whitney Houston
9	Prince
10	David Bowie

The Top 10 is based on estimated UK record sales from 1980 to 1989. The top performer, Madonna, scored 21 Top 10 hit singles (including six No. 1s), while all five of her albums were Top Tenners, two of them topping the album charts, an achievement that far outstrips that of any other artist of the decade.

Music Quiz

1 What is Madonna's full name?
2 What is the connection between The Monkees, The Kinks and David Bowie?
3 What was comedian Billy Connolly's 1975 No. 1 hit record?
4 Who is the senior member of the Rolling Stones?
5 In 1965 Gerry Dorsey adopted the name of a German classical composer who had died in 1921. Who was he?
6 What were jazz musician Duke Ellington's first names?
7 What is regarded as the most frequently sung song?
8 What was Elton John's only No.1 record of the 1970s and 1980s?
9 In which year were The Beatles awarded the MBE?
10 What singer was born Steven Giorgiou and is now called Yusef Islam?

THE TOP 10 CLASSICAL COMPOSERS

	Composer	Performances
1	Beethoven	$62\frac{1}{4}$
2	Mozart	56
3	Mahler	$32\frac{1}{4}$
4	Haydn	32
5	Dvořák	$20\frac{1}{2}$
6	Shostakovich	18
7	Schubert	$17\frac{1}{2}$
8	Tchaikovsky	16
9	Mendelssohn	15
10	Brahms	14

David Chesterman has been writing to *The Times* every year since 1952, reporting on the 10 composers whose symphonies have been most performed at the Royal Albert, Royal Festival, Barbican and Queen Elizabeth Halls and at St John's, Smith Square, London. His analysis is based on the number of times each composer's work is played, with individual movements counted as fractions of the whole symphony. Beethoven has remained at the top of the list for many years, although in 1989 Mozart's Symphony No. 41 was the most-played with 14 performances. Other composers, such as Bruckner, Sibelius and Berlioz, have made occasional appearances in the list, but the members of this musical élite have remained fairly constant during the 1980s, with some jockeying for position among the Top 10 composers.

BOTTOM LEFT Dvořák, performed $20\frac{1}{2}$ times in London in 1989.

ABOVE Mozart appears in the Top 10 of Classical Composers and 'Your Hundred Best Tunes'.

THE TOP 10 OF 'YOUR HUNDRED BEST TUNES'

	Composer	'Tune'
1	Georges Bizet	In the Depths of the Temple (from *The Pearl Fishers*)
2	Giuseppi Verdi	Chorus of the Hebrew Slaves (from *Nabucco*)
3	Gregorio Allegri	*Miserere*
4	Max Bruch	Violin Concerto No. 1 in G Minor (Adagio)
5	Johann Pachelbel	Canon in D
6	Ludwig van Beethoven	Symphony No. 6 ('Pastoral') (last movement)
7	Wolfgang Amadeus Mozart	Piano Concerto No. 21 (Andante)
8	Christoph Willibald von Gluck	Lament: What is Life? (from *Orfeo ed Euridice*)
9	Stephen Adams	*The Holy City*
10	Sir Edward Elgar	Nimrod (from *Enigma Variations*)

BBC Radio 2's 'Your Hundred Best Tunes' first went on the air as 'The Hundred Best Tunes in the World' on 22 November 1959, and is still broadcast every Sunday night by its original presenter, Alan Keith. The Top 10 comes from the programme's listeners' poll of all-time favourites.

THE TOP 10 CLASSICAL ALBUMS OF 1989 IN THE UK*

Artist	Album
1 Various artists	The Classical Experience
2 Nigel Kennedy/English Chamber Orchestra	Vivaldi: *The Four Seasons*
3 Placido Domingo	The Essential Domingo
4 London Symphony Orchestra	Classic Rock – The Living Years
5 Justin Hayward/ Mike Batt/London Philharmonic Orchestra	Classic Blue
6 José Carreras	José Carreras Sings Andrew Lloyd Webber
7 Virtuosi of England	Vivaldi: *The Four Seasons*
8 Luciano Pavarotti	The New Pavarotti Collection Live
9 Luciano Pavarotti	The Pavarotti Collection
10 Placido Domingo	Goya – A Life In Song

*Including full-, mid- and budget-priced and
'crossover' (ie, classical music aimed at a popular
audience) albums.

ABOVE A scene from Bizet's
The Pearl Fishers, No. 1 in
'Your Hundred Best Tunes'.

TOP Placido Domingo
recorded two of the Top 10
classical albums of 1989.

THE 10 MOST POPULAR MUSICAL INSTRUMENTS STUDIED BY STUDENTS AT THE ROYAL COLLEGE OF MUSIC, LONDON

1	Piano
2	Violin
3	Voice
4	Cello
5	Viola
6	Horn
7	Flute
8	Clarinet
9	Oboe
10	Bassoon

Theatre

THE 10 LONGEST-RUNNING SHOWS OF ALL TIME ON BROADWAY

Show	Performances
1 A Chorus Line	6,137
2 Oh! Calcutta!	5,959
3 42nd Street	3,486
4 Grease	3,388
5 Fiddler on the Roof	3,242
6 Life with Father	3,224
7 Tobacco Road	3,182
8 Cats	3,125*
9 Hello Dolly!	2,844
10 My Fair Lady	2,717

Still running; total at 31 March 1990.

In 1989 *A Chorus Line* overtook *Oh! Calcutta!* to become the longest-running Broadway show of all time, but closed on 21 April 1990.

The Black and White Minstrel Show heads the list of longest-running musicals in the UK.

THE 10 LONGEST-RUNNING MUSICALS OF ALL TIME IN THE UK

Show	Performances
1 The Black and White Minstrel Show	6,464
2 Me and My Girl	4,363*
3 Oliver	4,125
4 Cats	3,722*
5 Jesus Christ, Superstar	3,357
6 Evita	2,900
7 Starlight Express	2,497*
8 The Sound of Music	2,386
9 Salad Days	2,283
10 My Fair Lady	2,281

Still running; total at 31 March 1990.

The *Black and White Minstrel Show* total includes both the original ten-year run (1962–72) and the 1973 revival.

Me and My Girl opened at the Victoria Palace on 16 December 1937 and, apart from a brief closure when war was declared in 1939, ran until 29 June 1940, by which time it had achieved 1,646 performances. Revivals in 1941, 1945–46, 1949–50 and 1985– have boosted the total to the present figure, making it the UK's longest-running musical comedy of all time.

Total performances of *Oliver* include runs at different theatres from 1960–66, 1967–68, 1977–80 and 1983–84.

On 12 May 1989 *Cats*, which opened in 1981, became the longest continuously running musical in British theatre history.

THE 10 LONGEST-RUNNING MUSICALS OF ALL TIME ON BROADWAY

Show	Performances
1 A Chorus Line	6,137
2 42nd Street	3,486
3 Grease	3,388
4 Fiddler on the Roof	3,242
5 Cats	3,125*
6 Hello Dolly!	2,844
7 My Fair Lady	2,717
8 Annie	2,377
9 Man of La Mancha	2,328
10 Oklahoma!	2,212

Still running; total at 31 March 1990.

LEFT *Me and My Girl*, the UK's longest-running musical comedy of all time.

OPPOSITE *Cats*, one of the longest-running shows on Broadway and in the UK.

THE 10 LONGEST-RUNNING NON-MUSICALS OF ALL TIME ON BROADWAY

Show	Performances
1 *Oh! Calcutta!*	5,959
2 *Life with Father*	3,224
3 *Tobacco Road*	3,182
4 *Abie's Irish Rose*	2,327
5 *Deathtrap*	1,792
6 *Gemini*	1,788
7 *Harvey*	1,775
8 *Born Yesterday*	1,642
9 *Mary, Mary*	1,572
10 *Voice of the Turtle*	1,557

More than half the longest-running non-musical shows on Broadway began their runs before the Second World War – in the case of *Abie's Irish Rose*, in 1922. The others all date from the period up to the 1970s, before the long-running musical completely dominated the Broadway stage.

THE 10 OLDEST LONDON THEATRES

Theatre	Date opened
1 Theatre Royal, Drury Lane	7 May 1663
2 Sadler's Wells, Rosebery Avenue	date unknown 1683
3 The Haymarket (Theatre Royal), Haymarket	29 December 1720
4 Royal Opera House, Covent Garden	7 December 1732
5 The Adelphi (originally Sans Pareil), Strand	27 November 1806
6 The Old Vic (originally Royal Coburg), Waterloo Road	11 May 1818
7 The Vaudeville, Strand	16 April 1870
8 The Criterion, Piccadilly Circus	21 March 1874
9 The Savoy, Strand	10 October 1881
10 The Comedy, Panton Street	15 October 1881

These are London's 10 oldest theatres still operating on their original sites – although most of them have been rebuilt, some several times.

THE 10 LONGEST-RUNNING SHOWS OF ALL TIME IN THE UK

Show	Performances
1 *The Mousetrap*	15,545*
2 *No Sex, Please – We're British*	6,761
3 *The Black and White Minstrel Show*	6,464
4 *Me and My Girl*	4,363*
5 *Oliver*	4,125
6 *Oh! Calcutta!*	3,918
7 *Cats*	3,722*
8 *Jesus Christ, Superstar*	3,357
9 *Life with Father*	3,213
10 *Evita*	2,900

Still running; total at 31 March 1990.

All the longest-running shows in the UK have been London productions. *The Mousetrap* opened on 25 November 1952 at the Ambassador's Theatre. After 8,862 performances it transferred to St Martin's Theatre where it re-opened on 25 March 1974. It is not the only play in the world to have run continuously since the 1950s: Eugene Ionesco's *The Bald Prima Donna* has been on in Paris since 1953.

AMBASSADORS THEATRE, West St. Cambridge Circus, W.C.2
Sole Proprietors: Ambassadors Theatre Ltd.   Lessees: J. W. Pemberton & Co. Ltd.
Managing Directors: W. G. Curtis & H. J. Malden.
Licensed by the Lord Chamberlain to J. F. H. Jay.

Monday to Friday: 7.30   Saturday: 5.15 and 8.0   Tuesday: 2.30 | BOX OFFICE
Stalls: 15/-, 10/6, 8/6;   Dress Circle: 15/-, 10/6, 8/6, 5/6;   Pit (unreserved): 3/6. | Temple Bar 1171

Peter Saunders presents

Richard Attenborough
Sheila Sim in

THE MOUSETRAP
by Agatha Christie

With
Jessica Spencer
Aubrey Dexter
Mignon O'Doherty
Allan McClelland
John Paul
and
Martin Miller

Décor by Roger Furse

DIRECTED BY PETER COTES

Opened in 1952 and still going strong.

The Coliseum, London's second largest theatre.

THE 10 LARGEST THEATRES IN LONDON

Theatre	Seats
1 Apollo Victoria	2,572
2 London Coliseum	2,358
3 London Palladium	2,317
4 Theatre Royal, Drury Lane	2,245
5 Royal Opera House	2,095
6 Dominion	2,007
7 Prince Edward Theatre	1,666
8 Victoria Palace	1,565
9 Sadler's Wells	1,499
10 Royal Adelphi Theatre	1,481

The Hammersmith Odeon has 3,483 seats, but is used for rock concerts and other non-theatrical events. Among London's newest theatres, neither the Olivier at the National Theatre (1,160 seats) nor the Barbican (1,166 seats) rank in the Top 10. London also boasts several large concert halls, including the Royal Festival Hall (3,111 seats), Barbican Hall (2,047 seats) and the Royal Albert Hall, which can accommodate up to 7,000 depending on the nature of the performance. The recently opened London Arena is the largest, seating 12,500. The largest theatre – and the largest stage – in the UK is the Blackpool Opera House with a capacity of 2,975.

THE 10 LONGEST-RUNNING NON-MUSICALS OF ALL TIME IN THE UK

Show	Performances
1 The Mousetrap	15,545*
2 No Sex, Please – We're British	6,761
3 Oh! Calcutta!	3,918
4 Life with Father	3,213
5 Run for Your Wife	2,638*
6 There's a Girl in My Soup	2,547
7 Pyjama Tops	2,498
8 Sleuth	2,359
9 Boeing Boeing	2,035
10 Blithe Spirit	1,997

*Still running; total at 31 March 1990.

Oh! Calcutta! is included here as it is regarded as a review with music, rather than a musical.

Theatre Quiz

1 Where in a theatre would you find a 'scruto'?
2 Who wrote the comedies *Entertaining Mr Sloan*, *Loot* and *What the Butler Saw*?
3 Who was the first British actor to be made a peer?
4 The first ever musical containing a nude scene opened in London in 1968. What was it called?
5 What type of hat derives from a play of the same name?
6 What is Noh theatre?
7 From which children's play does the phrase 'in the doghouse' derive?
8 Who wrote the lyrics for *West Side Story*?
9 What London theatre burned down in 1613 while Shakespeare's *Henry VIII* was being performed?
10 What London theatre, the home of Gilbert and Sullivan operas, was gutted by fire in 1990?

The play *Blithe Spirit* clocked up almost 2,000 performances before giving up the ghost.

Film

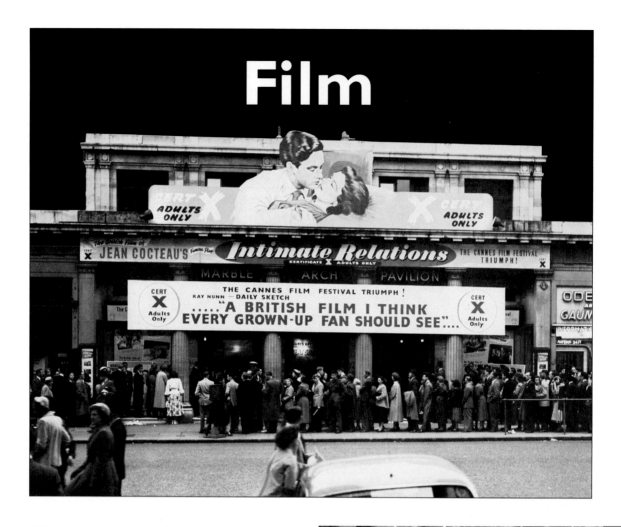

THE 10 MOST EXPENSIVE FILMS EVER MADE

	Film	Year	Production cost ($)
1	Who Framed Roger Rabbit?	1988	70,000,000
2	Rambo III	1988	58,000,000
3=	Superman	1978	55,000,000
3=	Superman II	1981	55,000,000
3=	Ishtar	1987	55,000,000
3=	Tango and Cash	1989	55,000,000
7	The Adventures of Baron Munchausen	1988	52,000,000
8	Annie	1982	51,500,000
9	The Cotton Club	1984	51,000,000
10=	Batman	1989	50,000,000
10=	Santa Claus – The Movie	1985	50,000,000

Bunny money: *Who Framed Roger Rabbit?* cost $70,000,000 to make, ranking it as the most expensive film of all time.

As further information emerges, the amounts and order of this list have undergone revision: *Who Framed Roger Rabbit?*, for example, was previously estimated to have cost $53,000,000, but it appears to have cost over 30 per cent more, while the final figures for several other films have been similarly increased. By the end of its release year *Tango and Cash* had recouped only $17,000,000 in rental fees – less than a third of its estimated production cost – but it is too early to state whether it yet qualifies as a 'film flop'.

THE 10 BIGGEST FILM FLOPS OF ALL TIME

	Film	Year	Loss ($)
1	The Adventures of Baron Munchausen	1988	48,100,000
2	Ishtar	1987	47,300,000
3	Inchon	1981	44,100,000
4	The Cotton Club	1984	38,100,000
5	Santa Claus – The Movie	1985	37,000,000
6	Heaven's Gate	1980	34,200,000
7	Pirates	1986	30,300,000
8	Rambo III	1988	30,000,000
9	Raise the Titantic	1980	29,200,000
10	Revolution	1985	27,000,000

Based on North American (USA and Canada) rental receipts balanced against production cost. The loss incurred by *Inchon* is even greater than previously rumoured. Financed by the Moonies religious sect, it portrays Laurence Olivier as General MacArthur receiving divine guidance during the Korean War, and was described by Jack Kroll of *Newsweek* as 'The worst film ever made, a turkey the size of Godzilla'. The losses on *Heaven's Gate*, however, previously estimated as $42,000,000, have been re-assessed at a lower figure that is believed to be more precise, while *Baron Munchausen* now emerges as the all-time greatest flop, although it and other major loss-making films are progressively recovering some of their deficits through worldwide distribution, video and television showings.

THE TOP 10 FILM-PRODUCING COUNTRIES

	Country	Films produced
1	India	806
2	USA	578
3	Japan	286
4	USSR	156
5	China	140
6	Thailand	134
7	France	133
8	Hong Kong	130
9	Italy	116
10	Turkey	96

The list is of full-length (generally at least 1,600 m/5,250 ft) feature films, based on UNESCO statistics for films produced in 1987, the latest year for which complete international figures are available. In the same year, the British film industry produced 51 full-length films.

India is the world's top film-producing country.

THE 10 LEADING FILM-GOING COUNTRIES

	Country	Annual cinema visits per inhabitant
1	USSR	14.8
2	Singapore	12.5
3	Hong Kong	12.3
4	Bulgaria	9.5
5	Iceland	9.4
6	North Korea	9.2
7	Romania	9.1
8	India	5.9
9	Vietnam	5.8
10	Hungary	5.3

The popularity of films on a country-by-country basis can be roughly measured by analysing the average number of visits to the cinema per head of the population. This produces one of the very few world lists in which Iceland appears, while the USA (with 4.6 visits per inhabitant) and the UK (1.3) do not.

Baron Munchausen lost a staggering $48,100,000.

THE 10 COUNTRIES WITH THE MOST CINEMAS

	Country	Cinemas
1	USSR	176,172
2	USA	23,555
3	India	8,221
4	France	5,063
5	Italy	4,143
6	West Germany	3,252
7	Bulgaria	3,028
8	Czechoslovakia	2,634
9	Spain	2,234
10	Mexico	2,226

This list is based on UNESCO's figures for indoor cinemas equipped to show 35 mm films – the format used for most feature films. In addition, the USSR has 1,547, India 4,511, France 1,679 and Bulgaria 223 cinemas showing 16 mm film. The total for the USSR seems almost incredible, but UNESCO has been reporting similarly huge figures for many years, a reflection of the value placed on film in the Soviet Union as a medium of entertainment and political ideology. The UK, with 1,226 cinemas, is 17th in the world league, after East Germany, Japan, Indonesia, North Korea, Poland and Brazil.

ABOVE One of the USSR's 176,172 cinemas.

RIGHT *The Ten Commandments*, the top film of the 1950s.

Although an enormous international success, *Batman* was relegated to third position at the UK box office in 1989.

THE TOP 10 FILMS AT THE UK BOX OFFICE IN 1989

	Film	Box office gross (£)
1	Indiana Jones and the Last Crusade	15,932,168
2	Who Framed Roger Rabbit?	15,612,005
3	Batman	12,034,291
4	Rain Man	9,660,125
5	The Naked Gun	7,740,553
6	Licence to Kill	7,550,989
7	Lethal Weapon 2	6,745,293
8	Twins	6,550,839
9	Dead Poets Society	5,871,252
10	Cocktail	5,752,439

THE 10 MOST SUCCESSFUL FILMS RELEASED IN THE 1940s

	Film	Year
1	Bambi	1942
2	Cinderella	1949
3	Pinocchio	1940
4	Song of the South	1946
5	Fantasia	1940
6	Samson and Delilah	1949
7=	Duel in the Sun	1946
7=	The Best Years of Our Lives	1946
9	This is the Army	1943
10	The Bells of St Mary's	1945

THE 10 MOST SUCCESSFUL FILMS RELEASED IN THE 1950s

	Film	Year
1	The Ten Commandments	1957
2	Lady and the Tramp	1955
3	Peter Pan	1953
4	Ben Hur	1959
5	Around the World in 80 Days	1957
6	Sleeping Beauty	1959
7 =	South Pacific	1958
7 =	The Robe	1953
9	Bridge on the River Kwai	1958
10	Giant	1956

Star Wars, the star film of the 1970s and the second most successful film of all time.

THE 10 MOST SUCCESSFUL FILMS RELEASED IN THE 1960s

	Film	Year
1	The Sound of Music	1965
2	Dr Zhivago	1965
3	Butch Cassidy and the Sundance Kid	1969
4	Mary Poppins	1964
5	The Graduate	1968
6	The Jungle Book	1967
7	101 Dalmations	1961
8	Thunderball	1965
9	Funny Girl	1968
10	Cleopatra	1963

Maria (Julie Andrews) and the Trapp children in *The Sound of Music*, the most successful film of the 1960s.

THE 10 MOST SUCCESSFUL FILMS RELEASED IN THE 1970s

	Film	Year
1	Star Wars	1977
2	Jaws	1975
3	Grease	1978
4	The Exorcist	1973
5	The Godfather	1972
6	Superman	1978
7	Close Encounters of the Third Kind	1977*
8	The Sting	1973
9	Saturday Night Fever	1977
10	National Lampoon's Animal House	1978

*Close Encounters' *place in the Top 10 derives from the success of its original release and the 1980 'Special Edition'.*

THE 10 MOST SUCCESSFUL FILMS RELEASED IN THE 1980s

	Film	Year
1	E.T.	1982
2	Return of the Jedi	1983
3	Batman	1989
4	The Empire Strikes Back	1980
5	Ghostbusters	1984
6	Raiders of the Lost Ark	1981
7	Indiana Jones and the Last Crusade	1989
8	Indiana Jones and the Temple of Doom	1984
9	Beverly Hills Cop	1984
10	Back to the Future	1985

THE TOP 10 FILMS OF THE 1980s IN THE UK

	Film	Released
1	Crocodile Dundee	1986
2	E.T.	1982
3	Who Framed Roger Rabbit?	1988
4	Indiana Jones and the Last Crusade	1989
5	Fatal Attraction	1987
6	Return of the Jedi	1983
7	Ghostbusters	1984
8	Crocodile Dundee II	1988
9	Batman	1989
10	The Empire Strikes Back	1980

TOP 10 FILM LISTS

Films that appear in the various lists of '10 Most Successful' are ranked according to the total rental fees paid to distributors by cinemas in North America (USA and Canada). This is regarded by the film industry as a reliable guide to what a film has earned in those markets, while as a rough rule of thumb – also used by the industry – doubling the North American rental receipts gives a very approximate world total.

It should be noted that rental income is not the same as 'box-office gross', which is another commonly used way of comparing the success of films. While the latter method is certainly valid over a short period – for example, to compare films released in the same year – it indicates what the cinemas earned rather than the films themselves and, of course, varies according to ticket price.

Inflation is a key factor in calculating 'success', whichever method of assessment is used: as cinema ticket prices go up, so do box office income *and* the rental fees charged by distributors. This means that the biggest earners tend to be among the most recent releases. If inflation is taken into account, the most successful film ever would be *Gone With the Wind*; while it has earned actual rental fees of almost $80,000,000, inflation since the film's release in 1939 makes this worth over $500,000,000 in today's money.

Attempts have been made to compile precise comparative lists by building in factors for increases in ticket prices and inflation, but with such changes taking place so frequently in recent years, and with a total lack of uniformity in box office prices even in one country, it is virtually impossible to achieve consistent or meaningful results, and rental fees remain the most satisfactory index for comparing the success of one film against another. However, even the dollar rental amounts are extremely volatile, with new information constantly emerging about not only newly released films but also many older ones. The order of those in the various Top 10 lists should therefore be taken only as a guide based on currently best available evidence. Actual amounts are given only for the 'All-Time Film Rental Blockbusters' category, as an indication of the exceptional earning power of this élite group of films. To place it in perspective, of all the films ever made, fewer than 70 have earned total rental fees of more than $50,000,000.

Finally, it must not be forgotten that over recent years additional income has been derived by distributors from sales of video recordings and TV broadcasting rights. As this is not generally included in rental fees, it may alter the overall earnings of certain films, and hence their order in the Top 10 lists.

ABOVE LEFT *E.T.*, the top film of the 1980s and all time.

RIGHT Harrison Ford, star of six out of the 10 all-time blockbusters.

THE 10 ALL-TIME FILM RENTAL BLOCKBUSTERS

Film	Year	Total rental ($)
1 E.T.	1982	228,500,000
2 Star Wars	1977	193,500,000
3 Return of the Jedi	1983	168,000,000
4 Batman	1989	150,500,000
5 The Empire Strikes Back	1980	141,500,000
6 Ghostbusters	1984	130,000,000
7 Jaws	1975	129,500,000
8 Raiders of the Lost Ark	1981	115,500,000
9 Indiana Jones and the Last Crusade	1989	115,500,000
10 Indiana Jones and the Temple of Doom	1984	109,000,000

Since many of the most recently released films are also among the highest earners, this list is identical to The 10 Most Successful Films Released in the 1980s, with the exception of *Star Wars* and *Jaws*, the two most successful films of the 1970s that have also earned a place in the all-time list.

The hugely successful 1989 releases of *Batman* and *Indiana Jones and the Last Crusade* revised the previous order, ousting *Beverly Hills Cop* (1984) and *Back to the Future* (1985). *Last Crusade* has earned only very slightly less than *Raiders of the Lost Ark* (although rounding-off makes them appear identical), and seems set to overtake it during 1990.

Two men, Steven Spielberg (born 1946) and George Lucas (born 1945), continue to dominate the all-time list. Steven Spielberg directed Nos. 1, 7, 8 and 10 and co-produced 1, and George Lucas directed No. 2 and co-produced 3, 5, 8, 9 and 10. The actor Harrison Ford (born 1942) also appeared in all of the Lucas films.

RIGHT Marilyn Monroe –
with Tony Curtis in drag in
the bath – from *Some Like
it Hot*.

BOTTOM *Octopussy*, most
successful of the long-
running Bond films.

THE 10 MOST SUCCESSFUL JAMES BOND FILMS

	Film	Year
1	Octopussy	1983
2	Moonraker	1979
3	Thunderball	1965
4	Never Say Never Again	1983
5	The Living Daylights	1987
6	For Your Eyes Only	1981
7	A View to a Kill	1985
8	The Spy Who Loved Me	1977
9	Goldfinger	1964
10	Diamonds Are Forever	1967

Of the 10 most successful James Bond films,
Roger Moore starred as Bond in five (Nos. 1, 2, 6, 7
and 8), Sean Connery in four (3, 4, 9 and 10) and
Timothy Dalton in one (5). Dalton also appeared in
Licence to Kill (1989), which is on the way to entering
the Top 10. The first Bond film, *Dr No* (1963), has
earned the least.

THE 10 MOST SUCCESSFUL MARILYN MONROE FILMS*

	Film	Year
1	Some Like it Hot	1959
2	How to Marry a Millionaire	1953
3	The Seven Year Itch	1955
4	Gentlemen Prefer Blondes	1953
5	There's No Business Like Show Business	1954
6	Bus Stop	1956
7	The Misfits	1961
8	River of No Return	1954
9	All About Eve	1950
10	The Prince and the Showgirl	1957

*Includes films in which she appeared or starred.

THE 10 MOST SUCCESSFUL ALFRED HITCHCOCK FILMS

	Film	Year
1	Psycho	1960
2	Rear Window	1954
3	North by Northwest	1959
4	Family Plot	1976
5	Torn Curtain	1966
6	Frenzy	1972
7	Vertigo	1958
8	The Man Who Knew Too Much	1956
9	The Birds	1963
10	Spellbound	1945

THE 10 MOST SUCCESSFUL WOODY ALLEN FILMS

Film	Year
1 *Annie Hall*	1977
2 *Hannah and Her Sisters*	1986
3 *Manhattan*	1979
4 *Casino Royale*	1967
5 *Everything You Ever Wanted to Know About Sex, But Were Afraid to Ask*	1972
6 *What's New Pussycat?*	1965
7 *Sleeper*	1973
8 *Love and Death*	1975
9 *Zelig*	1983
10 *Radio Days*	1987

The list includes films which Woody Allen has either written, starred in or directed.

Film Quiz

1 Who played James Bond in the film *Casino Royale*?
2 Arthur Miller wrote the script of the last film in which his wife appeared. What was it and who was she?
3 British films won Oscars for Best Film in 1982 and 1983. What were they?
4 What was James Stewart's companion Harvey in the 1950 film of this name?
5 Where was Alfred Hitchcock born?
6 What film used the slogan, 'We are not alone'?
7 *I Am A Camera*, based on stories by Christopher Isherwood, was performed as a play in 1951, filmed in 1955 and made into a cinema musical in 1972. What was the musical's title?
8 Who ends what film with the words, 'After all, tomorrow is another day'?
9 What was the film name of Marion Morrison?
10 Who played eight parts in the 1949 film *Kind Hearts and Coronets*?

LEFT Diane Keaton and Woody Allen in a scene from *Annie Hall*, Allen's most successful film.

BELOW James Stewart snaps Raymond Burr in *Rear Window*.

THE 10 MOST SUCCESSFUL WAR FILMS OF ALL TIME

Film	Year
1 Platoon	1986
2 Good Morning, Vietnam	1987
3 Apocalypse Now	1979
4 M*A*S*H	1970
5 Patton	1970
6 The Deer Hunter	1978
7 Full Metal Jacket	1987
8 Midway	1976
9 The Dirty Dozen	1967
10 A Bridge Too Far	1977

THE 10 MOST SUCCESSFUL SCIENCE-FICTION AND FANTASY FILMS OF ALL TIME

Film	Year
1 E.T.	1982
2 Star Wars	1977
3 Return of the Jedi	1983
4 Batman	1989
5 The Empire Strikes Back	1980
6 Ghostbusters	1984
7 Back to the Future	1985
8 Superman	1978
9 Close Encounters of the Third Kind	1977/80
10 Gremlins	1984

Reflecting our taste for escapist fantasy adventures, the first six in this list also appear in the All-Time Top 10, and all 10 are among the 24 most successful films of all time. Films released in 1989 include *Batman*, the phenomenal success of which rocketed it into the No. 4 position, with three further contenders just outside the Top 10 achieving rentals in excess of $60,000,000: *Honey, I Shrunk the Kids*, *Back to the Future Part II* and *Ghostbusters II*.

ABOVE Eddie Murphy's *Beverly Hills Cop* is the No. 1 action comedy.

TOP RIGHT *Platoon*, the most successful war film.

BOTTOM RIGHT *Back to the Future*, No. 7 science-fiction film.

THE 10 MOST SUCCESSFUL COMEDY FILMS OF ALL TIME

Film	Year
1 Beverly Hills Cop	1984
2 Tootsie	1982
3 Three Men and a Baby	1987
4 Beverly Hills Cop II	1987
5 The Sting	1973
6 National Lampoon's Animal House	1978
7 Crocodile Dundee	1986
8 Coming to America	1988
9 Nine to Five	1980
10 Smokey and the Bandit	1977

THE 10 MOST SUCCESSFUL WESTERNS OF ALL TIME

	Film	Year
1	Butch Cassidy and the Sundance Kid	1969
2	Jeremiah Johnson	1972
3	How the West Was Won	1962
4	Pale Rider	1985
5	Young Guns	1988
6 =	Little Big Man	1970
6 =	Bronco Billy	1980
8	True Grit	1969
9	The Outlaw Josey Wales	1976
10	Duel in the Sun	1946

THE 10 MOST SUCCESSFUL MUSICAL FILMS OF ALL TIME

	Film	Year
1	Grease	1978
2	The Sound of Music	1965
3	Saturday Night Fever	1977
4	American Graffiti	1973
5	The Best Little Whorehouse in Texas	1982
6	Mary Poppins	1964
7	Fiddler on the Roof	1971
8	Annie	1982
9	A Star is Born	1976
10	Flashdance	1983

Traditional musicals (films in which the cast actually sing) and films in which a musical soundtrack is a component of the film are included. Several other musical films have also each earned in excess of $30,000,000 in US film rentals, including *The Coal Miner's Daughter* (1980), *The Rocky Horror Picture Show* (1975), *Footloose* (1984), *The Blues Brothers* (1980) and *Purple Rain* (1984).

Robert Redford and Paul Newman in *Butch Cassidy and the Sundance Kid*, the most successful western of all time.

THE 10 MOST SUCCESSFUL HORROR FILMS OF ALL TIME

	Film	Year
1	The Exorcist	1973
2	Poltergeist	1982
3	King Kong	1976
4	The Amityville Horror	1979
5	Predator	1987
6	The Shining	1980
7	The Abyss	1988
8	The Omen	1976
9	Pet Sematary	1989
10	A Nightmare on Elm Street IV	1988

ABOVE Hiding under the bedclothes in *Poltergeist*.

TOP John Travolta and Olivia Newton-John in *Grease*.

THE 10 MOST SUCCESSFUL PRE-WAR FILMS

	Film	Year
1	Gone With the Wind	1939
2	Snow White and the Seven Dwarfs	1937
3	The Birth of a Nation	1915
4	The Big Parade	1925
5	King Kong	1933
6	The Wizard of Oz	1939
7	Ben Hur	1926
8	The Singing Fool	1928
9 =	The Covered Wagon	1923
9 =	The Jazz Singer	1927
9 =	Cavalcade	1933

The Wizard of Oz and Gone With the Wind, which has headed this list for many years, both celebrated their 50th anniversaries in 1989, the extra publicity generated by these events further enhancing their rental income.

Nos. 1, 2 and 6 were filmed in Technicolor. No. 7, despite its early date, contains a colour sequence. Nos. 3, 4 and 7 are silent films, and The Jazz Singer is hailed as 'the first talkie'.

THE 10 LEAST DISASTROUS DISASTER FILMS OF ALL TIME

	Film	Year
1	The Towering Inferno	1975
2	Airport	1970
3	The Poseidon Adventure	1972
4	Earthquake	1974
5	Airport 1975	1974
6	Airport '77	1977
7	The Hindenburg	1975
8	Black Sunday	1977
9	Rollercoaster	1977
10	Two-Minute Warning	1976

A towering success – The Towering Inferno was the most successful ever disaster film.

THE 10 MOST SUCCESSFUL ANIMATED FILMS OF ALL TIME

	Film	Year
1	Who Framed Roger Rabbit?	1988
2	Snow White and the Seven Dwarfs	1937
3	Bambi	1942
4	Cinderella	1949
5	Lady and the Tramp	1955
6	The Jungle Book	1967
7	101 Dalmatians	1961
8	Pinocchio	1940
9	The Rescuers	1977
10	Song of the South	1946

All except No. 1 were made by the Disney studio. Nos. 1 and 10 are part animation, part live action.

Honey, I Shrunk the Kids, the No. 1 children's film.

THE 10 MOST SUCCESSFUL CHILDREN'S FILMS OF ALL TIME*

	Film	Year
1	Honey, I Shrunk the Kids	1989
2	Karate Kid Part II	1986
3	Mary Poppins	1964
4	Karate Kid Part I	1984
5	War Games	1983
6	The Muppet Movie	1979
7	The Goonies	1985
8	Willow	1988
9	Dark Crystal	1982
10	The Love Bug	1969

*Excluding animated films.

Radio, TV & Video

THE 10 LONGEST-RUNNING PROGRAMMES ON BBC TELEVISION

Programme	First shown
1 Come Dancing	29 September 1950
2 Panorama	11 November 1953
3 The Sky at Night	24 April 1957
4 Grandstand	11 October 1958
5 Blue Peter	16 October 1958
6 Songs of Praise	1 October 1961
7 Dr Who	23 November 1963
8 Top of the Pops	1 January 1964
9 Horizon	2 May 1964
10 Match of the Day	22 August 1964

Patrick Moore, star-gazing on BBC Television's 'The Sky at Night' since 1957.

Only programmes that are still current are listed. Several other BBC programmes, such as 'The Good Old Days' (1953–83), ran for many years but are now defunct. 'The Sky at Night' has the additional distinction of having had the same presenter, Patrick Moore, since its first programme.

THE TOP 10 BBC 1 AUDIENCES, 1989

	Programme	Day	Date	Audience
1	EastEnders	Thu/Sun	23/26 February	24,080,000†*
2	Film: *Crocodile Dundee*	Mon	25 December	21,770,000
3	Neighbours	Tue	4 April	20,920,000†*
4	Only Fools and Horses	Mon	25 December	20,120,000*
5	Bread	Mon	25 December	16,510,000*
6	Russ Abbot Christmas Show	Mon	25 December	15,010,000
7=	'Allo 'Allo	Sat	25 February	14,730,000*
7=	The Good Life	Tue	4 April	14,730,000*
9	Antiques Roadshow	Sun	26 February	14,330,000*
10	Tyson v Bruno	Sun	26 February	14,300,000

The 1989 Wimbledon Men's Final achieved the top BBC2 viewing figure of the year.

THE TOP 10 BBC 2 AUDIENCES, 1989

	Programme	Day	Date	Audience
1	Wimbledon Men's Final	Sun	9 July	11,710,000*
2	World Cup Football	Wed	11 October	7,560,000
3	40 Minutes	Thu/Sun	16/19 March	7,270,000†*
4	Blackeyes	Wed	30 November	7,150,000*
5	M*A*S*H	Wed	29 November	6,970,000*
6	Film: *A Deadly Puzzle*	Mon	22 May	6,720,000
7	Naked Video	Thu	19 January	6,550,000*
8	Snooker	Sun	30 April	6,420,000*
9	Film: *Weird Science*	Sun	17 December	6,340,000
10	Film: *Risky Business*	Sun	22 October	6,300,000

THE TOP 10 ITV AUDIENCES, 1989

	Programme	Day	Date	Audience
1	Coronation Street	Wed/Sun	15/19 March	26,930,000†*
2	Blind Date	Sat	18 November	16,860,000*
3	Forever Green	Sun	12 March	15,750,000*
4	Inspector Morse	Wed	25 January	15,490,000*
5	Film: *The Man With the Golden Gun*	Mon	27 March	15,480,000
6	Royal Variety Performance	Sat	25 November	15,470,000
7	Beadle's About	Sat	18 November	15,390,000*
8	The Heroes	Sun	2 April	15,100,000*
9	This Is Your Life	Wed	22 February	15,080,000*
10	The Bill	Tue/Fri	25/28 April	14,900,000†*

†*Aggregates two screenings of the same programme.*
*Highest total of series.
All audience figures based on programmes of 15 minutes or longer.

THE TOP 10 CHANNEL 4 AUDIENCES, 1989

	Programme	Day	Date	Audience
1	Film: *Mona Lisa*	Thu	23 February	7,820,000
2	Brookside	Mon/Sat	30 January/ 4 February	7,680,000†*
3	Behaving Badly	Mon/Sat	20/25 February	6,280,000†*
4	Treasure Hunt	Thu	6 April	6,150,000*
5	The Cosby Show	Sun	15 January & 26 February	6,100,000*
6	Roseanne	Fri	9 June	5,470,000*
7	Film: *Starcrossed*	Mon	13 February	5,450,000
8	Hill Street Blues	Tue	4 April	5,440,000*
9	Film: *Johnny Bull*	Mon	6 February	5,150,000
10	Film: *Avanti!*	Mon	20 March	5,030,000

ABOVE *Mona Lisa*, the No. 1 Channel 4 programme of 1989.

BELOW *The Man With the Golden Gun*, ITV's top film of 1989.

As the viewing figures show, BBC 1 captured a substantial share of the 1989 Christmas audience. The soaps – 'EastEnders', 'Neighbours', 'Coronation Street' and 'Brookside' – maintain their dominant positions in the ratings, although only 'Coronation Street' increased its audience figure on 1988. American imports such as 'The Cosby Show' and reruns of 'M*A*S*H' and 'Hill Street Blues' remain popular, and the Royal Variety Performance, the Wimbledon Men's Final and snooker make their usual annual appearance in the charts. Major feature films also attract large audiences – *The Man With the Golden Gun* was actually watched by more people in 1989 than when it was shown in 1988. 'Treasure Hunt' lost ground (it was No. 1 in the Channel 4 ratings the previous year), but 'Blind Date' increased its viewing figure by nearly 2,000,000. If, as some critics claim, television is dominated by quiz programmes, it is salient that not one appears in any channel's 1989 Top 10.

TV Quiz

1 Were the first BBC television programmes broadcast from Alexandra Palace in 1926, 1936 or 1946?
2 What was the name of the character played in *M*A*S*H* by Loretta Swit?
3 What was the subject of the 1957 April Fool's Day hoax on BBC television's *Panorama*?
4 In what year was colour television inaugurated in the UK?
5 What is the postcode of the imaginary London borough of 'Walford' in which *EastEnders* is located?
6 Did *Coronation Street* first appear in 1955, 1960 or 1965?
7 In television, what does the abbreviation 'OB' stand for?
8 Who is the longest-serving British children's TV personality?
9 What is the American version of *Till Death Us Do Part* called, and what is the name of the Alf Garnett character?
10 What British television series starred, at different times, Honor Blackman, Diana Rigg and Joanna Lumley?

THE 10 BIGGEST EVER TV AUDIENCES IN THE USA

Programme	Date	Households Total	%
1 M*A*S*H Special	28 Feb 1983	50,150,000	60.2
2 Dallas	21 Nov 1980	41,470,000	53.3
3 Roots Part 8	30 Jan 1977	36,380,000	51.1
4 Super Bowl XVI	24 Jan 1982	40,020,000	49.1
5 Super Bowl XVII	30 Jan 1983	40,480,000	48.6
6 Super Bowl XX	26 Jan 1986	41,490,000	48.3
7 Gone With the Wind Pt. 1	7 Nov 1976	33,960,000	47.7
8 Gone With the Wind Pt. 2	8 Nov 1976	33,750,000	47.4
9 Super Bowl XII	15 Jan 1978	34,410,000	47.2
10 Super Bowl XIII	21 Jan 1979	35,090,000	47.1

THE 10 BIGGEST EVER TV AUDIENCES IN THE UK

Programme	Date	Audience
1 Royal Wedding of HRH Prince Charles to Lady Diana Spencer	29 Jul 1981	39,000,000
2 Brazil v England: 1970 World Cup	10 Jun 1970	32,500,000
3= Chelsea v Leeds: Cup Final Replay	28 Apr 1970	32,000,000
3= England v West Germany: 1966 World Cup Final	30 Jul 1966	32,000,000
5 EastEnders Christmas Episode	25 Dec 1987	30,000,000
6 Morecambe and Wise Christmas Show	25 Dec 1977	28,000,000
7= Dallas	22 Nov 1980	27,000,000
7= World Heavyweight Boxing Championship: Joe Frazier v Muhammad Ali	8 Mar 1971	27,000,000
9 To The Manor Born (last episode)	11 Nov 1979	24,000,000
10 Live And Let Die (James Bond film)	20 Jan 1980	23,500,000

In the last edition of *The Top 10 of Everything* we ranked the Top 10 TV programmes according to households viewing. However, as more and more households acquire television sets, the most recently screened programmes tend to be watched by larger audiences, which distorts the historical picture. This year we are therefore listing the Top 10 according to *percentage* of households viewing. The last ever episode of 'M*A*S*H' remains at No.1, with both the largest number and highest percentage of households watching while 'Dallas' rises from 3rd to 2nd place. Several Super Bowl games remain in the Top 10, but earlier programmes with high-percentage audience figures, such as 'Roots' and *Gone With the Wind*, also make an appearance. Among other popular programmes in the Top 50 are several episodes of the 1960s series 'Beverly Hillbillies', the 'Thornbirds' serial, the films *Airport* and *Love Story*, the 1970 Academy Awards ceremony and the 1961 Miss America Pageant.

The episode of 'Dallas' revealing who shot J.R. is the only programme in the Top 10 on both sides of the Atlantic. It was shown one day later in the UK. Had it been shown on the same day, in view of the time difference between the USA and UK, the British audience would have seen it first and could thus telephone their friends in the States and spoil it for them; instead, it worked the other way round ...

THE TOP 10 TELEVISION-OWNING COUNTRIES

Country	TV sets per 1,000 population
1 Bermuda	833
2 USA	811
3 West Germany	754
4 Oman	739
5 Monaco	667
6 Guam	638
7 St Pierre and Miquelon	625
8 Japan	587
9 Canada	577
10 US Virgin Islands	565

The UK (with 434 sets per 1,000) is 14th after Australia (483), Austria (480) and the Netherlands (469). The very high densities in the most affluent countries contrast sharply with the position in most parts of the Third World. In Ethiopia, for example, there is the equivalent of 1.6 television sets per 1,000 population, and in Mali, where there are only about 2,000 television sets in the entire country, the figure is 0.2 per 1,000.

THE TOP 10 RADIO-OWNING COUNTRIES

Country	Radio sets per 1,000 population
1 USA	2,119
2 Guam	1,381
3 Australia	1,270
4 Bermuda	1,250
5 UK	1,145
6 Gibraltar	1,143
7 American Samoa	1,113
8 Netherlands Antilles	1,053
9 Monaco	1,007
10 Norfolk Island	1,000

As these figures show, there are just nine countries in the world where there are more radio sets than people. The prevalence of radios in island communities is particularly marked, perhaps indicating something of the value placed on the radio as a means of maintaining contact with the rest of the world.

OPPOSITE The last 'M*A*S*H', seen in 60.2 per cent of US homes.

ABOVE The Royal Wedding holds the UK TV audience record.

ABOVE *Dirty Dancing*, the UK's bestselling video of all time.

BELOW RIGHT *Crocodile Dundee*, most-rented video in the UK.

THE 10 ALL-TIME BESTSELLING VIDEOS IN THE UK

1 *Dirty Dancing*

2 *Callanetics*

3 *Watch With Mother*

4 *Jane Fonda's New Workout*

5 *Pinocchio*

6 *Crocodile Dundee*

7 *Making Michael Jackson's 'Thriller'*

8 U2, *Rattle and Hum*

9 Michael Jackson, *The Legend Continues*

10 Kylie Minogue, *The Videos*

The under-£10 video sales market has boomed in the UK from a business worth some £15,000,000 in 1985 to a staggering £300,000,000 in 1989. Originally dominated by music titles, the biggest sellers have shifted towards highly-publicized fitness tapes and a small number of feature films that are regarded as possessing a 're-watchability factor'.

THE 10 BESTSELLING MUSIC VIDEOS IN THE UK

1 *Making Michael Jackson's 'Thriller'*

2 U2, *Rattle and Hum*

3 Michael Jackson, *The Legend Continues*

4 Kylie Minogue, *The Videos*

5 Cliff Richard, *Private Collection*

6 Jason Donovan, *The Videos*

7 Kylie Minogue, *The Videos, Vol. 2*

8 Phil Collins, *The Singles Collection*

9 *Queen's Greatest Flix*

10 *Bros Live: The Big Push Tour*

Making Michael Jackson's 'Thriller' was the first music video to sell in large numbers, and continues to achieve volume sales years after its release. Most of the other Top 10 bestsellers date from 1988–89 and reflect the huge expansion of the video sales market during those years.

THE 10 MOST-RENTED VIDEOS OF ALL TIME IN THE UK

1 *Crocodile Dundee*

2 *Dirty Dancing*

3 *A Fish Called Wanda*

4 *Robocop*

5 *E.T.*

6 *Back to the Future*

7 *Police Academy*

8 *Beverly Hills Cop*

9 *Raiders of the Lost Ark*

10 *Lethal Weapon*

THE TOP 10 VIDEO RENTALS IN THE UK IN 1989

1 *Fatal Attraction*

2 *Crocodile Dundee II*

3 *A Fish Called Wanda*

4 *Three Men and a Baby*

5 *Good Morning, Vietnam*

6 *Buster*

7 *Coming to America*

8 *Beetlejuice*

9 *Die Hard*

10 *The Running Man*

ABOVE Jamie Lee Curtis and John Cleese in *A Fish Called Wanda*, the top US video rental of 1989.

THE TOP 10 VIDEO RENTALS IN THE USA IN 1989

1 *A Fish Called Wanda*

2 *Die Hard*

3 *Rain Man*

4 *Coming to America*

5 *Big*

6 *Twins*

7 *The Accused*

8 *Beaches*

9 *Tequila Sunrise*

10 *Cocktail*

The time of the year when a video is released affects its ability to qualify for the Top 10 rentals of that year. Certain 1989 US video releases, such as *Batman* and *Ghostbusters II*, for example, do not rank in the Top 10 because they were released late in the year (20 and 27 November respectively), while among those that do feature in the Top 10, *Rain Man*, which was not released until 4 September, will almost certainly out-rent *A Fish Called Wanda*, which was released on 27 February.

THE 10 ALL-TIME BESTSELLING CHILDREN'S VIDEOS IN THE UK

1 *Watch With Mother*

2 *Pinocchio*

3 *Thomas the Tank Engine: The Deputation*

4 *Postman Pat I*

5 *Rupert and the Frog Song*

6 *Sleeping Beauty*

7 *Robin Hood*

8 *Dumbo*

9 *The Sword in the Stone*

10 *Thomas the Tank Engine: Thomas, Percy and the Coal*

It seems likely that the hugely successful BBC *Watch With Mother* video, containing vintage episodes of Bill and Ben, The Woodentops and other favourites from the 1950s, was bought more by and for nostalgic adults than their offspring. Nos. 2, 6, 7, 8 and 9 are all animated versions of familiar stories produced by Walt Disney. Under Disney's cinema release policy, the videos of *Pinocchio* and *Sleeping Beauty* were available for a limited period and will not be released again for several years, when they will reappear for the next 'Disney generation'.

THE TOP 10 MUSICALS ON VIDEO IN THE UK

Film	Year released
1 *Grease*	1978
2 *The Sound of Music*	1965
3 *The Little Shop of Horrors*	1986
4 *Calamity Jane*	1953
5 *South Pacific*	1958
6 *The Gay Divorcee*	1934
7 *Seven Brides for Seven Brothers*	1954
8 *Flying Down to Rio*	1933
9 *Bugsy Malone*	1977
10 *The Wizard of Oz*	1939

Industry, Commerce & Communications

THE 10 RETAILERS WITH THE MOST OUTLETS IN THE UK

Retailer	Outlets
1 Sears (including Selfridges, Freeman Hardy & Willis, Dolcis, Olympus, etc)	3,599
2 Burton (including Top Shop, Dorothy Perkins, Debenhams, etc)	2,365
3 Gallaher (including Dollond & Aitchison, etc)	2,321
4 Kingfisher (Woolworths)	1,970
5 Thorn EMI (including Rumbelows, HMV, DER, etc)	1,733
6 Boots	1,330
7 Dixons (including Currys, etc)	1,326
8 Dewhurst butchers	1,250
9 Associated British Foods	1,176
10 Argyll (including Safeway, etc)	1,167

Includes concessions (shops within stores, etc).

THE TOP 10 RETAILERS IN THE UK

Retailer	Annual sales (£)
1 J. Sainsbury	5,152,000,000
2 Tesco	4,718,000,000
3 Marks & Spencer	4,425,000,000
4 Asda Group	3,514,000,000
5 Argyll Group	3,501,000,000
6 Gateway Corporation	2,994,000,000
7 Kingfisher	2,776,000,000
8 The Boots Company	2,711,000,000
9 Sears	1,767,000,000
10 John Lewis Partnership	1,754,000,000

Based on *The Retail Rankings* (1990) published by The Corporate Intelligence Group Ltd.

THE 10 BESTSELLING DUTY-FREE PRODUCTS

Product	Sales (US$)
1 Women's fragrances	1,440,000,000
2 Cigarettes	1,430,000,000
3 Scotch whisky	1,125,000,000
4 Women's cosmetics and toiletries	750,000,000
5 Cognac	730,000,000
6 Leather goods	650,000,000
7 Men's fragrances and toiletries	530,000,000
8 Confectionery	470,000,000
9 Accessories	435,000,000
10 Watches	380,000,000

Total world sales of duty-free goods in 1988 were estimated to have reached $11,500,000,000.

BELOW Checkout at Sainsbury's. Including all its activities, the firm is the UK's leading retailer.

RIGHT Heathrow, the top duty-free shop in the UK.

THE TOP 10 DUTY-FREE SHOPS IN THE WORLD

Shop location	Annual sales (US$)
1 Honolulu Airport	450,000,000
2 London Heathrow Airport	220,000,000
3 Hong Kong Airport	215,000,000
4 Amsterdam Schiphol Airport	165,000,000
5 Singapore Airport	160,000,000
6 Paris Charles de Gaulle Airport	152,000,000
7 Taipei Airport	140,000,000
8 Frankfurt Airport	139,000,000
9 Viking Line Ferries (Finland)	120,000,000
10 London Gatwick Airport	118,000,000

All but one of the world's Top 10 duty-free shops are in airports. Although Honolulu handles fewer than 12 per cent of the number of international passengers that pass through London Heathrow (2,200,000 compared with Heathrow's almost 19,000,000), they tend to be very high-spending. As a result, Honolulu is not only the top airport duty-free shop in terms of total annual sales, but also in sales per passenger, which average $204.55, while Heathrow's are only $11.72 per passenger.

THE TOP 10 DUTY-FREE SHOPS IN THE UK

Shop location	Annual sales (US$)
1 London Heathrow Airport	220,000,000
2 London Gatwick Airport	118,000,000
3 Sealink Ferries	87,000,000
4 P & O Ferries	83,000,000
5 Britannia Airways (charter airline)	43,500,000
6 Manchester Ringway Airport	40,000,000
7 British Airways	35,000,000
8 Dan-Air (charter airline)	31,500,000
9 Monarch Airlines (charter airline)	24,000,000
10 Sally Line (ferry operator)	21,000,000

INDUSTRY, COMMERCE & COMMUNICATIONS

THE TOP 10 SUPERMARKET GROUPS*

Group	Annual sales (£)
1 Tesco	4,718,000,000
2 J. Sainsbury	4,688,000,000**
3 Gateway Corporation	3,817,000,000
4 Argyll Group	3,390,000,000
5 Asda	2,521,000,000
6 Kwik Save	1,181,000,000
7 Waitrose	851,000,000
8 Iceland (including Bejam)	634,000,000
9 William Morrison	604,000,000
10 William Low	304,000,000

*Excluding Co-ops.
**Excluding Savacentre.

Based on *The Retail Rankings* (1990) published by The Corporate Intelligence Group Ltd.

THE TOP 10 GROCERY BRANDS IN GREAT BRITAIN

Brand (product)	Manufacturer	Annual sales (£)
1 Persil (washing powder)	Lever Bros	192,100,000
2 Nescafé (instant coffee)	Nestlé	188,400,000
3 Whiskas (catfood)	Pedigree Petfoods	180,800,000
4 Ariel (washing powder)	Procter & Gamble	171,800,000
5 Andrex (toilet paper)	Scott	164,800,000
6 Coca-Cola (soft drink)	Coca-Cola	141,800,000
7 PG Tips (tea)	Brooke Bond Foods (Unilever)	115,800,000
8 Chum (dogfood)	Pedigree Petfoods	104,100,000
9 Heinz Baked Beans	H.J. Heinz	94,000,000
10 Flora (margarine)	Van den Berghs & Jurgens (Unilever)	91,700,000

ABOVE Tesco is the UK's No. 1 supermarket.

BACKGROUND RIGHT Harrods, subject of a hard-fought takeover.

RIGHT Burton is the top UK clothing retailer.

BELOW Heinz Baked Beans are the ninth bestselling grocery line in Britain.

Both Britain's top two bestselling grocery lines originated in Europe and were the first in their fields: Persil, the first ever household detergent, went on the market in Germany on 6 June 1907. Its name may derive either from the parsley trademark of a French inventor ('persil' is French for parsley), or from two ingredients, *per*borate and *sil*icate, used by Professor Hermann Geissler and Dr Hermann Bauer, the German inventors of dry soap powder. The product has been made in Great Britain since 1909. Nescafé was the original instant coffee, first sold in 1938 by the Swiss firm, Nestlé. 'PG Tips' comes from the abbreviation of its earlier name, *Pre-Gestee*, referring to its supposed 'before digestion' medicinal properties: the tips are the best parts of tea leaves. The name Andrex stems from the location of the factory where it was first made in 1945: St Andrews Road, Walthamstow, London. It was originally called 'Androll' and changed to Andrex in 1954.

The COWBOY'S BREAKF[A]

with BACON

THE TOP 10 ACQUISITIONS AND MERGERS IN UK RETAILING IN THE 1980s

	Purchaser	Acquisition	Year	Value (£)*
1	Isosceles plc	Gateway	1989	2,200,000,000
2	Habitat Mothercare plc	British Home Stores	1985	1,500,000,000
3	Boots Company plc	Ward White	1989	900,000,000
4	Asda Group plc	61 Gateway stores	1989	700,000,000
5	Dee Corporation plc	Fine Fare/ Shoppers Paradise	1986	700,000,000
6	Argyll Group plc	Safeway	1987	700,000,000
7	Management buy-out	Magnet	1989	600,000,000
8=	Alfayed Investment Trust	House of Fraser (Harrods, etc)	1987	600,000,000
8=	Associated Dairies Group plc	MFI	1985	600,000,000
10	Burton Group plc	Debenhams	1985	600,000,000

*As a result of rounding-off, several values appear to be identical.

THE TOP 10 DEPARTMENT STORE GROUPS IN THE UK

	Group	Annual sales (£)
1	House of Fraser	992,000,000
2	John Lewis Partnership	903,000,000
3	Burton Group (Debenhams, etc)	706,000,000
4	Allders	284,000,000
5	Sears (Selfridges)	172,000,000
6	Fenwicks	132,000,000
7	London & Edinburgh Trust (Owen Owen)	103,000,000
8	Bentalls	75,000,000
9	James Beattie	62,000,000
10	Liberty	46,000,000

THE TOP 10 UK CLOTHING RETAILERS

	Retailer	Annual sales (£)
1	Burton Group	940,000,000
2	C & A/Brenninkmeyer	590,000,000
3	Sears	381,000,000
4	Storehouse (including Mothercare, Richards, Blazer, etc)	343,000,000
5	Next	259,000,000
6	Lewis Trust Group (including Chelsea Girl, etc)	179,000,000
7	Etam	141,000,000
8	Coats Viyella	100,000,000
9	Benetton	85,000,000
10	Mackays	61,000,000

Note: The annual sales figures for certain retailers that are specialist components of larger groups will be different from those of the group as a whole.

Based on *The Retail Rankings* (1990) published by The Corporate Intelligence Group Ltd.

THE 10 MOST DANGEROUS JOBS IN THE UK

1 Asbestos worker

2 Crews of boats, ships, railway trains and aircraft

3 Demolition contractor

4 Diver

5 Fireman

6 Miner

7 Oil/gas-rig worker

8 Steeplejack

9 Tunneller

10 Steel erector

Life assurance companies carefully base their premiums on actuarial statistics that take into account the likelihood of people in each job being involved in an accident that injures or kills them at work, or as a result of their contact with dangerous substances, such as asbestos dust. This does not mean that assurance companies will not provide cover for such professions, but the more risky the job, the higher the premium.

THE 10 MOST DANGEROUS JOBS IN THE USA

Job	Deaths per 100,000
1 Timber-cutters and loggers	129.0
2 Aircraft pilots	97.0
3 Asbestos and insulation workers	78.7
4 Structural metal workers	72.0
5 Electric power line and cable installers and repairers	50.7
6 Firefighters	48.8
7 Garbage collectors	40.0
8 Truck drivers	39.6
9 Bulldozer operators	39.3
10 Earth drillers	38.8

At least 240 people die every working day in the USA as a result of accidents at work or from diseases caused by their jobs. All the 10 riskiest jobs (except for pilots) are so-called 'blue-collar' or manual jobs. Other dangerous jobs that do not quite make the Top 10 are miners, taxi drivers and policemen. The risk attached to most 'white-collar' jobs is under 10 per 100,000, with some being placed extremely low – chance of death at work among embalmers and librarians, for example, is put at zero.

THE 10 MOST STRESSFUL JOBS IN THE USA

1	Firefighter
2	Racing car driver
3	Astronaut
4	Surgeon
5	National Football League player
6	Police officer
7	Osteopath
8	State police officer
9	Air traffic controller
10	Mayor

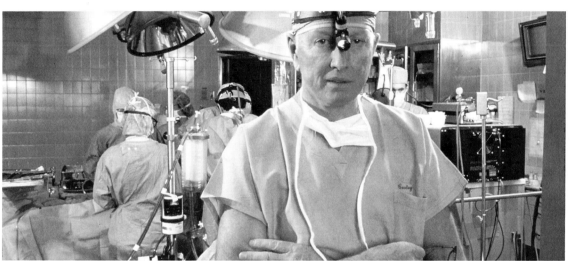

THE 10 BEST PAID JOBS IN THE USA

	Job	Average annual salary ($)
1	Lawyer	48,360
2	Airline pilot	42,796
3	Aerospace engineer	42,640
4	Doctor	42,380
5	Financial manager	40,976
6 =	Chemical engineer	40,820
6 =	Personnel/labour relations manager	40,820
8	Securities and financial services salesman	39,936
9	Education administrator	39,364
10	College professor	39,104

These are the average annual salaries for male employees in the highest-paid professions. Women – even those in the same professions – earn average salaries that are much lower than these (women doctors, for example, averaging $28,756), and only female lawyers (with an average of $40,248) earn salaries that qualify for the Top 10. Of course, in order to produce these averages, many employees of either sex (as well as self-employed people, who are not included) may earn considerably higher incomes than any of these.

OPPOSITE TOP & BOTTOM On top of the world – and almost at the top of the list of dangerous professions – a pilot and a structural metal worker.

TOP National Football League players rank fifth in the 10 most stressful jobs in the USA.
ABOVE A highly-paid US doctor.

THE 10 COUNTRIES WITH THE HIGHEST PROPORTION OF FARMERS

	Country	% in agriculture
1	Rwanda	91.6
2	Burundi	91.5
3	Niger	88.1
4	Burkina Faso	84.9
5	Mozambique	82.2
6	Uganda	82.0
7=	Mali	81.9
7=	Tanzania	81.9
9	Gambia	81.6
10	Lesotho	81.1

THE 10 COUNTRIES WITH THE LOWEST PROPORTION OF FARMERS

	Country	% in agriculture
1	Singapore	1.1
2	Hong Kong	1.3
3=	Bahrain	1.9
3=	Kuwait	1.9
5	Belgium/Luxembourg	2.0
6	UK	2.1
7	USA	2.5
8	Qatar	2.8
9	United Arab Emirates	2.9
10	Puerto Rico	3.1

This list is based on a study of the number of people dependent on agriculture for their livelihood as a proportion of the 'economically active' (ie, excluding children, retired, unemployed, etc) population of the country. Of Rwanda's total population of 6,754,000, for example, 3,320,000 are economically active and 3,041,000 of them work on the land, giving the world's highest proportion of 91.6 per cent. The world average is 47.4 per cent, but many countries have figures far below this as the following list shows:

Of the UK's economically active population of 28,229,000 (roughly half the total population), only 593,000 are engaged in agriculture.

BELOW Rwanda's markets serve the country with the world's highest proportion dependent on the land.

RIGHT Stamps celebrating 150 years of the RSPCA's activities as Britain's leading animal charity.

BRITAIN'S TOP 10 FUND-RAISING CHARITIES

	Charity	Voluntary income (£)
1	Oxfam	40,986,000
2	National Trust	40,556,000
3	Royal National Lifeboat Institution	37,725,000
4	Imperial Cancer Research Fund	32,075,000
5	Cancer Research Campaign	31,016,000
6	Salvation Army	26,076,000
7	Barnardos	25,311,000
8	Save the Children Fund	24,133,000
9	Guide Dogs for the Blind Association	19,923,000
10	Spastics Society	18,532,000

There are over 165,000 registered charities in England and Wales alone. The order of the Top 10 is for *voluntary* income only. Most charities also receive income from other sources, such as rents and interest on investments. In 1988, for example, the *total* income of the National Trust from all sources was £85,295,000 with £20,506,000 from rents and investments, and that of the Salvation Army was £70,759,000. In the same year, the voluntary income of all charities was between £3,000,000,000 and £4,500,000,000 and their total income approximately £15,000,000,000, or £26 for every person in the UK. The order of the largest ones and the amounts donated to them have changed dramatically over recent years. The experience of Band Aid is perhaps the most striking: in 1984–85 it was the No. 1 charity with total income of £56,500,000, but by 1988 it was down to No. 392, raising just £179,000.

ABOVE Oxfam is Britain's top fund-raising charity.

1840·RSPCA·1990

1840·RSPCA·1990

1840·RSPCA·1990

1840·RSPCA·1990

BRITAIN'S TOP 10 ANIMAL CHARITIES

	Charity	Income (£) Voluntary	Total
1	Royal Society for the Prevention of Cruelty to Animals (RSPCA)	16,861,000	21,715,000
2	People's Dispensary for Sick Animals (PDSA)	11,390,000	13,568,000
3	Royal Society for the Protection of Birds (RSPB)	10,131,000	13,194,000
4	World Wide Fund for Nature	7,741,000	8,932,000
5	Donkey Sanctuary	2,932,000	3,145,000
6	Wildfowl Trust	976,000	3,032,000
7	Battersea Dogs Home	1,522,000	2,882,000
8	National Canine Defence League	2,226,000	2,534,000
9	Scottish Society for the Prevention of Cruelty to Animals (SSPCA)	1,400,000	2,325,000
10	Cats Protection League	1,503,000	1,911,000

THE TOP 10 CHILDREN'S CHARITIES IN THE UK

Charity	Income (£)	
	Voluntary	Total
1 Barnardos	25,311,000	59,010,000
2 Spastics Society	18,532,000	46,559,000
3 Save the Children Fund	24,133,000	35,963,000
4 National Children's Home	7,788,000	30,467,000
5 National Society for the Prevention of Cruelty to Children	16,709,000	20,336,000
6 United Nations International Children's Emergency Fund	3,935,000	19,859,000
7 Church of England Children's Society	9,619,000	17,659,000
8 Action Aid	12,887,000	15,212,000
9 Great Ormond Street Hospital Redevelopment Appeal	9,032,000	9,699,000
10 Scottish Council for Spastics	1,289,000	8,166,000

The Top 10 includes some charities that aid adults as well as children.

THE 10 LEADING CARBON DIOXIDE PRODUCERS IN THE WORLD

1 USA
2 USSR
3 China
4 Japan
5 West Germany
6 UK
7 India
8 Poland
9 Canada
10 France

The Carbon Dioxide Information Analysis Center at Oak Ridge, Tennessee, monitors CO_2 emissions from three principal sources – fossil fuel burning, cement manufacturing and gas flaring. It found that between 1950 and 1987 the USSR, China, Japan, India and France more than doubled their emissions while those of West Germany, the UK and Canada were reduced. The USA, although still the worst offender, reduced its output from over 40 per cent of the world's total to just over 20 per cent. The USA's annual production of carbon is equivalent to over $4\frac{1}{2}$ tons per person, exceeded only by South Africa, which belches out the equivalent of over 5 tons per inhabitant.

THE 10 LEADING SULPHUR DIOXIDE PRODUCERS IN THE EC

Country	Annual SO_2 emissions (tonnes)
1 UK	3,863,000
2 Spain	2,543,000
3 West Germany	2,223,000
4 Italy	2,075,000
5 France	1,517,000
6 Belgium	610,000
7 Greece	546,000
8 Portugal	286,000
9 Netherlands	274,000
10 Denmark	248,000

Based on the most recent statistics available for emissions of sulphur dioxide – the principal cause of acid rain – from fuel combustion in EC factories and power stations during the 1980s. During the decade, emissions by all countries declined: the UK's production was estimated at 5,310,000 tonnes in 1975 and further reductions are planned so that the level in the year 2003 will be 60 per cent less than that in 1980.

THE 10 COMMONEST TYPES OF LITTER

1 Cigarette ends
2 Paper items
3 Matchsticks
4 Ring pulls
5 Plastic cups
6 Sweet wrappers
7 Glass bottles
8 Bottle tops
9 Tickets and stickers
10 Metal cans

Based on a survey conducted by the Tidy Britain Group, which counted the number of items in each category in typical samplings of litter deposited on Britain's streets.

INDUSTRY, COMMERCE & COMMUNICATIONS

What a load of rubbish! Debris at the end of a pop concert.

THE TOP 10 PERSONAL ENVIRONMENTAL IMPROVEMENT ACTIVITIES

	Activity	% already undertaking
1	Use of ozone-friendly aerosols	64
2	Picking up other people's litter	52
3	Avoiding use of pesticides in the garden	42
4	Taking bottles to a bottle bank	40
5=	Cutting down on the use of electricity	38
5=	Collecting old newspapers for recycling	38
7	Using alternative transport to the car	28
8=	Using recycled paper	25
8=	Making compost out of kitchen waste	25
10	Using unleaded petrol	22

Based on a 1989 Department of the Environment Survey of Public Attitudes to the Environment conducted in England and Wales in which people were asked what environment-improving activities they already undertake. When interviewees were also asked what activities they would consider, the largest number, 59 per cent, claimed they would use recycled paper and the same number would buy phosphate-free washing powder, although only 9 per cent said they already used it.

BOTTOM LEFT Industrial waste and raw sewage discharged into rivers – among our major environmental concerns.

ABOVE The increasing use of bottle banks marks our growing awareness of the benefits of recycling.

THE TOP 10 ENVIRONMENTAL CONCERNS

	Environmental problem	Total % worried
1	Chemicals put into rivers and the sea	91
2	Sewage contamination of beaches and bathing water	89
3	Oil spills at sea and oil on beaches	86
4	Destruction of the ozone layer	83
5	Loss of wildlife and habitats, destruction of species	82
6	Radioactive waste	81
7	Insecticides, fertilizers and chemical sprays	80
8	Destruction of tropical forests	76
9	Acid rain	75
10=	Traffic exhaust fumes	74
10=	Litter and rubbish	74

Based on a 1989 Department of the Environment Survey of Public Attitudes to the Environment conducted in England and Wales in which people were asked how worried they were about environmental problems. Interviewees were asked whether they were 'very worried' or 'quite worried', and the list combines the two degrees of concern.

THE 10 BESTSELLING ELECTRICAL APPLIANCES IN THE UK*

1 Colour televisions
2 Audio systems and separates
3 Videocassette recorders
4 Washing machines
5 Fridges and fridge-freezers
6 Vacuum cleaners
7 Microwave ovens
8 Camcorders
9 Washer/dryers
10 Freestanding cookers

*Based on total retail value.

During 1989, a number of health scares relating to the safety of microwave ovens depressed their previously high sales. In the same year, high interest rates reduced consumer spending in all sectors of the market, although certain areas of growth were observed, especially in FST (Flat Square Tube) televisions and compact disc players. Camcorders (video cameras and recorders), which had been on the market for barely a year, entered the Top 10 for the first time. However, their position in the list is less a reflection of the total volume of sales than the fact that they are very expensive, few costing less than £1,000.

The long-running Ideal Home Exhibition remains perennially popular.

THE TOP 10 EXHIBITIONS AND EVENTS AT EARLS COURT AND OLYMPIA IN THE 1980s

1 Daily Mail Ideal Home Exhibition
2 Motorfair
3 The Royal Tournament
4 London International Boat Show
5 Billy Graham Mission '89
6 Daily Mail International Ski Show
7 Caravan and Holiday Show
8 Opera
9 Personal Computer Show
10 Crufts Dog Show

THE 10 PRINCIPAL CATEGORIES OF CONSUMER SPENDING IN THE UK

Item	Average weekly expenditure £ p
1 Food	38.28
2 Housing	35.81
3 Motoring expenditure	25.31
4 Leisure services (cinema, sports events, holidays, etc)	18.13
5 Household goods (furniture, etc)	15.01
6 Clothing and footwear	14.52
7 Fuel, light and power	10.48
8 Household services (insurance, telephone, postage, etc)	9.80
9 Leisure goods (television, video, books, newspapers, toys, etc)	9.61
10 Alcoholic drinks	9.19

This list is based on a Government survey of family expenditure during 1988. With the addition of certain other categories (personal goods and services, fares and other travel costs, tobacco and miscellaneous items), the average family's total weekly spending was reckoned to be £204.41.

PHONE NUMBERS

THE 10 COUNTRIES WITH THE MOST TELEPHONES

	Country	Telephones
1	USA	126,725,000
2	Japan	49,247,000
3	USSR	28,184,000
4	West Germany	27,552,453
5	France	24,461,808
6	UK	23,290,000
7	Italy	19,104,828
8	Canada	13,444,317
9	Spain	10,236,408
10	South Korea	8,785,165

'Number, please?' Many British telephone exchanges remained manually operated until long after the introduction of automatic exchanges in 1912.

It is estimated that there are some 454,622,000 telephones in use in the world, of which 186,839,000 are in Europe, 163,520,000 in North and South America, 88,763,000 in Asia, 8,644,000 in Oceania and 6,856,000 in Africa.

Ranking countries according to number of telephones per 1,000 produces the following list:

	Country	Telephones per 1,000 population
1	Monaco	733
2	Sweden	657
3	Switzerland	535
4	Denmark	529
5	Canada	524
6	USA	520
7	Finland	480
8	Iceland	470
9	Norway	465
10	West Germany	450
	UK	*409*

There are many countries in the world with fewer than 10 telephones per 1,000 population, including China (7 phones per 1,000), Pakistan (6), India (5) and Indonesia (4), and most of Africa – Niger, for example, has only 1.4 phones per 1,000.

The figure for Monaco varies according to what source is used – one actually gives more phones than inhabitants! If we take Monaco out altogether and move all the others up, France enters the list in 10th position with 440 phones per 1,000.

THE 10 COUNTRIES WITH THE MOST PUBLIC TELEPHONES

	Country	Public phones per 1,000	Total public phones
1	USA	7.12	1,736,645
2	Japan	6.78	828,000
3	Italy	7.69	440,903
4	France	3.53	196,109
5	Brazil	1.27	180,122
6	West Germany	2.67	163,030
7	Republic of Korea	3.81	160,165
8	Canada	5.93	152,115
9	Taiwan	5.01	97,952
10	UK	1.42	80,800

Ranking countries according to number of public phones per 1,000 produces a different order:

1	Singapore	9.58
2	Switzerland	9.24
3	Italy	7.69
4	USA	7.12
5	Japan	6.78
6	Canada	5.93
7	Taiwan	5.01
8	Austria	3.85
9	Finland	3.84
10	South Korea	3.81

THE 10 MOST-DIALLED UK TELEPHONE SERVICES

Service	Provider
1 123 ('Speaking Clock')	British Telecom
2 Rapid Raceline (horse racing results)	William Hill Leisure
3 Rapid Cricketline	William Hill Leisure
4 Turfcall (horse racing results)	British Telecom Supercall
5 Racecall (horse racing results)	Telephone Information Services
6 F.I.S.T. (Fantasy Interactive Scenarios by Telephone – fantasy game)	Computerdial
7 F.T. Cityline (financial data)	*Financial Times*
8 Russell Grant Horoscope	Computerdial
9 *The Sun* Justin Toper Horoscope	Legion Telecommunications
10 Weathercall	Telephone Information Services

The Top 10 covers charged services only, not those to the operator, directory enquiries and other (as yet) free facilities. British Telecom will not reveal how many people dial 123 (formerly 'TIM'), but it is estimated that some of the leading services generate up to 50,000,000 calls each per annum. The total value of the telephone information market, some 225,000,000 calls a year, is reckoned to be in excess of £130,000,000.

The expansion in the use of cellular mobile phones is one component of the communications revolution of the 1980s.

THE 10 COUNTRIES THAT MAKE THE MOST INTERNATIONAL PHONE CALLS

Country	Calls per head	Total calls
1 USA	2.3	566,998,000
2 West Germany	8.4	514,931,000
3 UK	4.9	280,000,000
4 Canada	7.4	190,000,000
5 Switzerland	28.1	183,950,000
6 Italy	2.9	164,316,000
7 Netherlands	10.8	159,000,000
8 Belgium	12.3	121,700,000
9 Spain	3.0	117,299,000
10 Japan	0.8	96,083,000

After Switzerland, Denmark, which does not even appear in the Top 10, makes the second highest number of international calls per person (14.8).

THE TOP 10 CELLULAR MOBILE PHONE USERS

Country	Mobile phones
1 USA	2,069,000
2 UK	498,000
3 Sweden	243,000
4 Japan	210,000
5 Canada	196,000
6 Norway	152,000
7 Finland	105,000
8 Denmark	102,000
9 West Germany	99,000
10 France	98,000

Phone Quiz

1 How was Elisha Gray not quite the inventor of the telephone?
2 Did the telephone dial come into use in the UK in 1903, 1913, or 1923?
3 Who had a No. 5 hit in the UK in 1978 with 'Hanging On The Telephone'?
4 When was the 999 emergency telephone service introduced in the UK?
5 Who was anxious to 'phone home' in a 1982 film?
6 In the UK, where would you get through to if you dialled 071–930 4832?
7 Who was the first European monarch to speak on the telephone?
8 What British actress appeared in the 1967 film, *Up The Junction*, and in a long-running series of commercials for British Telecom?
9 The architect of Liverpool Cathedral and Battersea Power Station also designed the traditional British telephone box. Who was he?
10 Prior to the introduction of '123', what number was dialled in the London area for the speaking clock?

THE 10 LARGEST COMPANIES IN GREAT BRITAIN (BY SHARE CAPITAL)

Company	Share capital (£)
1 BP	17,702,000,000
2 British Telecom	17,539,000,000
3 Shell	15,282,000,000
4 BAT	12,039,000,000
5 Glaxo Holdings	10,854,000,000
6 British Gas	9,500,000,000
7 Hanson	8,777,000,000
8 BTR	7,569,000,000
9 ICI	7,525,000,000
10 GEC	6,408,000,000

BRITAIN'S TOP 10 COMPANIES

Company	Annual sales (£)
1 British Petroleum (petroleum products, oil and gas exploration)	25,851,204,000
2 ICI (chemicals, plastics, paints)	11,667,048,000
3 Electricity Council (electricity)	11,335,445,000
4 British Telecom (telecommunications)	11,071,012,000
5 BAT Industries (tobacco, financial services, paper and pulp, retailing)	7,875,434,000
6 British Gas (gas)	7,526,009,000
7 Hanson (conglomerate)	7,375,802,000
8 Unilever (consumer products, food)	6,366,566,000
9 Grand Metropolitan (hotels, food, drinks, leisure)	6,012,329,000
10 Ford (motor manufacture)	5,919,790,000

OPPOSITE 'The smile that says "You're welcome".' McDonald's, one of the UK's leading brand advertisers, practising *glasnost* in Moscow.

BELOW Macy's department stores, ninth on the list of largest private companies in the USA.

THE 10 LARGEST PRIVATE COMPANIES IN THE USA

Company	Nature of business	Annual revenue ($)
1 Cargill	International marketer, commodities	43,000,000,000
2 Koch Industries	Petroleum, gas, chemicals	16,000,000,000
3 R.J.R. Nabisco	Food, tobacco	14,000,000,000
4 Safeway Stores	Supermarkets	13,612,000,000
5 Continental Grain	Commodity trading, processing	13,500,000,000
6 United Parcel Service	Package delivery	11,000,000,000
7 Mars	Confectionery, petfood	8,541,000,000
8 Southland	Convenience stores	7,990,000,000
9 R.H. Macy	Department stores	7,000,000,000
10 Supermarkets General	Grocery shops	5,962,000,000

ABOVE Telecom Tower – one of the country's top buildings for one of its top companies.

A private company is one which does not have commonly traded stock – in other words, outsiders cannot buy shares in it.

THE TOP 10 BRAND ADVERTISERS IN THE UK

Company	Total advertising expenditure, 1989 (£)
1 Water Authorities	36,877,000
2 Halifax Building Society	26,595,000
3 Abbey National Building Society	22,171,000
4 Woolworth Stores	21,208,000
5 Sky	19,983,000
6 Midland Bank	17,997,000
7 NatWest Bank (personal)	17,739,000
8 McDonald's	16,945,000
9 MFI	16,940,000
10 Barclays Bank (personal)	16,404,000

The privatization of the Water Authorities in 1989 and Sky Television's campaign to attract subscribers brought both organizations into the Top 10 individual or 'brand' advertisers' list for the first time. The Water Authorities spent over £24,000,000 on television advertising alone – more than any other single advertiser in the year.

THE TOP 10 CORPORATE ADVERTISERS IN THE UK

Advertiser	Total advertising expenditure, 1989 (£)
1 Unilever	133,060,000
2 HM Government	119,970,000
3 Procter & Gamble Ltd	76,510,000
4 Nestlé	72,320,000
5 Mars	67,810,000
6 Electricity Council	50,340,000
7 Kingfisher (Woolworths)	49,550,000
8 British Telecom	47,550,000
9 Kellogg's	45,180,000
10 Ford Motor Company	42,680,000

The high ranking of HM Government in the Top 10 results partly from its exceptional expenditure during the year of £36,877,000 on advertising the privatization of the Water Authorities, but also includes advertising on behalf of such bodies as the Departments of Health and Social Security, Trade and Industry and Employment, and National Savings.

THE 10 EUROPEAN COUNTRIES RECEIVING THE MOST DIRECT MAIL

Country	Average number of items per head per annum
1 Switzerland	96
2 Sweden	66
3 West Germany	59
4 Belgium	57
5 Netherlands	56
6 Norway	55
7= Denmark	45
7= Finland	45
7= France	45
10 UK	32

The amount of direct, or unsolicited mail (sometimes known as 'junk mail') advertising a wide range of goods and services has been inexorably increasing in recent years. However, when people in the USA were interviewed about their views on the subject, most said they would prefer to receive *more* rather than less junk mail. The latest trend is for 'junk faxes', which are a serious problem in the USA and on the increase elsewhere. The principal difference between junk mail and junk faxes is that whereas the costs of mail are borne by the sender, junk faxes are paid for in part by the often unwilling recipient in the cost of the paper consumed by the fax machine and by jamming the fax line, since while the machine is occupied in receiving the message, it is out of action for receiving or transmitting legitimate documents. Faxing a large quantity of blank pages to the sender has been suggested as a form of retaliation, but this could then escalate into fax warfare.

THE TOP 10 FAX COUNTRIES

Country	Fax machines
1 Japan	4,300,000
2 USA	2,420,000
3 UK	524,000
4 West Germany	520,000
5 Italy	458,000
6 France	310,000
7 Canada	265,000
8 Spain	204,000
9 Netherlands	189,000
10 Sweden	170,000

Facsimile transmission from one point to another was suggested in the early nineteenth century and developed in a primitive form soon after the invention of the telephone. The first practical machines came into use after World War II and were employed by the police and newspapers for transmitting photographs via telephone lines or radio. The technology was slow and the machines cumbersome until the Japanese pioneered their development as a quick means of sending handwritten documents, Japanese typewriters being notoriously slow and unwieldy. Their international proliferation during the 1980s has made considerable inroads into such long-established forms of communication as post and telex, and the ubiquitous 'fax' is being put to imaginative new uses, from faxed copies of works of art to ordering food from faxed menus.

THE TOP 10 EXHIBITIONS AT THE NEC, BIRMINGHAM

Exhibition	Highest recorded attendance
1 British International Motor Show	720,326
2 Interbuild	137,128
3 Boat, Caravan and Leisure Show	123,582
4 International Bike Show	122,000
5 IPEX – International Printing Exhibition	90,630
6 International Spring Fair (gift trade)	70,359
7 MACH – Machine Tool Exhibition	69,011
8 National Knitting Exhibition	55,000
9 Which Computer? Show	51,568
10 Holiday and Travel Fair	51,293

A creative use for the fax: assembling a faxed copy of a painting by David Hockney.

Wealth

THE TOP 10 GOLD PRODUCERS IN THE WORLD

Country	Annual production (tonnes)
1 South Africa	621.0
2 USSR	270.6*
3 USA	205.3
4 Australia	152.0
5 Canada	128.5
6 Brazil	100.2
7 China	59.1*
8 Philippines	42.7
9 Colombia	33.4
10 Papua New Guinea	32.6

Estimates.

In 1988, the non-Communist world mined a total of 1,538 tonnes of gold, of which South Africa produced over 40 per cent. By using improved mining and extraction methods and exploiting newly discovered deposits, most countries increased their production considerably: Australia's previous record annual production had stood at 119 tonnes since 1903, but in 1988 rocketed up to 152 tonnes, overtaking that of Canada, while Colombia pushed Papua New Guinea into 10th position.

THE 10 HIGHEST-EARNING ENTERTAINERS IN THE WORLD*

	Name	Profession	1988–89 income ($)
1	Steven Spielberg	Film producer/director	125,000,000
2	Mike Tyson	Boxer	71,000,000
3	Charles M. Schulz	'Peanuts' cartoonist	60,000,000
4	Oprah Winfrey	TV host/producer	55,000,000
5	Johnny Carson	TV host/producer	45,000,000
6	Sugar Ray Leonard	Boxer	42,000,000
7	Siegfried and Roy	Illusionists	26,000,000
8=	Jim Davis	'Garfield' cartoonist	25,000,000
8=	Andrew Lloyd Webber	Composer	25,000,000
10	Stephen King	Novelist/screenwriter	20,000,000

Other than actors and pop stars.
Used by permission of Forbes Magazine.

Based on *Forbes Magazine*'s survey of top entertainers' income in the years 1988 and 1989.

THE 10 HIGHEST-EARNING POP STARS IN THE WORLD

	Artist(s)	1988–89 income ($)
1	Michael Jackson	125,000,000
2	Pink Floyd	56,000,000
3	The Rolling Stones	55,000,000
4	George Michael	47,000,000
5	Julio Iglesias	46,000,000
6	Madonna	43,000,000
7=	Bruce Springsteen	40,000,000
7=	Bon Jovi	40,000,000
9	Prince	36,000,000
10	U2	33,000,000

Used by permission of Forbes Magazine.

Based on *Forbes Magazine*'s survey of top entertainers' income in the years 1988 and 1989. Several groups had enormously successful tours in this period: Pink Floyd's, for example, earned $135,000,000. Other high-earning groups include The Who ($32,000,000), Def Leppard ($30,000,000), Van Halen ($27,000,000), Grateful Dead ($25,000,000), Guns 'N' Roses ($24,000,000) and Aerosmith ($21,000,000), while among solo singers were Frank Sinatra ($26,000,000), Kenny Rogers ($23,000,000) and Rod Stewart ($21,000,000). In the same period, Whitney Houston, Tina Turner and Sting all failed to sustain their earlier huge earnings and thereby fell out of the Top 40.

THE TOP 10 OF EVERYTHING 1991

THE 10 HIGHEST-EARNING ACTORS IN THE WORLD

	Actor	1988–89 income ($)
1	William H. Cosby Jr	95,000,000
2	Eddie Murphy	57,000,000
3=	Sylvester Stallone	44,000,000
3=	Jack Nicholson	44,000,000
5	Arnold Schwarzenegger	41,000,000
6	Bill Murray	26,000,000
7	Jane Fonda	23,000,000
8	Tom Selleck	22,000,000
9=	Steve Martin	20,000,000
9=	Mel Gibson	20,000,000
9=	Michael J. Fox	20,000,000

Used by permission of Forbes Magazine.

Based on *Forbes Magazine*'s survey of top entertainers' income in the years 1988 and 1989. In this period, Jack Nicholson more than doubled his income – largely as a result of the success of the film *Batman* – while Paul Hogan, having previously earned almost $40,000,000 from the two *Crocodile Dundee* films, dropped out of the Top 40.

OPPOSITE
TOP Mike Tyson, second highest-earning entertainer in the world.
BOTTOM 1988–89 was a good year for Pink Floyd: the group has been performing since 1966.

BELOW Jack Nicholson, one of the world's top-earning actors.

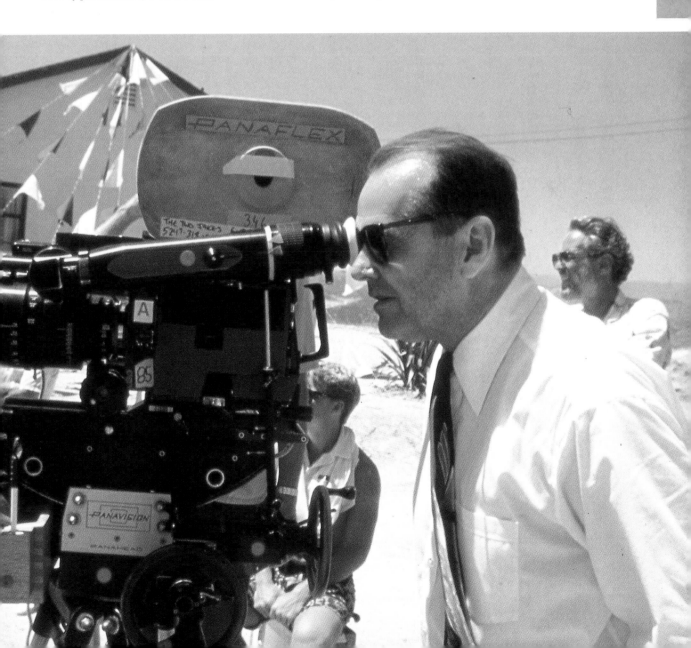

THE 10 RICHEST PEOPLE IN THE USA

In 1989, according to *Forbes Magazine*, at least 55 Americans were reckoned to be dollar billionaires – that is, with assets in excess of $1,000,000,000. They include both the inheritors of great family fortunes and self-made men, such as 33-year-old William Henry Gates III, the founder of Microsoft, the computer software corporation, whose wealth is estimated at $1,250,000,000. A placing in the Top 10 is extremely volatile, however: Samuel Moore Walton, who headed the list the previous year, decided to split his $9,000,000,000 fortune among his family and thus no longer appears in it, while those at positions 3, 4, 5 and 10 were not formerly eligible. The current 10 at the top of this enviable pile are:

1 John Werner Kluge $5,200,000,000 +

Founder of the Metromedia Company of Charlottesville, Virginia. The family of German-born Kluge settled in Detroit in 1922, where he worked on the Ford assembly line. He won a scholarship to Columbia University and gained a degree in economics. He started a radio station and in 1959, with partners, acquired the Metropolitan Broadcasting Company, developing it into Metromedia, a corporation that owns TV and radio stations and cellular telephone franchises, but with other properties as varied as the Chock Full O'Nuts Corporation and, formerly, the Harlem Globetrotters basketball team. Kluge has diversified his interests into such areas as films, printing and a chain of steak houses, and he owns a 78,000-acre estate in Scotland. Formerly the second wealthiest man in the USA, Kluge now occupies the premier position recently vacated by Samuel Moore Walton.

2 Warren Edward Buffett $4,200,000,000 +

Buffett was born and still lives in Omaha, Nebraska. His professional career started as a pinball service engineer, after which he published a horse race tip sheet. His diverse business interests include the major New England textile company, Berkshire Hathaway. He is reported to have left his fortune in trust to aid such causes as population control and nuclear disarmament.

3 Sumner Murray Redstone $2,880,000,000 +

A World War II Japanese codebreaker and then a lawyer, Redstone took over his father's drive-in movie chain and built it up into 400-screen National Amusements Inc, which acquired extensive and highly profitable TV and cable businesses, including MTV.

4 Ted Arison $2,860,000,000 +

The Palestinian-born son of an Israeli shipowner, Arison emigrated to the USA in 1952 and after a variety of ventures developed the cruise liner business, co-founding Carnival Cruise Lines, now the world's largest company of its kind.

5 Ronald Owen Perelman $2,750,000,000

Perelman is a wide-ranging entrepreneur who acquired Revlon, Max Factor and other cosmetics businesses, was the former owner of Technicolor and has professional interests that encompass firms from Marvel Comics to a camping goods company.

6 Samuel Irving Newhouse Jr and brother Donald Edward Newhouse $5,200,000,000 (shared)

The New York City based Newhouse brothers are owners of America's largest privately owned chain of newspapers, with interests that include cable television and book publishing. Samuel ('Si') Newhouse runs book publishers Random House and magazine publishers Condé Nast, the publishers of *Vogue*, often starting his working day at 4 a.m., while Donald controls their newspaper group.

7 Barbara Cox Anthony and sister Anne Cox Chambers $5,000,000,000 + (shared)

Daughters of a former schoolteacher who bought the *Dayton Daily News* in 1898. The family business grew into a media empire encompassing newspapers, magazines, TV and radio stations and many other interests. At one time Anne was US Ambassador to Belgium.

8 Henry Ross Perot $2,500,000,000

Son of a Texan horse-trader, Perot once sold saddles and served in the US Navy before becoming IBM's star salesman. In 1962, with $1,000, he founded Electronic Data Systems of Dallas. It crashed in 1970, losing a record $600,000,000 in a single day's trading, but Perot got the firm back on its feet and in 1984 sold it to General Motors for $991,000,000. A subsequent management dispute led to his being bought out in 1986 for $742,000,000. He now runs an investment company which has backed other high-tech entrepreneurs, such as Steve Jobs (the founder of Apple Computers) in the launch of NExT, Inc – to the tune of $20,000,000.

9 Jay Arthur Pritzker and Robert Alan Pritzker $4,700,000,000 + (shared)

Of Russian ancestry, the Pritzker brothers are Chicago financiers, the owners of Hyatt Hotels (run by Jay Pritzker's son Thomas), *McCall's* magazine, real estate and other interests.

10 A. Alfred Taubman $2,150,000,000

Taubman is a Michigan-based real estate magnate specializing in major developments such as shopping malls and department stores, and the owner of Sotheby's auction house.

RIGHT Michael D. Eisner, Chief Executive Officer of Walt Disney and the second highest-paid in the USA.

THE 10 HIGHEST-PAID CHIEF EXECUTIVE OFFICERS (CEOs) IN THE USA

CEO	Company	1988 salary +bonus (US$)
1 Paul B. Fireman	Reebok International	11,439,000
2 Michael D. Eisner	Walt Disney	7,506,000
3 Saul P. Steinberg	Reliance Group	4,498,000
4 Steven J. Ross	Warner Communications	4,481,000
5 Charles Lazarus	Toys 'Я' Us	4,429,000
6 S. Parker Gilbert	Morgan Stanley	4,425,000
7 John H. Gutfreund	Saloman	4,000,000
8 Thomas Spiegel	Columbia S & L Association	3,960,000
9 John A. Young	Hewlett-Packard	3,749,000
10 John B. Amos	American Family	3,700,000

These are the declared salaries of the CEOs of publicly quoted American companies as listed by *Forbes Magazine*. The fortunate Mr Fireman, the head of sports shoe manufacturers Reebok International, makes $31,340 a *day* or $1,306 for every hour of the year. Private firms are not obliged to reveal what they pay their personnel, and some could achieve higher incomes than these.

THE 10 COUNTRIES WITH THE MOST DOLLAR BILLIONAIRES*

	Country	Billionaires
1	USA	55
2	Japan	41
3	West Germany	20
4	Canada	9
5	UK	7
6 =	Italy	6
6 =	France	6
8 =	Hong Kong	5
8 =	Taiwan	5
8 =	Saudi Arabia	5

People with net worth of $1,000,000,000 or more.

Based on data published in *Forbes Magazine*.

THE 10 RICHEST STATES IN THE USA

State	Average annual income ($)
1 Connecticut	22,761
2 New Jersey	21,882
3 District of Columbia*	21,667
4 Massachusetts	20,701
5 Alaska	19,514
6 Maryland	19,314
7 New York	19,299
8 New Hampshire	19,016
9 California	18,855
10 Delaware	17,699

Not technically a state; if it is excluded, Virginia becomes No.10 ($17,640).

The average income in Mississippi is the lowest of all 50 states at $10,992.

THE 10 MOST INDEBTED COUNTRIES IN THE WORLD

	Country	Total debt (US$)
1	Brazil	112,700,000,000
2	Mexico	102,600,000,000
3	Argentina	61,900,000,000
4	Poland	40,100,000,000
5	Venezuela	34,100,000,000
6	Philippines	28,500,000,000
7	Morocco	20,800,000,000
8	Peru	19,900,000,000
9	Chile	18,500,000,000
10	Hungary	17,900,000,000

The World Bank monitors the level of countries' external borrowings. Their 1989 figures indicate that the Top 10, and a further nine or ten countries, all of which are classified as 'severely indebted', have debts so great that they are often unable even to repay the interest on the loan, let alone the principal amount borrowed. In recent years, some banks have 'written off' certain loans that were unlikely ever to be repaid. Although Brazil's external debt is the highest in total, it is equivalent to less than $800 for every man, woman and child in the country, while several other countries have debts of more than $1,000 per head of population: that of Mexico is over $1,200 and Argentina's almost $2,000.

BOTTOM LEFT Tiny Rowland, second highest-paid UK director.

ABOVE A shanty town in Brazil, the world's leading debtor nation.

THE 10 HIGHEST-PAID DIRECTORS OF PUBLIC COMPANIES IN THE UK

	Name/company	Annual salary (£)
1	Lord Hanson (Hanson plc)	1,534,000
2	Tiny Rowland (Lonrho plc)	1,015,000
3	Unnamed director (Robert Fleming)	1,014,000
4	Unnamed director (Palmerston Holdings plc)	911,608
5	Mitchell Fromstein (Blue Arrow Personnel Services Ltd)	910,000
6	Sir Ralph Halpern (Burton Group plc)	899,000
7	Sir John Nott (Lazard Bros & Co Ltd)	885,000
8	Unnamed director (J. Rothschild Holdings plc)	802,000
9	Richard Giordano (British Oxygen Co Ltd)	796,557
10	Unnamed director (F.K.I. Babcock)	773,319

The designation 'unnamed director' is applied to those declared anonymously in their company's accounts as 'highest paid'.

THE 10 RICHEST BRITISH PEOPLE

This list is based on round-figure estimates of 'realisable' wealth – assets that their owner could dispose of if he so wished. In the previous edition of *The Top 10 of Everything*, the Queen was excluded because so much of her wealth derives from assets such as the Crown Estates and the royal art collection, components of the British national heritage that she manages but will ultimately pass on to her successor: it is inconceivable, for instance, that the Crown Jewels, the royal yacht or Buckingham Palace would ever be sold. However, recent assessments have indicated that based solely on the Queen's privately owned assets – unlikely though it may be that she would ever liquidate them – she ranks as the wealthiest British person and the richest woman in the world. The list includes only British citizens (though not necessarily residents), although there are several very wealthy foreigners living in the UK who would rank in the Top 10, among them Gad and Hans Rausing (Swedish – shared £2,000,000,000 +), John Paul Getty III (American – £1,500,000,000) and George Stavros Livanos (Greek – £1,000,000,000).

| 1 | Her Majesty Queen Elizabeth II | £6,700,000,000 |

The Queen's private fortune is held in jewellery, art, racehorses, land, property in the UK (including Balmoral Castle and Sandringham), Europe and the USA and shares worth an estimated £2,500,000.

| 2 | The Duke of Westminster | £4,300,000,000 |

Gerald Grosvenor owns 300 acres in Mayfair and Belgravia (part of which was once a cabbage-patch, acquired in 1677 as the dowry of the 12-year-old bride of Sir Thomas Grosvenor), Eaton Hall near Chester and its 13,000-acre estate (from which he commutes in his Squirrel helicopter) and 100,000 acres of Scottish forest, as well as property around the world.

| 3 | The Sainsbury Family | £2,125,000,000 |

Founded in 1869 and expanded as high-street grocers, Sainsbury's were among the first to develop American-style supermarkets in the UK. Today Lord (Alan) Sainsbury, Sir Robert Sainsbury, Sir John Sainsbury and David Sainsbury own the majority of the shares in the chain which has an annual turnover in excess of £5,000,000,000. The family has financed the extension to the National Gallery, London, to be known as the Sainsbury Wing.

| 4= | Sir John Moores | £1,700,000,000 |

Originally a post office messenger, Sir John Moores was in 1923 founder and remains the owner of Littlewoods, Britain's largest private company which operates Littlewoods Football Pools and the Littlewoods retail and mail-order stores group.

| 4= | Garfield Weston | £1,700,000,000 |

Weston's family emigrated to Canada over a century ago and made a fortune in the bakery business. Galen Weston runs the Canadian company, while his elder brother Garfield is today Chairman of the British arm of the firm, Associated British Foods, bakers of Sunblest bread and owners of other well-known brands.

| 6 | Lord Samuel and Edmund Vestey | £1,500,000,000 |

Running a business built up during the nineteenth century from a cattle-ranching and meat-shipping business, cousins Lord Samuel and Edmund Vestey's company, Union International plc, is today the world's largest retail butcher.

| 7 | Robert Maxwell | £1,100,000,000 |

The son of a poor Czechoslovakian labourer, Robert Maxwell (whose name was originally Jan Ludwig Hoch) distinguished himself in the British army during World War II and went on to found a global printing and publishing empire that today, as Maxwell Communications Corporation, includes Mirror Group Newspapers, Macdonald Publishers and Pergamon Press in the UK and Macmillan in the USA.

| 8 | Sir James Goldsmith | £875,000,000 |

Principally a financier, Sir James was the one-time owner of a diverse group of businesses ranging from food companies to the French newspaper, *L'Express* – as well as 2,500,000 acres of American forests.

| 9 | Sir Adrian and Sir John Swire | £700,000,000 |

The Swire brothers inherited a business started in the early nineteenth century and based on shipping. Today the John Swire Group includes Cathay Pacific Airline and extensive interests in property, hotels and insurance.

| 10 | Gerald Ronson | £550,000,000 |

Ronson's Heron Group owns garages and is involved in property development. After Littlewoods, it is Britain's largest privately owned company.

Although it is arguable whether she is the owner or custodian of much of her property, her known personal wealth makes HM The Queen the richest UK citizen.

Food & Drink

THE 10 LEADING CHOCOLATE-CONSUMING NATIONS IN THE WORLD

Country	Total consumption (tonnes)
1 USA	524,200
2 West Germany	186,000
3 USSR	159,600
4 UK	140,800
5 France	126,400
6 Japan	104,100
7 Italy	61,500
8 Brazil	55,800
9 Canada	52,500
10 Spain	51,200

In 1987–88 the world total consumption of cocoa, the principal ingredient of chocolate, was 1,917,000 tonnes. Like coffee, the consumption of chocolate tends to occur mainly in the Western world and in more affluent countries. Since some of the Top 10 consuming nations also have large populations, the figures for consumption per head present a somewhat different picture, led by those countries with a long-established tradition of manufacturing high-quality chocolate products:

Country	Consumption per head kg	lb oz
1 Switzerland	4.374	9 10
2 Belgium/Luxembourg	3.538	7 13
3 West Germany	3.039	6 11
4 Norway	2.983	6 9
5 Austria	2.863	6 5
6 UK	2.466	5 7
7 France	2.236	4 15
8 USA	2.128	4 11
9 Canada	2.023	4 7
10 Sweden	1.919	4 4

CADBURY'S TOP 10 CHOCOLATE PRODUCTS

1 Dairy Milk
2 Roses
3 Wispa
4 Flake
5 Crunchie
6 Milk Tray
7 Whole Nut
8 Fruit & Nut
9 Double Decker
10 Creme Eggs

The firms of Fry's and Cadbury's were founded in the early eighteenth and nineteenth centuries respectively by Quakers (who viewed drinking chocolate as a healthy alternative to alcohol) and merged in 1919. Many of their best-known products date back longer than one might suppose: Dairy Milk, famed for its 'glass-and-a-half' of full cream milk in every half pound' (the slogan of a campaign started in 1928) has been around since 1905, and Milk Tray since 1915. Flake, Fruit & Nut and Crunchie bars all date from the 1920s and Roses and Whole Nut from the 1930s. Wispa bars are made by machines that are capable of producing 1,680 per minute, while Creme Eggs, the 10th product on the list, are made at the rate of 1,100 a minute – and achieve sales of an astonishing 200,000,000 a year, or $3\frac{1}{2}$ for every inhabitant of the United Kingdom!

THE 10 BESTSELLING SWEETS IN THE UK

	Product	Manufacturer	Sales per annum (£)
1	KitKat	Rowntree	165,000,000
2	Mars Bar	Mars	150,000,000
3	Twix	Mars	97,000,000
4	Dairy Milk	Cadbury	86,000,000
5	Quality Street	Rowntree	56,000,000
6=	Maltesers	Mars	54,000,000
6=	Roses	Cadbury	54,000,000
8=	Wispa	Cadbury	50,000,000
8=	Flake	Cadbury	50,000,000
10	Milk Tray	Cadbury	46,000,000

It is estimated that there are over 1,000 different confectionery brands available in the UK, but a relatively small number account for a major proportion of sales. The Top 30 brands had a market value of some £1,400,000,000 in 1988, or around 43 per cent of the total, including imports. The two largest firms, Cadbury/Nestlé and Rowntree, each have approximately 22 per cent of this market; Mars is in third place with 18 per cent, followed by Terry's at 4 per cent and all the other companies, each with a very small percentage of the total.

The KitKat bar – for several years Britain's bestselling confectionery item – is also the 5th bestselling chocolate bar in both the USA and Japan. Of Britain's Top 20 bestselling sweets, only one – Polo Mints, at No. 17 (£33,000,000 per annum) – is not based on chocolate. Britain is one of the world's leading consumers of chocolate.

THE TOP 10 CHOCOLATE ADVERTISERS IN THE UK

	Company	Annual advertising expenditure (£)
1	Cadbury	23,051,000
2	Mars	19,450,000
3	Rowntree	17,785,000
4	Terry	4,010,000
5	Mackintosh	3,937,000
6	Nestlé	1,639,000
7	Ferrero Rocher	1,610,000
8	Suchard	1,149,000
9	Fry's	773,000
10	Barker & Dobson	622,000

THE TOP 10 FOOD AND DRINK ITEMS CONSUMED IN THE USA

Product	Average consumption per head per annum		
	kg	lb	oz
1 Meat	114.7	252	14
2 Milk and cream	107.1	236	3
3 Fruit	94.9	209	5
4 Vegetables	91.0	200	10
5 Beer	90.0	198	7
6 Grain products (bread, breakfast cereals, etc)	72.1	158	14
7 Sugar, honey and glucose	60.7	133	14
8 Potatoes	56.6	124	12
9 Oils and fats	29.5	65	0
10 Eggs	14.1	31	0

The USA is notable for its very high consumption of meat. Cheese comes 11th (10.7 kg/23 lb 10 oz) and low-calorie sweeteners 12th on the list (8.8 kg/19 lb 8 oz), the consumption per head of which is greater than that of fish (6.8 kg/15 lb).

THE TOP 10 MEAT-EATING NATIONS

	Consumption per head per annum		
	kg	lb	oz
1 USA	114.7	252	14
2 Australia	101.2	223	2
3 Hungary	99.8	220	0
4 Canada	97.8	215	10
5 East Germany	97.1	214	1
6 Denmark	96.2	212	1
7 Uruguay	95.2	209	14
8 Argentina	94.6	208	9
9 New Zealand	94.0	207	4
10 Belgium/Luxembourg	92.9	204	13
UK	*56.9*	*125*	*7*

Figures compiled by the Meat and Livestock Commission show a huge range of meat consumption around the world, from the countries featured in the Top 10 to Turkey where they eat less than 15 kg/33 lb of meat per head per year, while estimates by the United Nations Food and Agriculture Organization suggest that in very poor countries, such as India, meat consumption may be as little as 1.5 kg/3 lb per annum. Meat-eating is a reflection of various factors, principally wealth – in general, the richer the country, the more meat is eaten, although in recent years 'healthy eating' concerns of many Western countries have resulted in a deliberate decline in consumption. Availability is also significant – New Zealand's consumption of lamb is the world's highest at 27.2 kg/60 lb per head, while Argentineans eat 73.0 kg/161 lb and Uruguayans 65.0 kg/143 lb of beef per head. Culture also plays a role – as a result of dietary prohibitions, very little pork is eaten in the Middle East, and the Japanese eat only 39.9 kg/88 lb of meat, but larger quantities of fish than many other nations. The figures for Eastern European countries are from official sources, and those who have seen customers there queuing for small rationed quantities of meat may well question them. If Hungary and East Germany are excluded altogether from the Top 10, the 9th and 10th places are occupied by West Germany (89.6 kg/198 lb) and France (87.1 kg/192 lb). The United Kingdom's meat consumption is the second lowest in the EC, just beating that of Portugal (56.8 kg/125 lb).

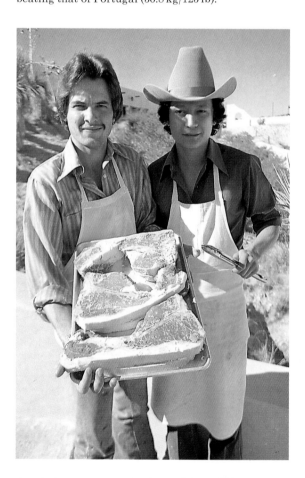

America's meat consumption is top of the world league.

THE TOP 10 FOOD AND DRINK ITEMS CONSUMED IN THE UK

Product	Average consumption per head per annum		
	kg	lb	oz
1 Milk and cream	133.1	293	7
2 Potatoes and potato products	113.1	249	5
3 Beer	109.0	240	0
4 Fruit	94.2	207	11
5 Vegetables	86.5	190	1
6 Grain products (bread, breakfast cereals, etc)	71.8	158	5
7 Meat	56.9	125	7
8 Sugar, honey and glucose	43.9	96	12
9 Oils and fats	22.7	50	1
10 Eggs	13.7	30	0

THE TOP 10 FOOD COMPANIES IN THE UK

Company	Best-known products	Annual sales (£)
1 Hillsdown Holdings	Buxted chickens, Blue Bird and Needlers confectionery	3,039,000,000
2 Associated British Foods	Sunblest bread, Ryvita	2,272,000,000
3 Unigate	St Ivel dairy products	2,165,000,000
4 Cadbury Schweppes	Cadbury's and Fry's chocolate, Coca-Cola, Schweppes soft drinks	2,031,000,000
5 United Biscuits	McVitie's and Crawfords biscuits, KP snacks, Wimpy and Pizzaland restaurants	1,955,000,000
6 Tate & Lyle	Sugar	1,819,000,000
7 Rank Hovis McDougall	Mother's Pride and Hovis bread, Mr Kipling cakes, McDougall's flour, Bisto	1,544,000,000
8 Rowntree	KitKat, Polo Mints and other confectionery	1,428,000,000
9 The Union International	Dewhurst butchers	1,213,000,000
10 Northern Foods	'Own-brand' foods for supermarkets, Bowyers meat products	1,009,000,000

TOP Unigate, the UK's third largest food company.

THE TOP 10 CALORIE-CONSUMING COUNTRIES

	Country	Average daily consumption
1	Belgium	3,850
2	East Germany	3,800
3	United Arab Emirates	3,713
4	Ireland	3,692
5	Greece	3,688
6	USA	3,642
7	Bulgaria	3,634
8	Libya	3,611
9	Yugoslavia	3,542
10	Hungary	3,541
	UK	3,218

The Calorie requirement of the average man is 2,700 and of a woman 2,500. Inactive people need less, while those engaged in heavy labour might require to increase, perhaps even to double these figures. Calories that are not consumed as energy turn to fat – which is why Calorie-counting is one of the key aspects of most diets. The high Calorie intake of certain countries, such as those in Eastern Europe, is a reflection of the high proportion of starchy foods, such as potatoes and bread, in the national diet; in many Western countries the high figures simply reflect over-eating. It should also be noted that these figures are averages – which means that at least part of the population of each country is pigging out at mega levels. While weight-watchers of the West guzzle their way through 30 per cent more than they need, the Calorie consumption in Bangladesh and some of the poorest African nations falls below 2,000, while in Ghana it drops to as little as 1,733.

JACOB'S BAKERY'S 10 BESTSELLING PRODUCTS

1 Club biscuits
2 Jacob's Cream Crackers
3 Famous Brands (a range of sweet biscuits – custard creams, bourbon, shortcake, etc)
4 Trio
5 Seasonal biscuits (Family Circle, Teatime, etc)
6 Ritz Crackers
7 Mrs Peek's Christmas Puddings
8 Twiglets
9 Teatime (400 gm box)
10 Ritz Cheese Sandwich

Based on sales by value.

SAINSBURY'S 10 BESTSELLING ORGANIC PRODUCTS

1 Potatoes
2 Carrots
3= Onions
3= Swedes
5 White cabbages
6 Red cabbages
7 Mushrooms
8 Green cabbages
9 Tomatoes
10 Oranges

Sainsbury's opened its first shop in 1869 and today is Britain's leading food retailer, with nearly 300 supermarkets, and annual sales of over £5,000,000,000. To the health-conscious consumer they offer a wide and increasing range of organically grown fruit and vegetables, of which these are the bestsellers by weight.

Increasingly popular: organic produce on sale in Sainsbury's.

The Real McCoy's and Hula Hoops, two KP bestsellers.

THE 10 BESTSELLING KP SNACKS

1 KP Nuts

2 KP Crisps

3 KP Hula Hoops

4 KP Skips

5 The Real McCoy's

6 KP Lower Fat Crisps

7 KP Discos

8 KP Dips

9 World Snacks

10 KP Crunchies

KP is so called after 'Kenyon Products', made by the original Yorkshire company, Kenyon Son and Craven.

McVITIE'S 10 BESTSELLING BISCUITS

1 Chocolate Homewheat

2 Digestive

3 Jaffa Cakes

4 Chocolate Hob-nobs

5 Rich Tea

6 Gold Bars

7 Ginger Nuts

8 Mini Cheddars

9 Hob-nob Bars

10 Fruit Jaspers

THE 10 MOST-ADVERTISED FOOD PRODUCTS IN THE UK

Product	Annual advertising expenditure (£)
1 Chocolate confectionery	76,465,000
2 Breakfast cereals	63,287,000
3 Coffee	46,222,000
4 Margarine	30,154,000
5 Sauces, pickles and salad cream	24,585,000
6 Crisps and snacks	23,192,000
7 Sugar confectionery	22,539,000
8 Tea	21,903,000
9 Biscuits	18,458,000
10 Milk and milk products	17,356,000

McVitie's Digestive biscuits are the single most popular biscuit in the UK, with annual sales approaching £50,000,000 out of a total UK biscuit market that is worth approximately £1,000,000,000 a year. They have been made to the same recipe since 1889 when Alexander Grant of McVitie's and Price of Edinburgh created the first one, giving it its name because it contains baking soda which is regarded as having properties that aid digestion. Homewheat biscuits, Digestives with a layer of chocolate, have been around since 1929. McVitie's advertising budget for their relatively newly launched Hob-nob Bars and Gold Bars alone is estimated at £5,500,000 for 1990.

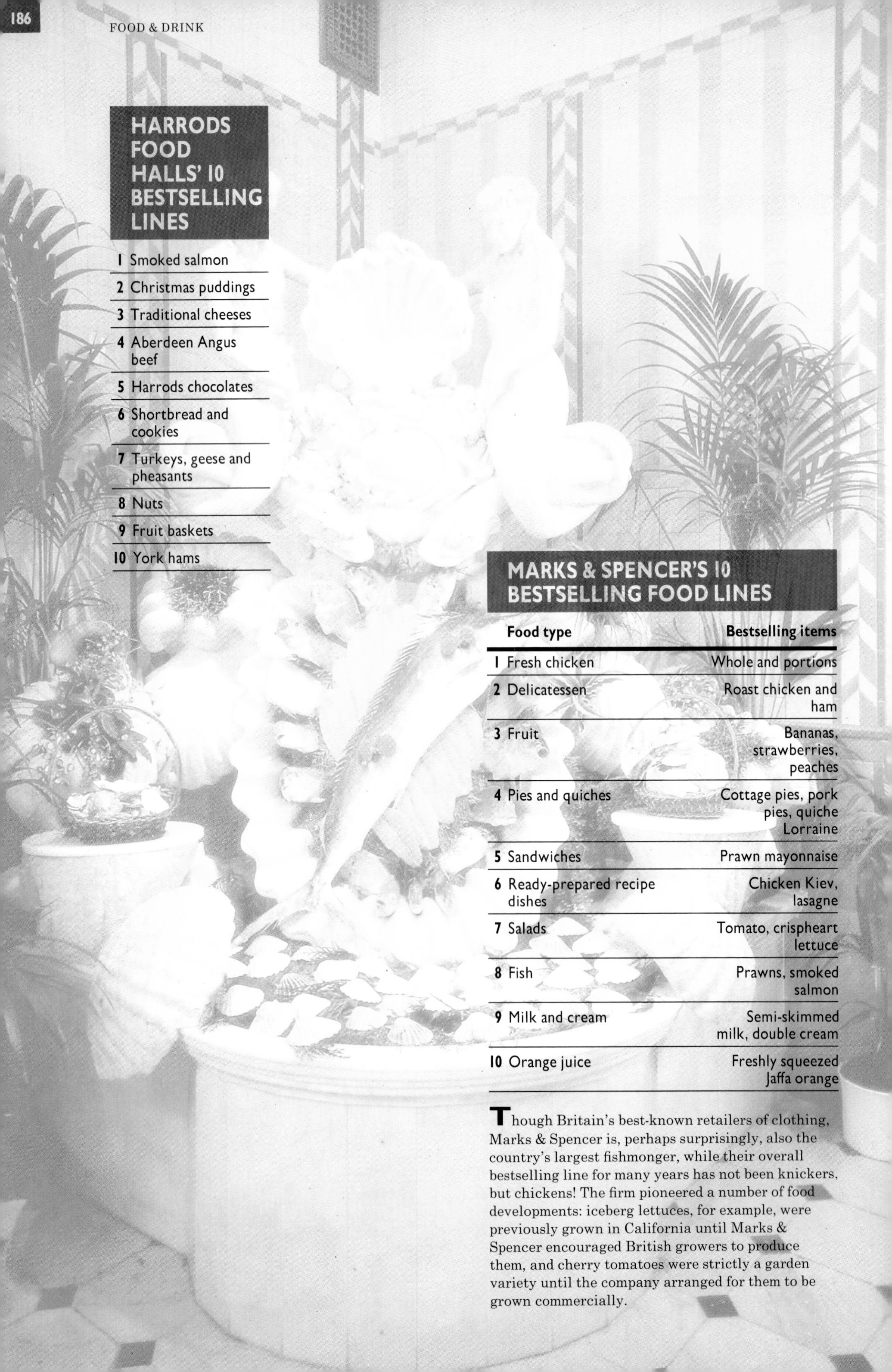

HARRODS FOOD HALLS' 10 BESTSELLING LINES

1 Smoked salmon
2 Christmas puddings
3 Traditional cheeses
4 Aberdeen Angus beef
5 Harrods chocolates
6 Shortbread and cookies
7 Turkeys, geese and pheasants
8 Nuts
9 Fruit baskets
10 York hams

MARKS & SPENCER'S 10 BESTSELLING FOOD LINES

Food type	Bestselling items
1 Fresh chicken	Whole and portions
2 Delicatessen	Roast chicken and ham
3 Fruit	Bananas, strawberries, peaches
4 Pies and quiches	Cottage pies, pork pies, quiche Lorraine
5 Sandwiches	Prawn mayonnaise
6 Ready-prepared recipe dishes	Chicken Kiev, lasagne
7 Salads	Tomato, crispheart lettuce
8 Fish	Prawns, smoked salmon
9 Milk and cream	Semi-skimmed milk, double cream
10 Orange juice	Freshly squeezed Jaffa orange

Though Britain's best-known retailers of clothing, Marks & Spencer is, perhaps surprisingly, also the country's largest fishmonger, while their overall bestselling line for many years has not been knickers, but chickens! The firm pioneered a number of food developments: iceberg lettuces, for example, were previously grown in California until Marks & Spencer encouraged British growers to produce them, and cherry tomatoes were strictly a garden variety until the company arranged for them to be grown commercially.

THE 10 BESTSELLING HEINZ SOUPS

1 Tomato

2 Chicken

3 Vegetable

4 Oxtail

5 Mushroom

6 Lentil

7 Mulligatawny

8 Minestrone

9 Scotch Broth

10 Farmhouse Vegetable

Henry John Heinz, the founder of the gigantic food processing and canning empire that bears his name, was born in Pittsburgh, Pennsylvania in 1844, of German immigrant parents. In 1869 he formed a partnership with a family friend, L.C. Noble, selling horseradish in clear glass jars (previously green glass disguised the dishonest practice of packing the horseradish out with turnip), beginning the Heinz reputation for quality and integrity. Their products were also sold on their lack of artificial flavourings and colourings long before these factors were thought desirable. Heinz & Noble steadily added other lines, including pickles. In 1876 with his brother John and cousin Frederick he formed F. & J. Heinz. One of their first products was ketchup – a staple product in every American household, but one previously made on a domestic scale, a task that involved the whole family stirring a huge cauldron over an open fire for an entire day.

The business was sufficiently well established by 1886 for the Heinz family to visit Europe, and H.J. sold the first Heinz products in Britain to Fortnum & Mason, the upmarket Piccadilly emporium, astonishing them by having the audacity to enter the store through the *front* door! The first branch office in London was opened in 1895, by which time the company had become H.J. Heinz & Co.

Why '57 Varieties'? In 1896, travelling on the New York Third Avenue railway, H.J. saw a sign advertising '21 Styles' of shoe. 'It set me to thinking,' he later recalled. 'I said to myself, "we do not have styles of products, but we do have *varieties* of products." Counting how many we had, I counted well beyond 57, but 57 kept coming back into my mind . . . 58 Varieties or 59 Varieties did not appeal to me at all – just "57 Varieties".' Henry got off the train and went straight to his printers where he designed the first 'Heinz 57' advertisement.

OPPOSITE Harrods Food Halls are a major tourist attraction.

LEFT Some of Marks & Spencer's bestselling food lines.

THE TOP 10 CONSUMERS OF PERRIER WATER

1 France
2 USA
3 UK
4 Belgium
5 Canada
6 West Germany
7 Switzerland
8 Netherlands
9 Australia
10 Italy

In 1903 St John Harmsworth, a wealthy Englishman on a tour of France, visited Vergèze, a spa town near Nimes. Its spring, Les Bouillons (believed to have been discovered by the Carthaginian soldier Hannibal in *c* 218 BC), was notable for the occurrence of carbon dioxide which is released from the rock, permeating through the water and making it 'naturally sparkling'. Harmsworth recognized the potential for selling the spa water and proceeded to buy the spring, naming it after Dr Louis Perrier, a local doctor, and bottling it in distinctive green bottles – said to have been modelled on the Indian clubs with which he exercised.

The company was sold back to the French in 1948, and Perrier maintained a reputation as a popular beverage in sophisticated circles. In 1960 in *For Your Eyes Only* Ian Fleming has James Bond drink it – 'He always stipulated Perrier...'. In the late 1970s a combination of increased health consciousness and ingenious advertising and marketing enabled Perrier to broaden its appeal and to achieve its world dominance of the burgeoning mineral water business. Perrier is now drunk in 120 countries around the world, and its name has become virtually synonymous with mineral water.

In the UK a decade ago, the total mineral water market was worth about £12,000,000 a year, of which Perrier's share was under 500,000 bottles. The market is now reckoned to be worth £250,000,000, with Perrier selling nearly 200,000,000 bottles, or almost half the total of 500,000,000 litres/879,876,500 pints consumed in the UK – some 9 litres/15 pints for every person in the country.

CADBURY SCHWEPPES' TOP 10 SOFT DRINKS

1 Schweppes Tonic
2 Canada Dry Ginger Ale
3 Sunkist Orange
4 Crush Orange
5 Motts Juices
6 Schweppes Ginger Ale
7 Kia-Ora (ready-to-drink orange)
8 Schweppes Lemonade
9 Rose's Lime Juice
10 Gini

German-born Jean Jacob Schweppe (1740–1821) moved to Geneva where he worked as a jeweller. An amateur scientist, he became interested in the manufacture of artificial mineral waters (which had been pioneered in England in 1741 by Dr William Brownrigg of Whitehaven). He moved to London in 1792 and in his Drury Lane factory began producing his own brand of soda water, forming Schweppe & Co (later Schweppes Ltd). By the 1870s the company was also making ginger ale and 'Indian Tonic Water' by adding quinine to sweetened soda water, after the style of the British in India who drank it as an antidote to malaria, thus beginning the fashion for gin and tonic. Kia-Ora, acquired by Schweppes in 1930, was originally marketed in Australia before being made in Great Britain. Its unusual name is Maori for 'good health'. Rose's Lime Juice joined the Schweppe group in 1957. Schweppes merged with Cadbury Brothers Ltd in 1969, forming Cadbury Schweppes.

Schweppes' advertising has always been memorable, from its 'Schweppervescence' campaign launched in 1946, through the late 1950s and early 1960s when the company's television advertisements featured Benny Hill, to their long-running series with actor William Franklyn, using just the 'Sch' sound of the name.

THE 10 BESTSELLING SOFT DRINKS IN THE USA

Brand	% of market
1 Coca-Cola	20.0
2 Pepsi-Cola	18.3
3 Diet Coke	8.9
4 Diet Pepsi	5.7
5 Dr Pepper	4.6
6 Sprite	3.6
7 Mountain Dew	3.5
8 7-Up	2.9
9 CF Diet Coke	2.4
10 CF Diet Pepsi	1.5

CF – Caffeine Free.

THE TOP 10 ALCOHOL-CONSUMING NATIONS

	Country	Annual consumption per head (100% alcohol)	
		lit	pt
1	France	13.3	23.4
2	Luxembourg	13.0	22.9
3	Spain	12.1	21.3
4=	Switzerland	11.0	19.4
4=	East Germany	11.0	19.4
6	Hungary	10.5	18.5
7=	West Germany	10.4	18.3
7=	Portugal	10.4	18.3
9	Belgium	10.0	17.6
10	Austria	9.9	17.4
21	USA	7.5	13.2
22	UK	7.4	13.0

Even though its total consumption has declined from its peak of 17.4 lit/30.6 pt per head, France has held its lead in this list for many years.

Coca-Cola is the USA's bestselling soft drink.

Food & Drink Quiz

1 Were bananas first sold in London in 1633, 1733 or 1833?
2 Which Australian opera singer had a dessert and a kind of bread named after her?
3 What is laver bread made from?
4 What is biltong?
5 From what fish does caviar come?
6 What is the food connection between Blanche Ames, Lord Lambourne and Willis Williams?
7 From what was chewing gum originally derived?
8 How big is the wine bottle known as a jeroboam?
9 Isabella Mayson, who died in 1865 aged just 29, the author of a famous cookery book, is better known by her married name. What was it?
10 What is poteen?

OPPOSITE Eau, what a success story! Perrier's distinctive bottles are sold all over the world.

THE WORLD'S TOP 10 CHAMPAGNE IMPORTERS

Country	Bottles imported
1 UK	22,792,260
2 USA	13,673,096
3 West Germany	12,950,831
4 Switzerland	9,318,286
5 Italy	9,108,946
6 Belgium	5,866,711
7 Netherlands	1,992,850
8 Australia	1,586,762
9 Canada	1,472,576
10 Japan	1,285,425

In 1989 an estimated record total of 248,913,509 bottles of champagne were produced. As usual, the French kept most of it for themselves and continued to lead the world as the leading champagne consumers, with a staggering 154,597,949 bottles drunk – equivalent to an annual consumption of almost 2.8 bottles for every man, woman and child in the country. But 94,315,560 bottles were exported and for many years the UK has led the world as the principal importer of champagne. Its import for 1989 represented a 10.38 per cent increase on 1988 and equals two-fifths of a bottle per head of the population. During the year, Japan increased its consumption by 66.65 per cent, entering the Top 10 for the first time and pushing Spain out of 10th position.

The French are the world's leading wine consumers.

Champagne, a bestselling drink for over 100 years.

THE TOP 10 WINE-PRODUCING COUNTRIES

Country	Annual production (tonnes)
1 Italy	6,390,000
2 France	6,379,000
3 Spain	2,267,000
4 Argentina	1,800,000
5 USA	1,740,000
6 USSR	1,500,000
7 Romania	1,000,000
8 West Germany	985,000
9 South Africa	850,000
10 Yugoslavia	576,000
World total	*27,336,000*

World wine production has steadily declined from a total 10 years ago of nearly 35,000,000 tonnes. The production of certain countries has also fallen dramatically – that of Portugal, for example, formerly No. 7 in the world list, from its peak of over 1,000,000 tonnes to 368,000 in 1988.

RIGHT The £105,000 1787 Château Lafite Jefferson wine bottle.

BOTTOM A Tuscan vineyard: Italy is the world's top wine producer.

THE TOP 10 WINE-DRINKING NATIONS

	Country	Litres per head	Equiv. 75 cl bottles
1	France	74.0	98.7
2	Italy	62.1	82.8
3	Luxembourg	58.3	77.7
4	Portugal	58.0	77.3
5	Argentina	55.8	74.4
6	Switzerland	49.9	66.5
7	Spain	47.4	63.2
8	Chile	35.0	46.7
9	Austria	32.9	43.9
10	Greece	32.0	42.7
26	UK	11.4	15.2
29	USA	8.6	11.5

THE 10 MOST EXPENSIVE BOTTLES OF WINE EVER SOLD AT AUCTION

	Wine	Price (£)
1	Château Lafite 1787 Sold by Christie's, London, 5 December 1985	105,000

The highest price ever paid for a bottle of red wine resulted from the bottle having been initialled by US President Thomas Jefferson. It was purchased by Christopher Forbes and is now on display in the Forbes Magazine Galleries, New York.

2	Château d'Yquem 1784 Sold by Christie's, London, 4 December 1986	39,600

The highest price ever paid for a bottle of white wine.

3	Château Lafite Rothschild 1832 (double magnum) Sold by International Wine Auctions, London, 9 April 1988	24,000
4	Château Lafite 1806 Sold by Sotheby's, Geneva, 13 November 1988 (SF 57,200)	21,700
5	Château Lafite 1811 (tappit-hen – equivalent to three bottles) Sold by Christie's, London, 23 June 1988	20,000
6	Château Margaux 1784 (half-bottle) Sold by Christie's, at Vin Expo, Bordeaux, France, 26 June 1987	18,000

The highest price ever paid for a half-bottle.

7	Château d'Yquem 1811 Sold by Christie's, London, 1 December 1988	15,000
8	Château Lafite Rothschild 1806 Sold at a Heublein Auction, San Francisco, 24 May 1979 ($28,000)	14,000
9	Château Lafite 1822 Sold at a Heublein Auction, San Francisco, 28 May 1980 ($31,000)	13,400
10	Château Lafite Rothschild 1811 Sold by International Wine Auctions, London, 26 June 1985	12,000

Rare bottles of wine have also been sold privately for sums in excess of £25,000.

On 25 April 1989, No.6, also initialled by Thomas Jefferson and now with an asking price of $500,000/ £304,878, was smashed by a waiter's tray while on display at a tasting in the Four Seasons restaurant, New York. A small quantity of the wine was salvaged, but was declared virtually undrinkable.

THE WORLD'S TOP 10 BEER BRANDS

Brand	Company/country	Annual sales lit	pt
1 Budweiser	Anheuser-Busch, USA	60,000,000,000	105,600,000
2 Kirin Beer	Kirin Brewing Co Ltd, Japan	25,000,000,000	44,000,000
3 Miller Lite	Miller Brewing Co, USA	23,000,000,000	40,500,000
4 Heineken	Heineken NV, Netherlands	15,600,000,000	27,500,000
5 Antartica	Companhia Antartica Paulista, Brazil	13,000,000,000	22,900,000
6 Brahma Chopp	Companhia Cervejaria Brahma, Brazil	12,500,000,000	22,000,000
7 Miller High Life	Miller Brewing Co, USA	11,600,000,000	20,400,000
8 Polar	Cerveceria Polar CA, Venezuela	10,800,000,000	19,000,000
9 Coors Lite	Adolph Coors Co, USA	9,800,000,000	17,200,000
10 Castle Lager	South African Breweries Ltd	9,500,000,000	16,700,000
20 Guinness	Guinness plc, Ireland	7,200,000,000	12,700,000

The Munich Beer Festival: the Germans are the world's greatest beer drinkers.

THE TOP 10 COFFEE ADVERTISERS IN THE UK

Company	Annual advertising expenditure (£)
1 Nescafé	24,737,000
2 Maxwell House	9,859,000
3 Brooke Bond	3,714,000
4 Café Hag	2,396,000
5 Birds Mellow	1,646,000
6 Kenco	1,610,000
7 Lyons	1,060,000
8 Master Blend	840,000
9 Melitta	202,000
10 Verdona	103,000

THE TOP 10 COFFEE-DRINKING NATIONS

Country	Annual consumption per head kg	lb oz		cups*
1 Finland	11.68	25	12	1,752
2 Sweden	11.08	24	7	1,662
3 Denmark	10.20	22	8	1,530
4 Netherlands	9.89	21	4	1,484
5 Norway	9.19	20	4	1,379
6 West Germany	8.26	18	3	1,239
7 Austria	8.01	17	11	1,202
8 Switzerland	7.88	17	6	1,170
9 Belgium/Luxembourg	7.06	15	9	1,059
10 France	5.78	12	12	867
12 USA	4.40	9	11	660
17 UK	2.45	5	6	368

*Based on 150 cups per kg/2.2 lb.

Since the last edition, the total consumption of many countries has declined, including that of Finland, the leading consumer throughout the 1980s, which fell from 1,892 cups to 1,752. Norway has slipped down from 3rd to 5th position, but West Germany has overtaken Austria, and Italy has pushed the USA from 11th to 12th position. UK total consumption is slightly down, but its position has risen from 18th to 17th. The average Finn now drinks less than five cups of coffee a day compared with just one for the UK. As the table of Top 10 Tea-Drinking Nations shows, the Brits remain a nation of tea-drinkers.

Refreshing the parts other beers cannot reach: Heineken is the fourth bestselling beer in the world.

THE TOP 10 BEER-DRINKING NATIONS

	Country	Annual consumption per head	
		lit	pt
1 =	West Germany	143.0	251.6
1 =	East Germany	143.0	251.6
3	Czechoslovakia	130.0	228.7
4	Denmark	119.9	211.0
5	Belgium	118.6	208.7
6	Austria	117.8	207.3
7	Luxembourg	115.8	203.8
8	New Zealand	115.2	202.7
9	Australia	113.1	199.0
10	UK	111.2	195.7

THE 10 LEADING TEA-DRINKING NATIONS

	Country	Average annual consumption per head			
		kg	lb	oz	cups*
1	Qatar	3.21	7	1	1,412
2	Irish Republic	3.09	6	13	1,360
3	UK	2.81	6	3	1,236
4	Turkey	2.72	6	0	1,197
5	Iraq	2.51	5	9	1,104
6	Kuwait	2.23	4	15	981
7	Tunisia	1.82	4	13	801
8	New Zealand	1.71	3	12	752
9	Hong Kong	1.63	3	8	717
10	Bahrein	1.45	3	3	638

*Based on 440 cups per kg/2.2 lb.

Within Europe, consumption of tea varies enormously from the 1,360 cups per head recorded for Ireland down to just 26 cups in Italy, one of the lowest in the world. The average USA citizen drinks fewer than 150 cups a year.

THE TOP 10 TEA ADVERTISERS IN THE UK

	Company	Annual advertising expenditure (£)
1	Brooke Bond	11,388,000
2	Tetley	4,501,000
3	Typhoo	4,173,000
4	Twining	423,000
5	Lift	341,000
6	Lyons	244,000
7	Taylor	227,000
8	Ridgeway	200,000
9	Jackson	154,000
10	Nabarne	100,000

Britain remains one of the world's top tea-drinkers.

Crime & Punishment

THE 10 COMMONEST MOTORING OFFENCES IN THE UK

Offence	% of motoring offences
1 Driving while uninsured	13.53
2 Speeding	10.78
3 Failing to pay road tax	9.38
4 Drink-driving	6.41
5 Careless driving	5.38
6 Driving without a licence	3.58
7 Defective tyres	3.42
8 Driving without L-plates	3.26
9 Unaccompanied L-driver	2.52
10 Driving while disqualified	2.22

THE 10 COMMONEST REPORTED CRIMINAL OFFENCES IN ENGLAND AND WALES

Offence	Number*
1 Theft from a vehicle	620,600
2 Criminal damage	593,900
3 Burglary in a dwelling	441,000
4 Burglary in other buildings	376,800
5 Theft or unauthorized taking of a vehicle	366,700
6 Theft from a shop	216,200
7 Violence against the person	158,200
8 Fraud and forgery	133,900
9 Theft of a pedal cycle	108,800
10 Handling stolen goods	49,300

*Notified to police.

Based on Home Office statistics for 1988.

THE 10 COMMONEST RELATIONSHIPS OF HOMICIDE VICTIMS TO SUSPECTS IN ENGLAND AND WALES

Relationship	Victims
1 Male stranger	122
2 Male friend or acquaintance	89
3 Wife, ex-wife or female cohabitant	87
4 Son	51
5 Daughter	34
6 Female stranger	30
7 Female friend or acquaintance	27
8 Husband, ex-husband or male cohabitant	21
9 Female lover, ex-lover or lover's spouse	20
10 Mother	13

Based on Home Office statistics for 1988.

TOP RIGHT Unpaid diplomatic parking fines are an enduring problem.

THE 10 DIPLOMATIC MISSIONS WITH THE MOST UNPAID PARKING FINES

	Mission	Total unpaid fines	
		1988	1989
1	USSR	656	599
2	Saudi Arabia	357	287
3	Ivory Coast	300	272
4=	Egypt	668	261
4=	Cameroon	311	261
6	Poland	340	244
7	Pakistan	228	243
8	Sudan	286	238
9	United Arab Emirates	122	231
10	Korea	175	216

For many years diplomats used their immunity from prosecution to avoid paying parking fines. In 1984 they managed to clock up a record 108,845 unpaid tickets. Since 1985, however, this practice has been challenged and pressure brought to bear on the offending embassies and international organizations to make their staffs behave responsibly. The total in 1989 was 7,831, a 22 per cent reduction on the 1988 figure of 10,079.

THE 10 COMMONEST OFFENCES IN ENGLAND AND WALES

Offence	Offenders found guilty
1 Motoring offences	745,200
2 Theft and handling stolen goods	163,400
3 Wireless Telegraphy Acts (failure to have TV licence, etc)	124,300
4 Revenue laws (tax evasion, etc)	113,400
5 Wounding	50,900
6 Burglary	48,400
7 Criminal and malicious damage	47,000
8 Drunkenness	45,300
9 Assault	11,500
10 Railway offences (travelling without a ticket, etc)	9,200

This list includes both indictable offences (those normally calling for a trial before a jury) and summary offences (usually tried before a magistrates' court). Some, such as certain criminal damage offences, may be either indictable or summary. There are also groups of less specific offences lumped together as 'breach of local and other regulations' and 'other summary offences' which in total make up large numbers. It should be noted that direct comparisons cannot be made with offences under Scottish legal jurisdiction, which employs different categories of offence, some bearing a ring of the age in which they were established, including 'theft by opening lockfast places' and 'lewd and libidinous practices'.

THE 10 LARGEST PRISONS IN ENGLAND AND WALES

Prison	Inmates
1 Strangeways, Manchester	1,508*
2 Wandsworth, London	1,465
3 Walton, Liverpool	1,266
4 Armley, Leeds	1,094
5 Brixton, London	975
6 Wormwood Scrubs, London	958
7 Durham (male and female)	948
8 Winston Green, Birmingham	905
9 Pentonville, London	846
10 Lindholme, Doncaster	778

Temporarily uninhabitable as a result of damage caused by prisoners rioting.

The total population of the 10 largest prisons was 11,595 in 1988. On 31 December 1989 it had been reduced to 10,743, a fall of 7 per cent.

ABOVE Wormwood Scrubs, one of England's largest prisons.

BELOW Pedro Alonso López, the 'Colombian Monster'.

Prison **Q**uiz

Identify these prisoners who wrote while in jail:

1 In Bedford prison for 11 years for preaching without a licence, he wrote *The Pilgrim's Progress*.

2 Jailed for debt in Newgate Prison, he wrote *Fanny Hill*.

3 While imprisoned in Spain in 1597, he began *Don Quixote*.

4 He wrote his *Hymn to the Pillory* while in jail in 1703, and later wrote *Robinson Crusoe*.

5 He wrote his *History of the World* in the Tower of London.

6 While serving nine months of a five-year sentence in Landsberg prison, he wrote *Mein Kampf*.

7 In prison in Genoa, he wrote a book about his extensive travels in China.

8 He wrote a poem, *The Ballad of Reading Gaol*, while imprisoned there.

9 This American author began writing short stories while in prison for embezzlement.

10 The Cavalier poet who penned the song *To Althea*, which contains the line, 'Stone walls do not a prison make'.

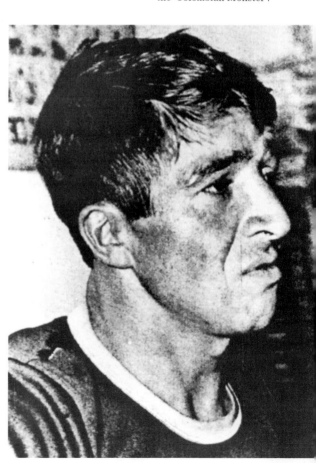

THE 10 MOST PROLIFIC MURDERERS IN THE WORLD

1 Behram
The leader of the Thug cult in India, in the period 1790–1840, he was reputed to have committed over 931 ritual strangulations.

2 Countess Erszebet Bathory
In the period up to 1610 in Hungary, Bathory (1560–1614), known as 'Countess Dracula', murdered 300–650 girls, in the belief that drinking their blood would prevent her from ageing. She was eventually arrested in 1611. Tried and found guilty, she died on 21 August 1614 walled up in her castle.

3 William Estel Brown
On 17 July 1961 Brown admitted that on 18 March 1937 he had deliberately loosened the gas pipes in his school basement in New London, Texas, thereby causing an explosion that killed 282 children and 24 teachers.

4 Pedro Alonso López
Known as the 'Colombian Monster' and the 'Monster of the Andes', up to his 1980 capture he murdered at least 300 young girls in Colombia, Ecuador and Peru. He was caught by Ayacucho Indians in Peru, whose children he had been abducting, and escorted to Ecuador by a female missionary. He was arrested and led police to 53 graves; further bodies were revealed when a river flooded, but others were devoured by wild animals or buried under roads and on construction sites and were never discovered. López was convicted and sentenced to life imprisonment.

5 Gilles de Rais
A fabulously wealthy French aristocrat, de Rais (b.1404) was accused of having kidnapped and killed between 60 and 200 children. He was strangled and his body burnt at Nantes on 25 October 1440.

6 Herman Webster Mudgett
Also known as 'H.H. Holmes', Mudgett (b.1860) was believed to have lured over 150 women to his 63rd Street, Chicago, 'Castle', which was fully equipped for torturing and murdering them and disposing of the bodies. Arrested in 1894 and found guilty of murder, he confessed to killing 27. Mudgett, regarded as America's first mass murderer, was hanged on 7 May 1896.

7 Julio Gonzalez
On the morning of Sunday 27 March 1990, Gonzalez, a Cuban refugee who had lived in the USA for 10 years, allegedly firebombed Happy Land, an illegal discotheque in the Bronx, New York, killing 87.

8 Bruno Lüdke
Lüdke (b.1909) was a German who confessed to murdering 85 women between 1928 and 29 January 1943. Declared insane, he was incarcerated in a Vienna hospital where he was subjected to medical experiments, apparently dying on 8 April 1944 after a lethal injection.

9 Wou Bom-Kon
An off-duty policeman, on 26–27 April 1982 in South Korea he went on a drunken rampage with guns and grenades, killing 57 before blowing himself up with a grenade.

10 John Gilbert Graham
Graham placed a time bomb in his mother's luggage as she boarded an airliner in Denver, Colorado, on 1 November 1955. En route for San Francisco, it blew up killing all 44 on board. Graham was executed in the gas chamber of Colorado State Penitentiary.

Other possible contenders for this unenviable Top 10 include Ted Bundy who, after spending nine years on death row, was executed at Florida State Prison on 24 January 1989 for the murder of 12-year-old Kimberley Leach. During his last hours he confessed to 23 murders. Police linked him conclusively to the murders of 36 girls and he once admitted that he might have killed as many as 100 times.

On 13 March 1980 John Wayne Gacy (b. 1943) was sentenced to death by electrocution for the Chicago murders of 33 men. The sentence was never carried out and he is currently in prison.

At the end of World War I Fritz Haarman of Hanover, West Germany, may have murdered as many as 40 refugees in order to steal their clothes and sell their bodies as meat. He was charged with 27 murders and executed in 1924.

Dr Marcel Petiot is known to have killed at least 27 but admitted to 63 murders at his Paris house during World War II. He claimed that they were Nazi collaborators, but it is probable that they were wealthy Jews whom he robbed and killed after pretending to help them escape from occupied France.

Bella Gunness (née Grunt) (1859–1908) is said to have lured 16–28 suitors through 'Lonely Hearts' advertisements, as well as numerous others, to her La Porte, Indiana, farm, where – along with her two husbands – she murdered them. On 28 April 1908 she burned the farm down and either committed suicide or, according to some reports, faked her own death and disappeared.

The worst gun massacre in the USA took place on 19 July 1984 when 41-year-old James Huberty opened fire in a McDonald's restaurant in San Ysidro, California, killing 21 before being shot dead by police. A 22nd victim died from wounds the following day. In recent years several other incidents of this nature in the USA and Canada have resulted in the deaths of up to 16 people.

THE 10 MOST PROLIFIC MURDERERS IN THE UK

1   Mary Ann Cotton
Cotton (b.1832), a former nurse, is generally held to be Britain's worst mass murderer. Over a 20-year period, it seems probable that she disposed of 14–20 victims, including her husband, children and stepchildren by arsenic poisoning. She was hanged at Durham on 24 March 1873.

2   Dr William Palmer
Known as the 'Rugeley Poisoner', Palmer (b.1824) may have killed 13–16, including his wife, brother and children, in order to claim insurance, and various men whom he robbed to pay off his gambling debts. He was hanged at Stafford on 14 June 1856. The true number of his victims remains uncertain.

3= Bruce Lee
In 1981 Lee was convicted of arson that resulted in the deaths of 26 residents of an old people's home. He was later cleared by the Court of Appeal of 11 of the deaths. He is currently in a mental hospital.

3= William Burke and William Hare
Two Irishmen living in Edinburgh, Burke and Hare murdered at least 15 people in order to sell their bodies (for £8 to £14 each) to anatomists in the period before human dissection was legal. Burke was hanged on 28 January 1829 while Hare, having turned king's evidence against him, was released a week later and allegedly died a blind beggar in London in the 1860s.

3= Dennis Andrew Nilsen
Nilsen (b.1948) admitted to murdering 15 men between 1978 and 1983. On 4 November 1983 he was sentenced to life imprisonment on six charges of murder and two attempted murders.

3= Michael Ryan
On 19 August 1987 in Hungerford, Berkshire, Ryan (b.1960) shot 15 dead and wounded 15 others before shooting himself.

7   Peter Sutcliffe
Known as the 'Yorkshire Ripper', Sutcliffe (b.1946) was caught on 2 January 1981 and on 22 May 1981 found guilty of murdering 13 women and 7 attempted murders between 1975 and 1980. He was sentenced to life imprisonment on each charge and is currently in Parkhurst Prison.

8   Judith Minna Ward
Ward (b.1949) was found guilty of the 1974 bombing of an Army coach in Yorkshire, killing 12 soldiers.

9   Peter Thomas Anthony Manuel
Found guilty of murdering 7 people, it is likely that Manuel killed as many as 12. He was hanged at Barlinnie Prison on 11 July 1958.

10   John George Haigh
The so-called 'Acid Bath Murderer' may have killed up to 9 victims. He was hanged at Wandsworth Prison on 10 August 1949.

Other multiple murderers in British history include 'Jack the Ripper' (true identity and dates unknown), who in 1888 in Whitechapel, London, killed and mutilated six women, and John Reginald Halliday Christie who killed at least six women at 10 Rillington Place, London, and was hanged at Pentonville Prison on 15 July 1953. On 7 May 1981 John Thompson was found guilty on one specimen charge of murder by arson during an incident in which a total of 37 died at the Spanish Club, Denmark Street, London.

Mass-murderer Dennis Nilsen is led away by police.

THE 10 COMMONEST HOMICIDE WEAPONS IN THE USA

Weapon/homicide method	Victims
1 Handguns	8,278
2 Cutting and stabbing instruments	3,946
3 Blunt objects (hammers, clubs, etc)	1,143
4 'Personal weapons' (hands, feet, fists, etc)	1,139
5 Shotguns	1,117
6 Firearms (type not stated)	910
7 Rifles	764
8 Strangulation	335
9 Fire	258
10 Asphyxiation	72

In 1988, the year to which these figures relate, 'other weapons or weapons not stated' were used in 618 murders. Relatively less common methods included drowning (38 cases), explosives (35) and poison (15). The total number of murders for the year amounted to 18,269 – equivalent to one person in every 13,483 of the population.

THE 10 MOST DANGEROUS CITIES IN THE USA

City	Violent crimes per 100,000 population
1 Atlanta, Georgia	3,575.55
2 Newark, New Jersey	3,049.27
3 Flint, Michigan	2,732.82
4 St Louis, Missouri	2,465.03
5 Detroit, Michigan	2,374.59
6 New Haven, Connecticut	2,351.32
7 Orlando, Florida	2,291.98
8 Portland, Oregon	2,240.63
9 New York	2,217.64
10 Boston, Massachusetts	2,084.77

Atlanta, Georgia, is ranked as the most dangerous US city.

THE 10 COMMONEST HOMICIDE WEAPONS IN ENGLAND AND WALES

Weapon/homicide method	Victims
1 Sharp instrument	198
2 Hitting and kicking	129
3 Strangulation and asphyxiation	103
4 Blunt instrument	49
5 Shooting	43
6 Burning	21
7 Poison and drugs	15
8 Motor vehicle	9
9 Drowning	6
10 Explosives	2

According to Home Office statistics, there were 592 homicides in 1988 in England and Wales. In the light of police investigations and evidence presented in court, the provisional figure for the previous year – a peak of 635 – was reduced to 604. In addition to those in the list, 13 methods are described as 'other' and four of unknown cause. This is equivalent to approximately one homicide per 84,459 people – a sixth of the rate in the USA.

Military

THE 10 COUNTRIES SUFFERING THE GREATEST MILITARY LOSSES IN WORLD WAR I

Country	Killed
1 Germany	1,773,700
2 Russia	1,700,000
3 France	1,357,800
4 Austria–Hungary	1,200,000
5 British Empire*	908,371
6 Italy	650,000
7 Romania	335,706
8 Turkey	325,000
9 USA	116,516
10 Bulgaria	87,500

*Including Australia, Canada, India, New Zealand, South Africa, etc.

The number of battle fatalities and deaths from other causes among military personnel varied enormously from country to country: Romania's death rate was highest at 45 per cent of its total mobilized forces; Germany's was 16 per cent, Austria–Hungary's and Russia's 15 per cent and the British Empire's 10 per cent, with the USA's 2 per cent and Japan's 0.04 per cent among the lowest.

Trench warfare contributed to the huge casualty figures of World War I.

THE TOP 10 AIR ACES OF WORLD WAR I

	Pilot	Country	Kills claimed
1	Manfred von Richthofen	Germany	80
2	René Paul Fonck	France	75
3	Edward Mannock*	Great Britain	73
4	William Avery Bishop	Great Britain	72
5	Ernst Udet	Germany	62
6	Raymond Collishaw	Canada	60
7	James Thomas Byford McCudden*	Great Britain	57
8=	Anthony Wetherby Beauchamp-Proctor	Great Britain	54
8=	Donald Roderick MacLaren	Great Britain	54
8=	Georges-Marie Guynemer*	France	54

Killed in action.

Rittmeister Manfred Freiherr, Baron von Richthofen's claim of 80 kills has been disputed, since only 60 of them have been completely confirmed. Recent evidence has also suggested that Major Raymond Collishaw may have achieved as many as 81 kills, but that inter-service rivalries led to many of them not being confirmed. It certainly seems that he had more *witnessed* kills than any other flier (only 13 of Bishop's 72, for example, were actually witnessed).

If the German and French aces are excluded so that the list consists only of the Top 10 British Empire pilots belonging to the Royal Flying Corps, Royal Naval Air Service and (after 1 April 1918) the Royal Air Force, Mannock *et al* move up to occupy Nos. 1 to 5=, to which should be added:

7	William George Barker	53
8	Robert Alexander Little	47
9=	Philip Fletcher Fullard	46
9=	George Edward Henry McElroy	46

THE 10 GREATEST MERCHANT SHIPPING LOSSES IN WORLD WAR I

	Country	Vessels sunk Number	Tonnage
1	UK	2,038	6,797,802
2	Italy	228	720,064
3	France	213	651,583
4	USA	93	372,892
5	Germany	188	319,552
6	Greece	115	304,992
7	Denmark	126	205,002
8	Netherlands	74	194,483
9	Sweden	124	192,807
10	Spain	70	160,383

LEFT Manfred von Richthofen and BELOW Edward Mannock, respectively top German and British air aces of World War I.

THE TOP 10 US AIR ACES OF WORLD WAR I

	Pilot	Kills claimed
1	Eddie Rickenbacker	26
2	Frank Luke	21
3	Raoul Lufbery	17
4	George A. Vaughn	13
5=	Frank Kindley	12
5=	David E. Putnam	12
5=	Elliot W. Springs	12
8=	Reed G. Landis	10
8=	Michael Swaab	10
10=	L. A. Hamilton	9
10=	Chester Ellis Wright	9

LEFT Waterloo continues to attract numerous visitors.

RIGHT (inset) An officer is awarded his VC.

BOTTOM LEFT One of the many World War II cemeteries.

THE WORLD'S TOP 10 BATTLEFIELDS

	Battlefield	Battle date	Country
1	Gettysburg	1863	USA
2	Normandy Beaches	1944	France
3	Waterloo	1815	Belgium
4	The Somme	1916	France
5	Passchendaele	1917	Belgium
6	Arnhem	1944	Holland
7	The Alamo	1836	USA
8	Monte Cassino	1944	Italy
9	Verdun	1916	France
10	Rorke's Drift	1879	South Africa

Based on the battlefields most requested or visited by clients of Major and Mrs Holt's Battlefield Tours, a leading specialist tour operator offering a wide range of visits to important military sites all over the world.

THE 10 COUNTRIES SUFFERING THE GREATEST MILITARY LOSSES IN WORLD WAR II

	Country	Killed
1	USSR	13,600,000
2	Germany	3,300,000
3	China	1,324,516
4	Japan	1,140,429
5	British Empire* of which UK	357,116 264,000
6	Romania	350,000
7	Poland	320,000
8	Yugoslavia	305,000
9	USA	292,131
10	Italy	279,800

*Including Australia, Canada, India, New Zealand, etc.

The actual numbers killed in World War II have been the subject of intense argument for over 45 years. The immense level of the military casualty rate of the USSR in particular is hard to comprehend. It is included here at its likely lowest level, but most authorities now reckon that of the 30,000,000 Soviets who bore arms, perhaps as many as 8,500,000 died in action and up to 2,500,000 of wounds received in battle and disease. Some 5,800,000 were taken prisoner, of which a total as high as 3,300,000 may have died in captivity. It should also be borne in mind that these were *military* losses: to these should be added many untold millions of civilian war deaths, while recent estimates have suggested an additional figure of up to 25,000,000 civilian deaths as a result of Stalinist purges which began just before the war.

THE TOP 10 NATIONALITIES OF VC WINNERS DURING WORLD WAR II

	Nationality	VCs
1	British and Irish	109
2	Australian	19
3	Indian	17
4	Canadian	13
5	Nepalese (Gurkha)	10
6	New Zealander	8
7	South African	3
8=	Rhodesian	1
8=	Fijian	1
8=	Danish	1

THE 10 LARGEST ARMED FORCES OF WORLD WAR II

	Country	Personnel*
1	USSR	12,500,000
2	USA	12,364,000
3	Germany	10,000,000
4	Japan	6,095,000
5	France	5,700,000
6	UK	4,683,000
7	Italy	4,500,000
8	China	3,800,000
9	India	2,150,000
10	Poland	1,000,000

*Total at peak strength.

THE TOP 10 BRITISH AND COMMONWEALTH AIR ACES OF WORLD WAR II

	Pilot	Nationality	Kills claimed
1	Marmaduke Thomas St John Pattle	South African	41
2	James Edgar 'Johnny' Johnson	British	38
3	Adolf Gysbert 'Sailor' Malan	South African	35
4	Brendan 'Paddy' Finucane	Irish	32
5	George Frederick Beurling	Canadian	$31\frac{1}{3}$
6=	John Robert Daniel Braham	British	29
6=	Robert Roland Stanford Tuck	British	29
8	Neville Frederick Duke	British	$28\frac{5}{6}$
9	Clive Robert Caldwell	Australian	$28\frac{1}{2}$
10	Frank Reginald Carey	British	$28\frac{1}{3}$

Kills that are expressed as fractions refer to those that were shared with others, the number of fighters involved and the extent of each pilot's participation determining the proportion allocated to him. As a result of this precise reckoning, British pilot James Harry 'Ginger' Lacey, with 28 kills, misses sharing 10th place with Carey by just $\frac{1}{3}$ of a kill.

LEFT Scramble! Battle of Britain pilots race to their fighters.

RIGHT 'Paddy' Finucane is pointed out as the top Irish air ace.

BELOW The morning after: surveying Blitz-damaged homes in London.

OPPOSITE A Luftwaffe crew awaits the order to attack.

THE TOP 10 NATIONALITIES OF BATTLE OF BRITAIN PILOTS

	Nationality	Pilots
1	British (RAF 1,783; Fleet Air Arm 56) Total	1,839
2	Polish	143
3	New Zealander	94
4	Canadian	90
5	Czechoslovakian	87
6	Belgian	24
7	South African	23
8	Australian	21
9	French	13
10=	Irish	9
10=	American	9

THE 10 SQUADRONS WITH MOST KILLS DURING THE BATTLE OF BRITAIN

	Squadron	Kills
1	303	$126\frac{1}{2}$
2	602	102
3	603	98
4	92	$94\frac{2}{5}$
5	501	93
6	41	$92\frac{2}{5}$
7	609	$90\frac{1}{3}$
8	74	86
9	213	81
10	249	75

THE 10 MOST HEAVILY BOMBED LONDON BOROUGHS

	Borough	High-explosive bombs per 100 acres
1	Holborn	39.75
2	City	29.53
3	Westminster	28.85
4	Shoreditch	23.56
5	Southwark	23.35
6	Stepney	20.02
7	Finsbury	19.11
8	Chelsea	18.51
9	Bethnal Green	17.26
10	Bermondsey	17.16

During the 'Blitz', German bombing was concentrated on the centre of London and the Docks, but also caused enormous damage in adjacent boroughs, including the densely populated East End, and to a lesser extent, in the outer suburbs. About 15,000 people were killed and some 3,500,000 houses in London were bombed during World War II. The worst period was between 7 September 1940 and 11 May 1941 when an estimated 18,800 tons of high-explosive bombs were dropped. The last major raid, but one of the heaviest, occurred on Saturday 10 May 1941, when, in addition to 1,436 fatalities, many important buildings were gutted, including the churches of St Clement Danes, St Olave, Hart Street, and All Hallows, Barking, the House of Commons, Lambeth Palace Library, the Deanery of Westminster Abbey and the British Museum Library, destroying 150,000 books.

THE TOP 10 LUFTWAFFE ACES OF WORLD WAR II

	Pilot	Kills claimed
1	Eric Hartmann	352
2	Gerhard Barkhorn	301
3	Gunther Rall	275
4	Otto Kittel	267
5	Walther Nowotny	255
6	Wilhelm Batz	237
7	Erich Rudorffer	222
8	Heinrich Baer	220
9	Herman Graf	212
10	Heinrich Ehrler	209

These apparently high claims have been dismissed by some military historians as inflated for propaganda purposes.

THE 10 MOST HEAVILY BLITZED CITIES IN THE UK

City	Major raids	Tonnage of high explosive dropped
1 London	85	23,949
2 Liverpool/Birkenhead	8	1,957
3 Birmingham	8	1,852
4 Glasgow/Clydeside	5	1,329
5 Plymouth/Devonport	8	1,228
6 Bristol/Avonmouth	6	919
7 Coventry	2	818
8 Portsmouth	3	687
9 Southampton	4	647
10 Hull	3	593

THE 10 LONDON BOROUGHS RECEIVING THE MOST V1 HITS

	Borough	V1s
1	Croydon	141
2	Wandsworth	122
3	Lewisham	114
4	Camberwell	80
5	Woolwich	77
6	Lambeth	71
7	Beckenham	70
8	Orpington	63
9	West Ham	58
10	Coulsdon	54

A menacing V2 rocket is launched from Peenemünde, Germany.

THE 10 LONDON BOROUGHS RECEIVING THE MOST V2 HITS

	Borough	V2s
1	Woolwich	33
2	West Ham	27
3	Greenwich	22
4	Barking	21
5	Dagenham	19
6=	Erith	17
6=	Chislehurst	17
8	Waltham	15
9=	Wanstead	14
9=	East Ham	14

During 1944, V1 flying bombs destroyed approximately 24,000 houses in London and damaged a further 800,000 – particularly in the southern suburbs, which were the nearest to the V1 launch sites on the Channel coast of France. Casualty figures were also very high: in one incident, on Sunday 18 June, 121 members of the congregation were killed when a V1 hit the Guards Chapel at the Wellington Barracks during a service.

THE 10 COUNTIES RECEIVING THE MOST V1 HITS*

	County	V1s
1	Kent	1,444
2	Sussex	880
3	Essex	412
4	Surrey	295
5	Suffolk	93
6	Hertfordshire	82
7	Hampshire	80
8	Buckinghamshire	27
9	Norfolk	13
10	Berkshire	12

Excluding London.

The V1 was notoriously inaccurate: although most were targeted on London, one of them landed near Hitler's headquarters at Soissons, France, while others came down as far afield as Northampton.

THE 10 COUNTIES RECEIVING THE MOST V2 HITS

	County	V2s
1	London	517
2	Essex	378
3	Kent	64
4	Hertfordshire	34
5	Norfolk	29
6	Suffolk	13
7	Surrey	8
8	Sussex	4
9	Bedfordshire	3
10	Buckinghamshire	2

The last V2 to hit England exploded on Court Road, Orpington, Kent at 4.54 pm on 27 March 1945, killing one man – the last British civilian casualty of World War II.

Masterminded by Wernher von Braun, later leader of the US space programme, the 47 ft long V2 rocket was more accurate and more powerful than the V1, while its speed of 5,633 kph/3,500 mph made it virtually impossible to combat with anti-aircraft fire or to intercept with fighter aircraft. The first two were launched from Holland against Paris on 6 September 1944, and on 8 September the first two fell on London, followed by more than 1,000 over the next seven months, resulting in a total of 2,855 fatalities (an even larger number was directed at Belgium with 4,483 killed). On 25 November 1944 a V2 hit Woolworth's in Deptford, killing 160 shoppers, and on 8 March 1945 one hit Smithfield Market, killing 110. On 27 March one of the last V2s – and the last explosive of the war in London – hit a block of flats in Stepney, killing 134.

A V1 flying bomb descends over Fleet Street rooftops.

The Ink Spots' recording of 'Whispering Grass' was one of the hits of the Blitz.

THE TOP 10 SONGS OF THE BLITZ*

1	Whispering Grass
2	I'll Never Smile Again
3	All The Things You Are
4	Only Forever
5	Pennsylvania 6–5000
6	Just One Of Those Things
7	Room Five Hundred And Four
8	The Last Time I Saw Paris
9	I've Got Sixpence
10	A Nightingale Sang In Berkeley Square

*7 September 1940 – 11 May 1941.

THE TOP 10 MALE SINGERS OF 1940

1	Denny Dennis
2	Chick Henderson
3	Sam Browne
4	Al Bowlly
5	Jack Cooper
6	Leslie Douglas
7	Bob Mallin
8	Sam Costa
9	Dan Donovan
10	Brian Laurence

THE TOP 10 FEMALE SINGERS OF 1940

1	Vera Lynn
2	Evelyn Dall
3	Celia Lipton
4	Anne Lenner
5	Beryl Davis
6	Judy Shirley
7	Dolly Elsie
8	June Malo
9	Gwen Jones
10=	Rita Williams
10=	Molly O'Connor

BELOW Al Bowlly, one of the leading male singers of 1940.

ABOVE Vera Lynn, top female singer of 1940.

THE TOP 10 SONGS OF THE BATTLE OF BRITAIN*

1 So Deep Is The Night

2 You've Done Something To My Heart

3 Careless

4 It's A Lovely Day Tomorrow

5 I've Got My Eyes On You

6 If I Should Fall In Love Again

7 It's A Hap Hap Happy Day

8 In The Mood

9 Scatterbrain

10 The Lady Is A Tramp

*Peak period 13 August – 17 September 1940.

Ambrose, the No. 1 bandleader of 1940, with the Dorchester Girls.

THE TOP 10 UK DANCE BANDS OF 1940

1 Ambrose

2 Joe Loss

3 Billy Cotton

4 Oscar Rabin

5 Jack Harris

6 Harry Roy

7 Henry Hall

8 Eddie Carroll

9 Sidney Lipton

10 Ken Jones

A scene from *Pimpernel Smith*, the top film of World War II.

THE TOP 10 FILMS SHOWN IN LONDON DURING WORLD WAR II

1 *Pimpernel Smith*

2 *49th Parallel*

3 *Dangerous Moonlight*

4 *A Yank in the RAF*

5 *One of Our Aircraft is Missing*

6 *Pardon My Sarong*

7 *Beyond the Blue Horizon*

8 *The Road to Morocco*

9 *The Life and Death of Colonel Blimp*

10 *The Sullivans*

Of the 10 most successful films shown in Granada group cinemas during the period 1939–45, eight were war films.

THE 10 CITIES MOST BOMBED BY THE RAF AND USAF, 1939–45

	City	Estimated civilian fatalities
1	Dresden	100,000 +
2	Hamburg	55,000
3	Berlin	49,000
4	Cologne	20,000
5	Magdeburg	15,000
6	Kassel	13,000
7	Darmstadt	12,300
8 =	Heilbronn	7,500
8 =	Essen	7,500
10	Wuppertal	6,000

THE 10 SMALLEST ARMED FORCES OF WORLD WAR II

	Country	Personnel*
1	Costa Rica	400
2	Liberia	1,000
3 =	Honduras	3,000
3 =	Nicaragua	3,000
3 =	El Salvador	3,000
6	Haiti	3,500
7	Dominican Republic	4,000
8	Guatemala	5,000
9 =	Bolivia	8,000
9 =	Uruguay	8,000
9 =	Paraguay	8,000

*Total at peak strength.

As well as mobilizing very small armed forces, several South American countries entered World War II at a very late stage: Argentina, for example, did not declare war on Germany and Japan until 27 March 1945 – six weeks before Germany was defeated. The smallest European armed force was that of Denmark, with a maximum strength of 15,000.

THE TOP 10 V1 ACES

	Pilot	Nation-ality	V1s destroyed
1	Sqdn Ldr J. Berry	British	61⅓
2	Sqdn Ldr R. van Lierde	Belgian	40
3	Wg Cdr R. P. Beaumont	British	32
4	Wg Cdr E. D. Crew	British	31½
5	Flt Lt F. R. L. Mellersh	British	30
6	Sqdn Ldr A. E. Umbers	New Zealand	28
7	FO R. W. Cole	British	21⅔
8	Flt Lt A. R. Moore	British	21½
9=	FO H. Clapperton	British	21
9=	Sqdn Ldr R. Dryland	British	21
9=	Lt O. Burgwal	Dutch	21
9=	Flt Lt O. D. Eagleson	New Zealand	21

The first 10 V1 rockets (from the German, 'Vergeltungswaffe' – vengeance weapon) or 'flying bombs', popularly known as 'doodlebugs', were launched against England on 13 June 1944. Pilotless jet-propelled aircraft carrying one ton of high explosive, they had a top speed of 350–400 mph. Only one of the first wave reached its target and caused casualties – six killed in Bethnal Green, London – but in subsequent months a further 8,000 were launched. Many were erratic and strayed off course or crashed, and of those that continued towards London, a large proportion was brought down by barrage balloons, anti-aircraft fire and particularly by fighter pilots either shooting them down or flying alongside and 'tipping their wings' to send them off course. In the initial week of attack, some 33 per cent were destroyed, but within three months this figure had risen to 70 per cent, with only 9 per cent reaching London. On 28 August 1944, 97 of the 101 V1s that approached England were brought down.

ABOVE Wg Cdr R. P. Beaumont, a surviving V1 ace.

BOTTOM LEFT A US merchant ship falls victim in World War II.

THE 10 GREATEST MERCHANT SHIPPING LOSSES BY ALLIED AND NEUTRAL COUNTRIES IN WORLD WAR II

	Country	Vessels sunk Number	Tonnage
1	UK	4,786	21,194,000
2	USA	578	3,524,983
3	Norway	427	1,728,531
4	Netherlands	286	1,195,204
5	Greece	262	883,200
6	Panama	107	542,772
7	Sweden	204	481,864
8	France	90	334,140
9	Belgium	86	263,198
10	Brazil	30	122,896

The Axis powers' losses were:

Country	Vessels sunk Number	Tonnage
Japan	2,346	8,618,109
Germany	1,595	7,064,600
Italy	467	1,155,080

THE WORLD'S TOP 10 NAVIES

	Country	Manpower	Combat tonnage (1990)
1	USA	584,000	3,208,000
2	USSR	437,000	2,585,000
3	UK	57,000	336,000
4	China	227,000	325,000
5	Japan	44,000	242,000
6	France	63,000	229,000
7	India	46,000	170,000
8	Taiwan	35,000	121,000
9	Italy	51,000	113,000
10	Turkey	51,000	99,000

LEFT The US Navy's *Iowa* in action.

BELOW A Red Army parade: the USSR maintains the largest standing army in the world.

THE 10 SMALLEST ARMED FORCES IN THE WORLD*

	Country	Estimated total active forces (1990)
1	Belize	700
2	The Bahamas	750
3	Luxembourg	800
4	The Gambia	900
5	Cape Verde	1,200
6	The Seychelles	1,300
7	Equatorial Guinea	1,400
8	Malta	1,500
9	Trinidad and Tobago	2,650
10	Jamaica	2,800

Excluding countries not declaring a defence budget.

THE 10 LARGEST ARMED FORCES IN THE WORLD

	Country	Estimated total active forces (1990)
1	USSR	4,258,000
2	China	3,030,000
3	USA	2,124,900
4	India	1,260,000
5	Vietnam	1,249,000
6	North Korea	1,040,000
7	Iraq	1,000,000
8	Turkey	650,900
9	South Korea	650,000
10	Iran	604,000
	UK	*311,650*

Religion

THE TOP 10 ORGANIZED RELIGIONS

Religion	Followers
1 Christianity	1,669,520,440
2 Islam	880,555,210
3 Hinduism	663,495,450
4 Buddhism	311,836,170
5 Judaism	18,169,340
6 Sikhism	17,187,390
7 Confucianism	6,188,160
8 Baha'ism	4,691,890
9 Jainism	3,555,690
10 Shintoism	3,379,030

This list excludes the followers of various tribal and folk religions, new religions and shamanism which together total almost 400,000,000.

Christianity is the world's top organized religion.

THE TOP 10 RELIGIOUS AFFILIATIONS IN THE USA

Religion/organization	Membership
1 Roman Catholic Church	53,496,862
2 Southern Baptist Convention	14,722,617
3 United Methodist Church	9,124,575
4 Jews	5,943,700
5 National Baptist Convention, USA, Inc.	5,500,000
6 Evangelical Lutheran Church in America	5,288,230
7 Church of Jesus Christ of Latter-day Saints (Mormons)	3,860,000
8 Church of God in Christ	3,709,661
9 Presbyterian Church	2,967,781
10 National Baptist Convention of America	2,668,799

The total membership of all religious groups in the USA was estimated in 1989 at 143,830,806 – almost 59 per cent of the population.

The Jewish population of New York is over 63 per cent greater than Israel's.

THE 10 LARGEST JEWISH POPULATIONS IN THE WORLD

Country	Total Jewish population
1 USA	5,834,650
2 Israel	3,575,000
3 USSR	2,200,000
4 France	700,000
5 UK	385,000
6 Canada	304,000
7 Argentina	300,000
8 Brazil	175,000
9 South Africa	118,000
10 Australia	88,000

The Diaspora or scattering of Jewish people has been in progress for nearly 2,000 years, and as a result Jewish communities are found in virtually every country in the world. In 1939 it was estimated the total world Jewish population was 17,000,000. Some 6,000,000 fell victim to Nazi persecution, reducing it to about 11,000,000. In 1988 it was estimated to be 18,169,340.

Religion Quiz

1 Which of the following phrases is not found in the Bible: 'The four corners of the earth', 'A foregone conclusion', 'A wolf in sheep's clothing' or 'Nothing new under the sun'?
2 What is the popular name of the Society of Friends?
3 Who was the only English pope?
4 What member of a religious order had a No.7 hit in 1963 with 'Dominique'?
5 What is the commonest word in the Bible?
6 How many people were saved in Noah's Ark?
7 Who killed Cain?
8 Who founded the Mormons?
9 The sacred books of which religion are called the *Veda*?
10 What is the name most frequently adopted by popes?

Muslim worshippers at
Srinagar Mosque, India.

THE 10 LARGEST CHRISTIAN POPULATIONS IN THE WORLD

Country	Christians
1 USA	197,344,000
2 Brazil	118,856,000
3 USSR	96,726,500
4 Mexico	67,866,900
5 West Germany	57,557,300
6 UK	49,964,000
7 Philippines	49,201,700
8 Italy	47,104,500
9 France	44,110,800
10 Spain	35,932,700

Although Christian communities are found in almost every country in the world, it is more difficult to put a precise figure on nominal membership than on active participation. David Barrett's *World Christian Encyclopaedia* (1982) contained the most recent attempt to estimate global Christian populations, and the Top 10 is based on his findings.

THE 10 LARGEST MUSLIM POPULATIONS IN THE WORLD

Country	Total Muslim population
1 India	80,540,000
2 Pakistan	80,320,350
3 Bangladesh	72,848,640
4 Indonesia	67,213,000
5 Turkey	45,018,800
6 Iran	37,694,300
7 Egypt	34,648,360
8 Nigeria	32,668,000
9 USSR	30,297,000
10 Afghanistan	21,885,280

The phenomenal growth of Islam in recent years suggests that these figures, last compiled in the early 1980s, are already out of date, although the order of the Top 10 is probably unchanged. At the time they were prepared, the global Muslim population was said to be under 600,000,000; by 1987 a total figure of 860,388,300 was claimed by one authoritative source.

THE TOP 10 CHRISTIAN DENOMINATIONS IN THE WORLD

Denomination	Adherents
1 Roman Catholic	872,104,646
2 Slavonic Orthodox	92,523,987
3 United (including Lutheran/Reformed)	65,402,685
4 Pentecostal	58,999,862
5 Anglican	52,499,051
6 Baptist	50,321,923
7 Lutheran (excluding United)	44,899,837
8 Reformed (Presbyterian)	43,445,520
9 Methodist	31,718,508
10 Disciples (Restorationists)	8,783,192

The Top 10 is based on 1985 estimates supplied by MARC Europe, a Christian research and information organization. The Vatican's 1987 estimate increased the figure for Roman Catholics to 911,000,000 while retaining the 52,000,000 figure for Anglicans – which indicates something of the problem of arriving even at 'guesstimates' when it comes to global memberships.

Sports, Games & Pastimes

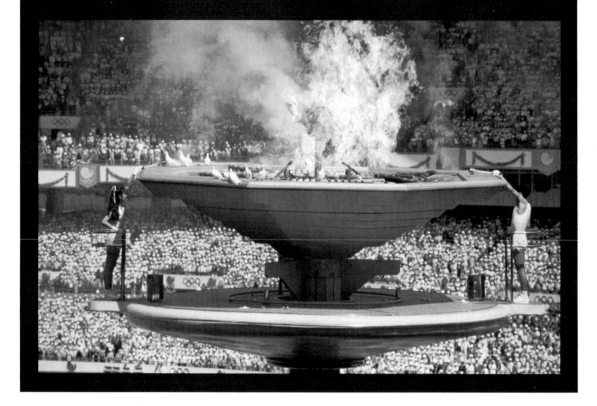

THE 10 MOST POPULAR LEISURE ACTIVITIES AMONG ADULTS IN THE UK

1 Watching television

2 Reading newspapers and general-interest magazines

3 Listening to music

4 Reading books

5 Reading special-interest magazines

6 Watching videos

7 Drinking alcohol at home

8 Visiting the pub

9 Gardening

10 Playing with children

Based on a 1989 survey conducted by the Henley Centre, a research organization. Those polled were asked to choose from 50 popular activities and the results ranked according to numbers claiming to participate in each.

THE TOP 10 WINNERS OF THE WIMBLEDON MEN'S SINGLES FINAL

	Player	Period	Wins
1	W. Renshaw	1881–89	7
2=	H.L. Doherty	1902–06	5
2=	Bjorn Borg	1976–80	5
4=	R.F. Doherty	1897–1900	4
4=	A.F. Wilding	1911–13	4
4=	Rod Laver	1961–69	4
7=	W. Baddeley	1891–95	3
7=	A.W. Gore	1901–09	3
7=	W.T. Tilden	1920–30	3
7=	F. J. Perry	1934–36	3
7=	John Newcombe	1967–71	3
7=	John McEnroe	1981–84	3
7=	Boris Becker	1985–89	3

LEFT Martina Navratilova, nine times Wimbledon winner.

OPPOSITE Watching TV has become the most popular leisure activity.

BELOW R.F. and H.L. Doherty, leading Wimbledon winners at the turn of the century.

THE TOP 10 WINNERS OF THE WIMBLEDON LADIES' SINGLES FINAL

	Player	Period	Wins
1	Martina Navratilova	1978–90	9
2	Helen Wills/Wills-Moody	1927–38	8
3=	Billie Jean King	1966–75	6
3=	Suzanne Lenglen	1919–23	6
5=	G.W. Hillyard	1889–1900	5
5=	L. Dod	1890–93	5
7=	R.L. Chambers	1910–14	4
7=	Louise Brough	1948–55	4
9=	C. Cooper	1895–98	3
9=	Maureen Connolly	1952–54	3
9=	Maria Bueno	1959–64	3

THE 10 COMMONEST FOOTBALL INJURIES

	Type of injury	% of injuries*
1	Twist, sprain, etc	52
2	Bruise	17
3 =	Fracture	8
3 =	Tear	8
5	Inflammation	6
6	Cut, laceration	4
7 =	Concussion	2
7 =	Dislocation	2
7 =	'Other'	2
10	Abrasion	less than 1

Figures rounded off.

Research carried out by Dr Klim McPherson and the late Sir Norman Chester during the 1984–85 football season studied reports of 1,364 injuries during training and matches. They found that more than a third of injuries occurred during training sessions, and that injuries caused without contact with another player were commonest (387 cases), with tackles second (288). There were 809 injuries caused by 'twists, etc'. Injuries to the upper leg are commonest (24% of the total), the knee second (20%) and ankle third (18%). They calculated that there is a 29% chance of one player being injured during a match and a 16% risk of any player being injured during a season.

THE TOP 10 GOAL-SCORERS IN 1988–89 ENGLISH FOOTBALL LEAGUE MATCHES

	Name	Club	Goals
1	Steve Bull	Wolverhampton Wanderers	37
2 =	Craig Maskell	Huddersfield Town	28
2 =	Phil Stant	Hereford United	28
4	Keith Edwards	Hull City	26
5 =	David Crown	Southend United	25
5 =	Kerry Dixon	Chelsea	25
7 =	Tony Daws	Scunthorpe United	24
7 =	Tommy Tynan	Plymouth Argyle	24
7 =	Ian Wright	Crystal Palace	24
10 =	Tony Agana	Sheffield United	23
10 =	Alan Smith	Arsenal	23

RIGHT Steve Bull (Wolves), top goal-scorer of the 1988–89 season.

BELOW The knee is the second most vulnerable location in the catalogue of football injuries.

THE 10 ENGLISH FOOTBALL LEAGUE CLUBS WITH THE MOST IN-GROUND ARRESTS IN THE 1987–88 SEASON

	Club	No. of arrests
1	Portsmouth	282
2	Southampton	208
3	Leeds United	184
4 =	Newcastle United	149
4 =	West Ham United	149
6	Scarborough	146
7 =	West Bromwich Albion	132
7 =	Wolverhampton Wanderers	132
9	Nottingham Forest	130
10	Huddersfield Town	126

THE TOP 10 TRANSFER FEES PAID FOR BRITISH PLAYERS

	Player	Sold by	To	Date	Amount (£ million)
1	Chris Waddle	Tottenham Hotspur	Marseille	Sep 89	4.3
2	Ian Rush	Liverpool	Juventus	Jun 87	3.2
3	Ian Rush	Juventus	Liverpool	Aug 88	2.8
4	Gary Lineker	Everton	Barcelona	Jun 86	2.75
5=	Mark Hughes	Manchester United	Barcelona	May 86	2.3
5=	Gary Pallister	Middlesbrough	Manchester United	Aug 89	2.3
7	Tony Cottee	West Ham United	Everton	Jul 88	2.2
8	Paul Gascoigne	Newcastle United	Tottenham Hotspur	Jul 88	2.0
9	Peter Beardsley	Newcastle United	Liverpool	Jul 87	1.9
10	Mark Hughes	Barcelona	Manchester United	May 88	1.8

Chris Waddle, believed to be the subject of the highest ever transfer fee.

Since none of the clubs or players will either confirm or deny them, the transfer fees quoted are 'best guesstimates'.

THE 10 ENGLISH FOOTBALL LEAGUE CLUBS WITH THE HIGHEST GROUND CAPACITY

	Club	Ground	Capacity
1	Manchester United	Old Trafford	50,837
2	Arsenal	Highbury	47,193
3	Manchester City	Maine Road	44,566
4	Everton	Goodison Park	42,889
5	Aston Villa	Villa Park	42,778
6	Sheffield Wednesday	Hillsborough	42,142
7	Liverpool	Anfield	39,285
8	Sheffield United	Bramall Lane	37,196
9	Chelsea	Stamford Bridge	36,364
10	Newcastle United	St James' Park	32,995

Most of the clubs have reduced their capacities from those of a year or so ago, as a result of new safety regulations.

THE 10 LARGEST FRESHWATER FISH CAUGHT BY ANGLERS IN GREAT BRITAIN (BY SPECIES)

Species	kg	gm	lb	oz	Angler/location/date
1 Salmon	29	29	64	0	Miss G.W. Ballantine, River Tay, Scotland, 1922
2 Pike	20	353	44	14	Michael G. Linton, Ardleigh Reservoir, Colchester, Essex, 1987
3 Carp	19	957	44	0	R. Walker, Redmire Pool, Herefordshire, 1952
4 Catfish	19	730	43	8	R.J. Bray, Wilstone Reservoir, Tring, Herts, 1970
5 Rainbow Trout	10	965	24	3	John Moore, Pennine Trout Fishery, Littleborough, Lancs, 1989
6 Sea Trout	10	205	22	8	Samuel Burgoyne, River Leven, Scotland, 1989
7 Brown Trout	8	880	19	4	J.A.F. Jackson, Loch Quoich, Inverness, Scotland, 1978
8 Zander	8	390	18	8	R.N. Meadows, Cambridge Stillwater, 1988
9 Common Bream	7	427	16	6	Anthony Bromley, Private fishery, Staffordshire, 1986
10 Grass Carp	7	257	16	0	K.R. Crow, Private lake, Canterbury, Kent, 1986

All fish in both freshwater and saltwater lists were rod-caught. All the saltwater fish were caught from boats. Comparative records exist for shore-caught fish, but they are generally much smaller.

THE 10 LARGEST SALTWATER FISH CAUGHT BY ANGLERS IN GREAT BRITAIN (BY SPECIES)

Species	kg	gm	lb	oz	Angler/location/date
1 Tunny	385	989	851	0	L. Mitchell Henry, Whitby, Yorks, 1933
2 Mako Shark	226	786	500	0	Mrs J.M. Yallop, off Eddystone Light, Cornwall, 1971
3 Porbeagle Shark	210	910	465	0	J. Potier, off Padstow, Cornwall, 1976
4 Thresher Shark	146	504	323	0	S. Mills, off Portsmouth, Hants, 1982
5 Halibut	106	136	234	0	C. Booth, Dunnet Head, off Scrabster, Highland, 1979
6 Common Skate	102	961	227	0	R. Banks, off Tobermory, Mull, 1986
7 Blue Shark	98	878	218	0	N. Sutcliffe, Looe, Cornwall, 1959
8 Opah	58	57	128	0	A.R. Blewett, Mounts Bay, Penzance, Cornwall, 1973
9 Conger	49	609	109	6	R.W. Potter, off Eddystone Light, Cornwall, 1976
10 Sunfish	48	986	108	0	T.F. Sisson, off Saundersfoot, Dyfed, 1976

Based on National Anglers' Council data.

THE FIRST 10 TEST CENTURIES SCORED BY ENGLAND BATSMEN

	Batsman	Score	Venue	Date
1	W. G. Grace	152	The Oval	6–8 Sep 1880
2	George Ulyett	149	Melbourne	10–14 Mar 1882
3	Allan Steel	135*	Sydney	17–21 Feb 1883
4	Allan Steel	148	Lord's	21–23 Jul 1884
5	Walter Read	117	The Oval	11–13 Aug 1884
6	W. Barnes	134	Adelaide	12–16 Dec 1884
7	John Briggs	121	Melbourne	1–5 Jan 1885
8	Arthur Shrewsbury	105*	Melbourne	21–25 Mar 1885
9	Arthur Shrewsbury	164	Lord's	19–21 Jul 1886
10	W. G. Grace	170	The Oval	12–14 Aug 1886

Not out.

All 10 were scored against Australia. W. G. Grace's two centuries were the only ones he scored in Test cricket.

THE TOP 10 BOWLERS IN A CAREER IN FIRST-CLASS CRICKET

	Player	Career	Total wickets
1	W. Rhodes	1898–1930	4,187
2	A.P. Freeman	1914–36	3,776
3	C.W.L. Parker	1903–35	3,278
4	J.T. Hearne	1888–1923	3,061
5	T.W.J. Goddard	1922–52	2,979
6	W.G. Grace	1865–1908	2,876
7	A. S. Kennedy	1907–36	2,874
8	D. Shackleton	1948–69	2,857
9	G.A.R. Lock	1946–71	2,844
10	F.J. Titmus	1949–82	2,830

THE 10 HIGHEST RUN-SCORERS IN A CAREER IN FIRST-CLASS CRICKET

	Player	Career	Total runs
1	J.B. Hobbs	1905–34	61,237
2	F.E. Woolley	1906–38	58,959
3	E.H. Hendren	1907–38	57,611
4	C.P. Mead	1905–36	55,061
5	W.G. Grace	1865–1908	54,896
6	W.R. Hammond	1920–51	50,551
7	H. Sutcliffe	1919–45	50,138
8	T.W. Graveney	1948–72	47,793
9	G. Boycott	1962–86	47,434
10	T.W. Hayward	1893–1914	43,551

ABOVE LEFT Jack Hobbs, highest run-scorer of all time.

RIGHT W. G. Grace features in all three Top 10 cricket lists.

THE 10 LOWEST FOUR-ROUND TOTALS IN THE BRITISH OPEN

	Player	Year	Venue	Finishing position	Score
1	Tom Watson (USA)	1977	Turnberry	1st	268
2	Jack Nicklaus (USA)	1977	Turnberry	2nd	269
3	Tom Watson (USA)	1980	Muirfield	1st	271
4	Seve Ballesteros (Spa)	1988	Lytham	1st	273
5 =	Lee Trevino (USA)	1980	Muirfield	2nd	275
5 =	Tom Watson (USA)	1983	Birkdale	1st	275
5 =	Nick Price (SAf)	1988	Lytham	2nd	275
5 =	Mark Calcavecchia (USA)	1989	Troon	1st	275
5 =	Wayne Grady (Aus)	1989	Troon	=2nd	275
5 =	Greg Norman (Aus)	1989	Troon	=2nd	275

The lowest four-round score by a British golfer was 278 by Dave Thomas at the 1958 Open at Lytham.

ABOVE Lytham ranks sixth among the most used British Open courses.

TOP RIGHT Seve Ballesteros wins the 1988 British Open with a four-round total of 273.

THE 10 MOST FREQUENT VENUES FOR THE BRITISH OPEN

	Course	Period	Occasions used
1 =	Prestwick	1860–1925	24
1 =	St Andrews	1873–1990	24
3	Muirfield	1892–1987	13
4	Sandwich	1894–1985	11
5	Hoylake	1897–1967	10
6	Lytham	1926–1988	8
7 =	Musselburgh	1874–1889	6
7 =	Birkdale	1954–1983	6
7 =	Troon	1923–1989	6
10	Carnoustie	1931–1975	5

Within a little over two years of Roger Bannister's capturing the imagination of the world by shattering the four minute mile barrier, the number of athletes to do so had risen to 10, although none had succeeded in lopping more than two seconds off the record. The time has been progressively reduced in subsequent years, however, by athletes such as Sebastian Coe. The world record is currently held by Steve Cram (GB) who at Oslo, Norway, on 27 July 1985 brought the time down to 3:46.32 – 13.8 seconds faster than Bannister.

THE 10 FASTEST MEN'S TIMES FOR THE LONDON MARATHON

	Runner	Country	Year	hr	Time min	sec
1	Steve Jones	UK	1985	2	8	16
2	Charlie Spedding	UK	1985	2	8	33
3	Douglas Wakiihuri	Kenya	1989	2	9	3
4	Steve Moneghetti	Australia	1989	2	9	6
5	Ahmed Salah	Djibouti	1989	2	9	9
6	Alister Hutton	UK	1985	2	9	16
7	Christoph Herle	West Germany	1985	2	9	23
8	Hugh Jones	UK	1982	2	9	24
9=	Mike Gratton	UK	1983	2	9	43
9=	Henrik Jorgensen	Denmark	1985	2	9	43
9=	Manuel Mattias	Portugal	1989	2	9	43

Douglas Wakiihuri of Kenya wins the 1989 London Marathon in the third fastest time.

THE 10 FASTEST WOMEN'S TIMES FOR THE LONDON MARATHON

	Runner	Country	Year	hr	Time min	sec
1	Ingrid Kristiansen	Norway	1985	2	21	6
2	Ingrid Kristiansen	Norway	1987	2	22	48
3	Ingrid Kristiansen	Norway	1984	2	24	26
4	Grete Waitz	Norway	1986	2	24	54
5	Grete Waitz	Norway	1983	2	25	29
6	Ingrid Kristiansen	Norway	1988	2	25	41
7	Veronique Marot	UK	1989	2	25	56
8	Wanda Panfil	Poland	1990	2	26	31
9	Priscilla Welch	UK	1987	2	26	51
10	Wanda Panfil	Poland	1989	2	27	5

Ingrid Kristiansen of Norway achieved four of the Top 10 record times in the London Marathon.

THE FIRST 10 ATHLETES TO RUN A MILE IN UNDER FOUR MINUTES

	Name	Country	Venue	Time	Date
1	Roger Bannister	GB	Oxford	3:59.4	6 May 1954
2	John Landy	Australia	Turku, Finland	3:57.9	21 Jun 1954
3=	Laszlo Tabori	Hungary	London	3:59.0	28 May 1955
3=	Chris Chataway	GB	London	3:59.8	28 May 1955
3=	Brian Hewson	GB	London	3:59.8	28 May 1955
6	Jim Bailey	Australia	Los Angeles	3:58.6	5 May 1956
7=	Ron Delany	Ireland	Compton, USA	3:59.4	1 Jun 1956
7=	Gunnar Nielsen	Denmark	Compton, USA	3:59.1	1 Jun 1956
9	Derek Ibbotson	GB	London	3:59.4	6 Aug 1956
10	István Rózsavölgyi	Hungary	Budapest	3:59.0	26 Aug 1956

Sub-4-minute-milers Bannister (in cap) and Chataway (left).

THE 10 MOST EXPENSIVE TOYS SOLD AT SOTHEBY'S, LONDON

	Toy	Year sold	Price (£)
1	Kämmer and Reinhardt bisque character doll, German, c1909	1989	90,200
2	William and Mary wooden doll, English, c1690	1987	67,000
3	Dual-plush Steiff Teddy bear, German, c1920 (see also 10 Most Expensive Teddy Bears)	1989	55,000
4	Tinplate clockwork battleship, Maine, by Märklin, German, c1904	1989	39,600
5	Tinplate clockwork paddleboat, Emily, by Märklin, German, c1902	1989	28,600
6	Tinplate Gauge I Rocket, by Märklin, German, c1909	1984	28,050
7	Gauge I armoured train set, by Märklin, German, c1902	1988	26,400
8=	Charles II oak baby house on stand, English, c1675	1988	25,300
8=	Tinplate live steam riverboat, 25 de Mayo, by Märklin, German, c1912	1990	25,300
10	Kämmer and Reinhardt bisque character doll, German, c1909	1986	24,200

W.H. SMITH'S TOP 10 GAMES

1	Pictionary
2	Trivial Pursuit
3	Pass the Pigs
4	Scrabble
5	Dingbats
6	Balderdash
7	Monopoly
8	Fun Water Games
9	Brit Quiz
10	Cluedo

The William and Mary doll held the world record price for a doll for just two years until toppled by the £90,200 Kämmer and Reinhardt doll. Toys by the German tinplate maker, Märklin, are regarded by collectors as the Rolls-Royce of toys, and similarly feature among the record prices of most of the world's auction houses.

Scrabble, Monopoly and Cluedo are long-standing bestsellers. Scrabble was invented in the USA by an unemployed architect, Alfred Butts. He developed it during the 1930s, changing its name successively from 'Lexiko' to 'It' and 'Criss-Cross'. It was further developed in the late 1940s by James Brunot, who decided on the name 'Scrabble' after rejecting several others that were in use for other products. By 1953 over 1,000,000 sets had been sold. Monopoly was also invented in the USA, in 1933 during the Depression, by Charles B. Darrow. It was for over 50 years the world's bestselling copyrighted board game, with over 100,000,000 sets produced in 23 languages – Russian being the latest addition, with a board based on the streets of Moscow. Cluedo has been consistently popular since it was first introduced in 1949. The other games are all relative newcomers, with Pictionary in 1989 knocking Trivial Pursuit off top spot.

Toys, Sports & Games Quiz

1 What is bezique?
2 How many halfpennies are used in the game of shove halfpenny?
3 When it was introduced in 1874 this sport was given the name 'sphairistike'. What is it now called?
4 What are zoetropes, praxinoscopes and phenakistoscopes?
5 What was the bestselling toy of 1981?
6 'Hurley-hacket' is an old Scottish sport. Is it a kind of croquet, hammer-throwing or tobogganing?
7 Where can Queen Mary's doll's house be seen?
8 How many balls are on a snooker table at the start of a game?
9 In what game are the terms nurdling, squopping and boondocking used?
10 What internationally popular toy is named after the Danish words for 'play well'?

ABOVE LEFT Emily, Sotheby's fifth most expensive toy.

BELOW Pictionary, bestselling game of 1989.

THE 10 MOST EXPENSIVE TEDDY BEARS SOLD AT AUCTION IN THE UK

	Bear	Price (£)
1	Dual-plush Steiff Teddy bear, c1920 Sotheby's, London, 19 September 1989.	55,000
	Although estimated at £700–£900, competitive bidding by several people pushed the price up to £40,000, with two battling for it up to the world record price	
2	Alfonzo, a red Steiff Teddy bear, c1906–09, once owned by Russian Princess Xenia Christie's, London, 18 May 1989	12,100
3	Apricot-coloured Steiff Teddy bear, c1904 Sotheby's, London, 31 January 1990	7,700
4	White plush Steiff Teddy bear, c1904 Sotheby's, London, 31 January 1990	6,050
5	Central seam Steiff Teddy bear, c1907 Christie's, London, 23 November 1989	4,180
6	Gold plush Steiff Teddy bear, c1905 Sotheby's, London, 16 February 1989	3,190
7	Gold plush Steiff Teddy bear, c1908 Sotheby's, London, 19 September 1989	2,970
8=	Noel, a black plush Steiff Teddy bear, c1910 Christie's, London, 21 September 1989	2,860
8=	White plush Steiff Teddy bear, c1921 Sotheby's, London, 31 January 1990	2,860
10	Long plush-covered Teddy bear Christie's, London, 21 September 1989	2,640

It is said that, while on a hunting trip, US President Theodore ('Teddy') Roosevelt refused to shoot a young bear. This became the subject of a famous cartoon by Clifford K. Berryman, published in the *Washington Post* on 16 November 1902. Immediately afterwards, Morris Michtom, a New York shopkeeper (and later founder of the Ideal Toy and Novelty Company) made stuffed bears and – with Roosevelt's permission – began advertising them as 'Teddy's Bears'. At about the same time, Margarete Steiff, a German toymaker, began making her first toy bears, exporting them to the USA to meet the demand 'Teddy's Bears' had created. In 1903 Steiff's factory produced 12,000 bears; by 1907, the figure had risen to 974,000. Steiff teddy bears are still made and are sold internationally, but it is the early examples that are most prized among collectors, so that all but one of the Top 10 are Steiffs.

Sylvanian Families, third bestselling toy of 1989.

THE 10 BESTSELLING TOYS OF 1989

	Toy	Manufacturer
1	The Real Ghostbusters	Tonka
2	Micromachines	Rainbow
3	Sylvanian Families	Tomy
4	Legoland Town	Lego
5	Fisher Price Preschool range	Fisher Price
6	Tomytime Preschool range	Tomy
7	Duplo	Lego
8	Transformers	Hasbro
9	Matchbox cars and accessories	Matchbox
10	Barbie dolls and accessories	Mattel

Based on data compiled by Nielsen Marketing Research from information supplied by 9,000 specialist toyshops, F.W. Woolworth, W.H. Smith, Argos and other retailers which together sell nearly 80 per cent of all toys sold in the UK. The Top 10 toys accounted for about 25 per cent of total toy sales during the year.

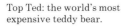

Top Ted: the world's most expensive teddy bear.

THE 10 MOST SUCCESSFUL FORMULA ONE RACING DRIVERS

	Driver	Country	Race wins
1	Alain Prost	France	39
2	Jackie Stewart	GB	27
3=	Jim Clark	GB	25
3=	Niki Lauda	Austria	25
5	Juan Manuel Fangio	Argentina	24
6=	Nelson Piquet	Brazil	20
6=	Ayrton Senna	Brazil	20
8	Stirling Moss	GB	16
9	Nigel Mansell	GB	15
10=	Jack Brabham	Aus	14
10=	Emerson Fittipaldi	Brazil	14
10=	Graham Hill	GB	14

Stirling Moss, who retired from Formula One racing after a crash in 1962, failed to become world champion, and Nigel Mansell is the only other driver in the Top 10 not to have won the title.

LEFT Alain Prost, the world's top Formula One driver.

ABOVE Cliff Thorburn's 147 break holds the record.

THE 10 BOXERS WITH THE MOST KOs IN A CAREER

	Name	Career	KOs
1	Archie Moore	1936–63	129
2	Young Stribling	1921–63	126
3	Billy Bird	1920–48	125
4	Sam Langford	1902–26	116
5	George Odwell	1930–45	114
6	Sugar Ray Robinson	1940–65	110
7	Sandy Saddler	1944–65	103
8	Henry Armstrong	1931–45	100
9	Jimmy Wilde	1911–23	99
10	Len Wickwar	1928–47	93

Although this is the most generally accepted Top 10, boxing historians disagree considerably on this subject, some, for example, including exhibition matches as well as professional bouts.

All 10 boxers were from the USA except Jimmy Wilde (1892–1969), who was Welsh.

THE 10 HIGHEST BREAKS IN THE EMBASSY WORLD PROFESSIONAL SNOOKER CHAMPIONSHIPS*

	Player	Year	Break
1	Cliff Thorburn v Terry Griffiths	1983	147
2	Doug Mountjoy v Ray Reardon	1981	145
3=	Willie Thorne v Alex Higgins	1982	143
3=	Bill Werbeniuk v Joe Johnson	1985	143
5	Bill Werbeniuk v John Virgo	1979	142
6	Stephen Hendry v Terry Griffiths	1989	141
7	Steve James v Rex Williams	1988	140
8=	Kirk Stevens v Perrie Mans	1983	139
8=	Stephen Hendry v Steve Davis	1989	139
10=	John Spencer v Perrie Mans	1978	138
10=	Rex Williams v Jimmy White	1984	138

*At the Crucible Theatre, Sheffield.

Air & Space

THE FIRST 10 PEOPLE IN SPACE

Name	Age	Date	Orbits	Duration hr:min	Spacecraft/ country
1 Fl Major Yuri Alekseyivich Gagarin	27	12 Apr 1961	1	1:48	Vostok I USSR
2 Major Gherman Stepanovich Titov	25	6–7 Aug 1961	17	25:18	Vostok II USSR
3 Lt-Col John Herschel Glenn	40	20 Feb 1962	3	4:56	Friendship 7 USA
4 Lt-Col Malcolm Scott Carpenter	37	24 May 1962	3	4:56	Aurora 7 USA
5 Major Andrian Grigoryevich Nikolayev	32	11–15 Aug 1962	64	94:22	Vostok III USSR
6 Col Pavel Romanovich Popovich	31	12–15 Aug 1962	48	70:57	Vostok IV USSR
7 Cdr Walter Marty Schirra	39	3 Oct 1962	6	9:13	Sigma 7 USA
8 Major Leroy Gordon Cooper	36	15–16 May 1963	22	34:19	Faith 7 USA
9 Lt-Col Valeri Fyodorovich Bykovsky	28	14–19 Jun 1963	81	119:06	Vostok V USSR
10 Jr Lt Valentina Vladimirovna Tereshkova	26	16–19 Jun 1963	48	70:50	Vostok VI USSR

John Glenn, off to become the first American in space.

No. 2 was the youngest ever astronaut, aged 25 years 329 days. No. 10 was the first woman in space. Among early pioneering flights, neither Alan Shepard (5 May 1961: *Freedom 7*) nor Gus Grissom (21 July 1961: *Liberty Bell 7*) actually entered space, achieving altitudes of only 185 km/115 miles and 190 km/118 miles respectively, and neither flight lasted more than 15 minutes. Glenn was the first American to orbit.

RIGHT 'Buzz' Aldrin, the second man on the Moon.

BELOW Valentina Tereshkova, tenth person and first woman in space.

THE FIRST 10 WOMEN IN SPACE

1 Valentina Vladimirovna Tereshkova (USSR)
16–19 June 1963 *Vostok VI*

Tereshkova was the first and youngest (26) woman in space.

2 Svetlana Savitskaya (USSR)
19 August 1982 *Soyuz T 7*

On 25 July 1984 Savitskaya also became the first woman to walk in space.

3 Sally Ride (USA)
18–24 June 1983 *STS-7 Challenger Shuttle*

Ride was the first American woman and the youngest (32) American in space. She also flew in the *STS-41-G Challenger Shuttle* (5–13 October 1984).

4 Judith A. Resnik (USA)
30 August – 5 September 1984
STS-41-D Discovery Shuttle

Resnik was killed in the *STS-51-L Challenger Shuttle* disaster of 28 January 1986.

5 Kathryn D. Sullivan (USA)
5–13 October 1984 *STS-41-G Challenger Shuttle*

Sullivan was the first American woman to walk in space.

6 Anna L. Fisher (USA)
8–16 November 1984 *STS-51-A Discovery Shuttle*

7 Margaret Rhea Seddon (USA)
12–19 April 1985 *STS-51-D Discovery Shuttle*

8 Shannon W. Lucid (USA)
17–24 June 1985 *STS-51-G Discovery Shuttle*

Lucid is the oldest (42) woman in space.

9 Loren Acton (USA)
29 July – 6 August 1985 *STS-51-F Challenger Shuttle*

10 Bonnie J. Dunbar (USA)
30 October – 6 November 1985
STS-61-A Challenger Shuttle

The only other woman in space to date was Mary L. Cleave (USA) who orbited in the *Atlantis Shuttle* from 26 November – 3 December 1985 and 4–8 April 1989, making a total of two Russian and nine American women.

Air & Space Quiz

1 Who was the first American woman to spacewalk?

2 The world's largest aeroplane was built and in 1947 piloted on a single flight by millionaire Howard Hughes. What was its name?

3 What was the name of the first animal in orbit?

4 To the nearest decade, when was the word 'astronaut' first used?

5 The Tornados had a No.1 hit in 1962 with a record named after a space satellite. What was it called?

6 What is the name of the spaceship's computer in *2001: A Space Odyssey*?

7 With what aviation invention is Frank Whittle associated?

8 Which astronaut said 'The Eagle has landed'?

9 What was the notable achievement of *Gossamer Albatross*?

10 What do US astronauts William Anders and Shannon Lucid have in common?

THE FIRST 10 MOONWALKERS

	Astronaut	Birthdate	Mission	Mission dates	Total EVA* hr: min
1	Neil A. Armstrong	5 Aug 30	Apollo 11	16–24 Jul 69	2:32
2	Edwin E. Aldrin	20 Jan 30	Apollo 11	16–24 Jul 69	2:15
3=	Charles Conrad Jr	2 Jun 30	Apollo 12	14–24 Nov 69	7:45
3=	Alan L. Bean	15 Mar 32	Apollo 12	14–24 Nov 69	7:45
5=	Alan B. Shepard	18 Nov 23	Apollo 14	31 Jan–9 Feb 71	9:23
5=	Edgar D. Mitchell	17 Sep 30	Apollo 14	31 Jan–9 Feb 71	9:23
7	David R. Scott	6 Jun 32	Apollo 15	26 Jul–7 Aug 71	19:08
8	James B. Irwin	17 Mar 30	Apollo 15	26 Jul–7 Aug 71	18:35
9=	John W. Young	24 Sep 30	Apollo 16	16–27 Apr 72	20:14
9=	Charles M. Duke	3 Oct 35	Apollo 16	16–27 Apr 72	20:14

'Colonel' Samuel Franklin Cody, American pilot of the first aeroplane to fly in England.

*Extravehicular activity (i.e. time spent out of the lunar module on the Moon's surface).

Eugene A. Cernan (b. 14 Mar 1934) and Harrison H. Schmitt (b. 3 Jul 1935) in Apollo 17 (7–19 Dec 1972) were the last and only other astronauts to date who have walked on the surface of the Moon; both spent a total of 22:04 in EVA.

The 12 moonwalkers brought back a total of 381 kg/840 lb of Moon rock samples.

THE FIRST 10 PEOPLE TO FLY IN HEAVIER-THAN-AIR AIRCRAFT

1 Orville Wright (1871–1948; American)
On 17 December 1903 at Kitty Hawk, North Carolina, Wright made the first ever manned flight in his Wright Flyer I. It lasted 12 seconds and covered a distance of 37 m/120 ft.

2 Wilbur Wright (1867–1912; American)
On the same day, Orville Wright's brother made his first flight in the Wright Flyer I (59 sec; 260 m/852 ft).

3 Alberto Santos-Dumont (1873–1932; Brazilian)
On 12 November 1906 at Bagatelle, France, in his Santos-Dumont 14-bis (21.2 sec; 220 m/722 ft).

4 Léon Delagrange (1873–1910; French)
On 5 November 1907 at Issy, France, in his Voisin-Delagrange I (40 sec; 500 m/1,640 ft).

5 Robert Esnault-Pelterie (1881–1957; French)
On 16 November 1907 at Buc, France in his REP I (55 sec; 600 m/1,968 ft).

6 Henri Farman (1874–1958; British – later French)
On 11 January 1908 at Issy, France, in his Voisin-Farman I (1 min 45 sec; distance not recorded). This was the first European flight of more than one minute; on 13 January Farman flew the first circle in Europe in the same aircraft.

7 Charles W. Furnas (1880–1941; American)
On 14 May 1908 at Dayton, Ohio, Wilbur Wright took Furnas, his mechanic, for a spin in the Wright Flyer III (29 sec; 600 m/1,968 ft). He was thus the first aeroplane passenger.

8 Louis Blériot (1872–1936; French)
On 29 June 1908 at Issy, France, in his Blériot VIII (50 sec; 700 m/2,297 ft). By 6 July 1908, Blériot had made a flight of 8 min 25 sec (distance not recorded); he flew across the English Channel on 25 July 1909.

9 Glenn Hammond Curtiss (1878–1930; American)
On 4 July 1908 at Hammondsport, New York, in an AEA June Bug (1 min 42.5 sec; 1,551 m/5,090 ft), the first official public flight in the USA.

10 Thérèse Peltier (French)
On 8 July 1908 at Turin, Italy, in a Voisin piloted by Delagrange. This short hop of 152 m/500 ft made her the first female aeroplane passenger.

While most of the fliers listed flew on numerous subsequent occasions and broke their first-time records, most other 'flights' of the 1906–08 period, other than those of the Wright brothers, were no more than short hops of a few seconds' duration; meanwhile, the Wrights were so far in advance of their competitors that they were flying under full control for more than an hour and over distances of 80 km/50 miles.

The first flight in Britain was by an American, Samuel Franklin Cody at Farnborough on 16 October 1908; it lasted barely 27 seconds and covered just 424 m/1,390 ft.

THE FIRST 10 TRANSATLANTIC FLIGHTS

1 16–27 May 1919*
Trepassy Harbor, Newfoundland to Lisbon, Portugal
US Navy/Curtiss flying boat *NC-4*.

Lt-Cdr Albert Cushing Read and a crew of five (Elmer Fowler Stone, Walter Hinton, James Lawrence Breese, Herbert Charles Rodd and Eugene Saylor Rhoads) crossed the Atlantic in a series of hops, refuelling at sea. The Atlantic leg was part of an even longer journey: a convoy of three flying boats, *NC-1*, *NC-3* and *NC-4*, left Rockaway, Long Island on 8 May, flying via the Azores to Portugal, but only *NC-4* completed the distance; its final destination, Plymouth, England, was reached on 31 May after covering a total distance of 7,591 km/4,717 miles.

2 14–15 June 1919
St John's, Newfoundland to Galway, Ireland
Twin Rolls-Royce-engined converted Vickers Vimy bomber.

British pilot Capt John Alcock and navigator Lt Arthur Whitten Brown achieved the first *non-stop* flight, ditching in a bog after their epic 16 hr 28 min journey. (The first non-stop east–west crossing of the North Atlantic, from Ireland to Newfoundland, was on 12–13 April 1928 by Hermann Köhl and his crew of two in a Junkers *W33* monoplane.)

3 2–6 July 1919
East Fortune, Scotland to Roosevelt Field, New York
British *R-34* airship.

Major George Herbert Scott and a crew of 30 (including the first ever transatlantic air stowaway, William Ballantyne) made the first east–west crossing. It was the first airship to do so and, when it returned to Pulham, England on 13 July, the first to complete a double crossing. The outward journey of 5,037 km/3,130 miles took 108 hr 12 min, and the return journey of 5,150 km/3,200 miles took 75 hr 3 min.

4 30 March – 5 June 1922
Lisbon, Portugal to Recife, Brazil
Fairey seaplane.

Portuguese pilots Admiral Coutinho and Commander Sacadura Cabral were the first to fly the South Atlantic in stages, though they replaced one damaged plane with another.

5 2–31 August 1924
Orkneys, Scotland to Labrador, Canada
Two Douglas seaplanes.

Lt Lowell H. Smith and L. P. Arnold in one biplane, and E. Nelson and J. Harding in another, set out and crossed the North Atlantic together in a series of hops via Iceland and Greenland.

6 12–15 October 1924
Friedrichshafen, Germany to Lakehurst, New Jersey

Los Angeles, a renamed German-built *ZR3* airship.

Piloted by its inventor, Dr Hugo Eckener, with 31 passengers and crew. The airship had been acquired as part of the German war reparations and remained in service with the US Navy until it was decommissioned in 1932.

7 22 January – 10 February 1926
Huelva, Spain to Recife, Brazil
Plus Ultra, a Dornier Wal twin-engined flying boat.

The crew of three Spaniards which included General Franco's brother Ramón with Julio Ruiz De Alda, Ensign Beran and mechanic Pablo Rada crossed the South Atlantic in stages.

8 8–24 February 1927
Cagliari, Sardinia to Recife, Brazil
Santa Maria, a Savoia-Marchetti S.55 flying boat.

Francesco Marquis de Pinedo, Capt Carlo del Prete and Lt Vitale Zacchetti crossed in stages as part of a goodwill trip to South America, from Fascist Italy.

9 16–17 March 1927
Lisbon, Portugal to Natal, Brazil
Dornier Wal flying boat.

Portuguese flyers Sarmento de Beires and Jorge de Castilho took the route via Casablanca.

10 28 April – 14 May 1927
Genoa, Italy to Natal, Brazil
Savoia-Marchetti flying boat.

A Brazilian crew of João De Barros, João Negrão, Newton Braga and Vasco Cinquini set out on 17 October 1926, flying in stages via the Canaries and Cape Verde Islands.

*All dates refer to the actual Atlantic legs of the journeys; some started earlier and ended beyond their first transatlantic landfalls.

Perhaps surprisingly, the most famous transatlantic flight of all, that of Capt Charles Lindbergh, rates at best 11th (or even lower if the return journey of the R.34 is counted as a separate crossing and those of Smith and Nelson as two independent flights). He was actually the 92nd individual to fly the Atlantic, but his remarkable achievement was that he was the first to cross *solo*. Lindbergh's epic journey took place on 20–21 May 1927 from Long Island, New York, to Paris, France in the *Spirit of St Louis*, a single-engined Ryan monoplane. The total distance covered was 5,810 km/3,610 miles in a time of 33 hr 29.5 min.

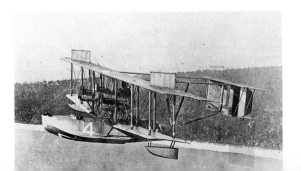

THE 10 LARGEST AIRLINES IN THE WORLD

	Airline	Country	Passengers per annum (approx.)
1	American Airlines	USA	64,000,000
2	United Airlines	USA	56,000,000
3	Continental Airlines	USA	37,000,000
4	Eastern Airlines	USA	35,000,000
5	TWA	USA	25,000,000
6	British Airways	UK	22,000,000
7	Japan Airlines	Japan	20,000,000
8	Lufthansa	West Germany	18,000,000
9=	Pan American	USA	15,000,000
9=	Iberia	Spain	15,000,000

American Airlines ranks as the world's top airline.

THE TOP 10 AIRLINES IN THE UK

Airline	Passengers per annum
1 British Airways	21,818,122
2 British Midland	2,311,130
3 Air UK	1,356,370
4 Dan Air	1,194,283
5 British Caledonian Airways	655,196
6 Air Europe	603,906
7 Virgin Atlantic Airways	595,576
8 Manx Airlines	513,244
9 Loganair	399,400
10 Aurigny Air Services	306,509

THE TOP 10 AIRLINES USING LONDON HEATHROW AIRPORT

Airline	Passengers per annum
1 British Airways	16,154,500
2 Pan American	2,173,600
3 British Midland	1,631,700
4 Air France	1,552,900
5 Lufthansa	1,207,300
6 Aer Lingus	1,174,700
7 Iberia	1,058,000
8 TWA	912,600
9 Swissair	790,700
10 Air Canada	681,500

ABOVE Pan American is the second greatest user of London Heathrow Airport.

Other airlines handle a total of 8,301,000 passengers, making a total of 35,638,500 passing through Britain's busiest airport.

OPPOSITE *NC-4* on one of the stages of the first ever transatlantic flight.

THE FIRST 10 MANNED BALLOON FLIGHTS*

1 The first 10 flights of the ballooning pioneers all took place within a year. The Montgolfier brothers, Joseph and Etienne, tested their first unmanned hot-air balloon in the French town of Annonay on 5 June 1783. They were then invited to demonstrate it to Louis XVI at Versailles. On 19 September 1783 it took off with the first ever airborne passengers – a sheep, a rooster and a duck. On 21 November 1783 François Laurent, Marquis d'Arlandes, and Jean-François Pilâtre de Rozier took off from the Bois de Boulogne, Paris, in a Montgolfier hot-air balloon. This first ever manned flight covered a distance of about 9 km/5½ miles in 23 minutes, landing safely near Gentilly. (On 15 June 1785 de Rozier and his passenger were killed near Boulogne when their hydrogen balloon burst into flames during an attempted Channel crossing, making them the first ever air fatalities.)

2 On 1 December 1783, watched by a crowd of 400,000, Jacques Alexandre César Charles and Nicholas-Louis Robert made the first ever flight in a hydrogen balloon. They took off from the Tuileries, Paris, and travelled about 43 km/27 miles north to Nesle in a time of about two hours. Charles then took off again alone, thus becoming the first solo flier.

3 On 19 January 1784 *La Flesselle*, a gigantic 40 m/131 ft high Montgolfier hot-air balloon named after its sponsor, the local Governor, ascended from Lyons piloted by Pilâtre de Rozier with Joseph Montgolfier, Prince Charles de Ligne and the Comtes de La Porte d'Anglefort, de Dampierre and de Laurencin – as well as the first ever aerial stowaway, a young man called Fontaine, who leaped in as it was taking off.

4 On 25 February 1784 the Chevalier Paolo Andreani and the brothers Augustino and Carlo Giuseppi Gerli (the builders of the balloon) made the first ever flight outside France, at Moncuco near Milan, Italy.

5 On 2 March 1784 Jean Pierre François Blanchard made his first flight in a hydrogen balloon from the Champ de Mars, Paris, after experimental hops during the preceding months.

6 On 14 April 1784 a Mr Rousseau and an unnamed 10-year-old drummer boy flew from Navan to Ratoath in Ireland, the first ascent in the British Isles.

7 On 25 April 1784 Guyton de Morveau, a French chemist, and L'Abbé Bertrand flew at Dijon.

8 On 8 May 1784 Bremond and Maret flew at Marseilles.

9 On 12 May 1784 Brun ascended at Chambéry.

10 On 15 May 1784 Adorne and an unnamed passenger took off but crash landed near Strasbourg.

Several of the balloonists listed also made subsequent flights, but in each instance only their first flights are included.

After the first 10 flights, the pace of ballooning accelerated rapidly. On 4 June 1784 a Monsieur Fleurand took as his passenger in a flight at Lyons a Mme Thiblé, an opera singer, who was thus the first woman to fly (the Marchioness de Montalembert and other aristocratic ladies had ascended on 20 May 1784, but in a tethered balloon). On 27 August James Tytler (known as 'Balloon Tytler'), a doctor and newspaper editor, took off from Comely Gardens, Edinburgh, achieving an altitude of 107 m/350 ft in a 0.8 km/½-mile hop in a homemade balloon – the first (and until Smeath in 1837, the only) hot-air balloon flight in Great Britain. On 15 September, watched by a crowd of 200,000, Vicenzo Lunardi ascended from the Artillery Company Ground, Moorfields, London, flying to Standon near Ware in Hertfordshire, the first ever balloon flight in England. (An attempt the previous month by a Dr Moret ended with the balloon catching fire and the crowd rioting.) Lunardi went on to make further flights in Edinburgh and Glasgow. On 4 October 1784 James Sadler flew a Montgolfier balloon at Oxford, thereby becoming the first English pilot.

On 7 January 1785 Jean-Pierre Blanchard achieved the first Channel crossing with Dr John Jeffries (the first American to fly). They also carried the first airmail letter. As they lost height, they had to reduce weight, so they threw almost everything overboard, including their clothes. On 23 March of the same year Rear-Admiral (later Admiral) Sir Edward Vernon flew with Count Francesco Zambeccari from Tottenham Court Road, London, to Horsham, Sussex. On 29 June a certain George Biggin, piloting Lunardi's balloon, took Letitia Sage, the first Englishwoman to fly, from St George's Fields, London to Harrow, Middlesex – despite some apparent concern that Miss Sage was rather overweight and that the balloon might not get airborne. On 9 January 1793 in Philadelphia, Blanchard made the first flight in America, watched by George Washington.

Accidents & Disasters

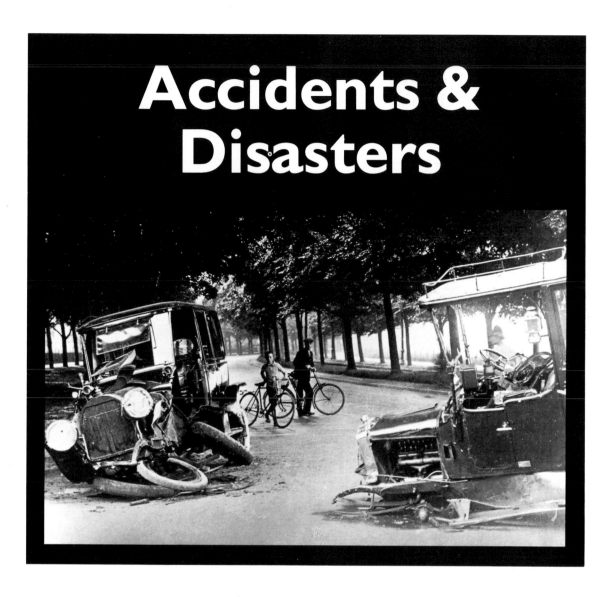

THE 10 WORST AIR DISASTERS IN THE WORLD

Incident	Killed
1 27 March 1977, Tenerife, Canary Islands: Two Boeing 747s (KLM and PanAm) collided on the runway.	583
2 12 August 1985, Mt Ogura, Japan: A JAL Boeing 747 on an internal flight from Tokyo to Osaka crashed, killing all but four on board in the worst-ever disaster involving only one aircraft.	520
3 3 March 1974, Paris, France: A Turkish Airlines DC-10 crashed at Ermenonville immediately after take-off.	346
4 23 June 1985, off the Irish coast: An Air India Boeing 747 on a flight from Vancouver to Delhi exploded in mid-air.	329
5 19 August 1980, Riyadh, Saudi Arabia: A Saudi Arabian Airlines Lockheed Tristar caught fire during an emergency landing.	301
6 3 July 1988, off the Iranian coast: An Iranian airliner was shot down in error by a missile fired by the USS *Vincennes*.	290
7 25 May 1979, Chicago, USA: An American Airlines DC-10 crashed on take-off.	275
8 21 December 1988, Lockerbie, Scotland: PanAm Flight 103 from London Heathrow to New York exploded in mid-air as a result of a terrorist bomb, killing 243 passengers, 16 crew and at least 11 on the ground in the UK's worst-ever air disaster.	270
9 1 September 1983, off the Siberian coast: A South Korean Boeing 747 that had strayed into Soviet airspace was shot down by a Soviet fighter.	269
10 28 November 1979, Mt Erebus, Antarctica: A New Zealand DC-10 crashed while on a sight-seeing trip.	257

THE 10 WORST AIR DISASTERS IN THE UK

	Incident	Killed
1	21 December 1988, Lockerbie, Scotland [see No. 8 on World's Worst Air Disasters]	270
2	18 June 1972, Staines, Middlesex A BEA Trident crashed after take-off.	118
3	12 March 1950, Siginstone, Glamorgan An Avro Tudor V crashed while attempting to land at Llandow; two saved.	81
4	23 August 1944, Freckelton, Lancashire A US Air Force B-24 crashed onto a school.	76
5	24 August 1921, off the coast near Hull Airship R38, sold by the British Government to the USA, broke in two on a training and test flight.	62
6	22 August 1985, Manchester A Boeing 737 caught fire on the ground.	55
7	5 January 1969, near Gatwick Airport An Ariana Afghan Airlines Boeing 727 crash-landed; the deaths include two on the ground.	50
8	8 January 1989, M1 Motorway A British Midland Boeing 737 attempting to land without engine power crashed on the M1 Motorway embankment near East Midlands Airport.	47
9=	6 November 1986, off Sumburgh, Shetland Islands A Chinook helicopter ferrying oil rig workers ditched in the sea.	45
9=	15 November 1957, Isle of Wight Following an engine fire, an Aquila Airlines Solent flying-boat struck a cliff.	45

In addition to disasters within the UK, a number of major air crashes involving British aircraft have occurred overseas. One of the earliest was that of British airship R101 which crashed near Beauvais, France, on 5 October 1930, killing 47. The biplane *City of Liverpool* crashed in Belgium on 28 March 1933, killing 13 (one passenger fell out before the crash, and sabotage was suspected). On 4 March 1962 a chartered Caledonian DC-7C crashed near Douala, Cameroon, with the loss of 111 lives; at the time, this was the worst disaster involving a British airliner and the worst in Africa. A BOAC Boeing 707 crashed on Mount Fuji, Japan, on 5 March 1966, killing 124, but the worst on record was the crash of a Dan-Air Boeing 727 at Santa Cruz de Tenerife, Canary Islands, on 25 April 1980 in which all 146 on board perished.

THE 10 WORST AIR DISASTERS IN THE USA

	Incident	Killed
1	25 May 1979, Chicago An American Airlines DC-10 crashed on take-off.	275
2	16 August 1987, Romulus, Michigan A Northwest Airlines Macdonald-Douglas-82 crashed after take-off.	156
3	9 July 1982, Kenner, Louisiana A PanAm Boeing 727 crashed after take-off, killing all on board and eight on the ground.	153
4	25 September 1955, San Diego A Pacific Southwest Boeing 727 collided in the air with a Cessna 172 light aircraft, killing 135 in the airliner, two in the Cessna and seven on the ground.	144
5	16 December 1960, New York A United Airlines DC-8 with 77 passengers and a crew of seven and a TransWorld Airlines Super Constellation with 39 passengers and four crew collided in a snowstorm. The DC-8 crashed in Brooklyn, killing eight on the ground, although one passenger survived; the Super Constellation crashed in Staten Island harbour, killing all on board.	134
6	2 August 1985, Dallas-Ft Worth Airport, Texas A Delta Airlines Boeing 747 crashed.	133
7	30 June 1956, Grand Canyon A United Airlines DC-7 and a TransWorld Airlines Super Constellation collided in the air.	128
8	24 June 1975, JFK Airport, New York An Eastern Airlines Boeing 727 crashed in a storm.	113
9	4 September 1971, Chilkoot Mountains, Alaska An Alaska Airlines Boeing 727 crashed.	111
10	30 December 1972, Everglades, near Miami, Florida An Eastern Airlines Lockheed TriStar crashed during landing, but 75 on board survived.	101

The 1988 Lockerbie crash [see No. 8 on World's Worst list] is the United States' worst air disaster not occurring within the US territory. The previous worst was the 12 December 1985 crash of a chartered Arrow Air DC-8 during take-off from Gander, Newfoundland, killing all 256 on board, including 248 members of the 101st US Airborne Division. A domestic incident that could potentially have resulted in a huge number of casualties, but in fact killed only 13, was the 28 July 1945 crash of a US Army bomber into the Empire State Building. The worst pre-war American air disaster was the 4 April 1933 crash into the sea off the New Jersey coast of the Akron dirigible airship, with the loss of 73 lives. The burning on 6 May 1937 of the German Zeppelin Hindenburg at Lakehurst, New Jersey, left 36 dead.

THE 10 WORST PRE-TWENTIETH CENTURY MARINE DISASTERS

Incident	Killed
1 *St George, Defence* and *Hero* British warships stranded off the Jutland coast, 24 December 1811	c2,000
2 *Sultana* A Mississippi River steamboat destroyed by boiler explosion near Memphis, 27 April 1865 – the USA's worst ever marine accident	1,547
3 *Royal George* British warship wrecked off Spithead, 29 August 1782 – the worst ever shipwreck off the British coast	800 +
4 *Princess Alice* Pleasure steamer in collision with *Bywell Castle* in the Thames near Woolwich, 3 September 1878	786
5 *Queen Charlotte* British warship burnt in Leghorn harbour, 17 March 1800	700 +
6 *Atlantic* British steamer wrecked off Nova Scotia, 1 April 1875	585
7 *Utopia* British steamer collided with British warship *Anson* off Gibraltar, 17 March 1891	562
8 *La Bourgogne* French steamer collided with British sailing vessel, *Cromartyshire*, off Nova Scotia, 4 July 1898	549
9 *Ertogrul* Turkish frigate wrecked off the Japanese coast, 19 September 1890	540
10 *City of Glasgow* British steamer, disappeared in the North Atlantic, March 1854	480

THE 10 WORST MARINE DISASTERS OF THE TWENTIETH CENTURY

Incident	Killed
1 *Wilhelm Gustloff* German liner torpedoed off Danzig by USSR submarine, *S-13*, 30 January 1945	c7,700
2 *Cap Arcona* German ship carrying concentration camp survivors bombed and sunk by British aircraft, 3 May 1945	c5,000
3 *Lancastria* British troop ship sunk of St Nazaire, 17 June 1940	c4,000
4 *Yamoto* Japanese battleship sunk off Kyushu Island, 7 April 1945	3,033
5 *Arisan Maru* Japanese vessel carrying American prisoners-of-war torpedoed by a US submarine in the South China Sea, 24 October 1944	c1,790
6 *Mont Blanc* French ammunition ship collided with Belgian steamer *Imo* and exploded, Halifax, Nova Scotia, 6 December 1917	1,600
7 *Titanic* British liner struck an iceberg in the North Atlantic, 14–15 April 1912 – the worst ever peacetime marine disaster	1,503
8 *Dona Paz* Ferry struck by oil tanker MV *Victor* in the Tabias Strait, Philippines, 20 December 1987; the loss of life may have been much higher (a figure of 3,000 has been suggested) due to excessive overcrowding, but no accurate records were kept	1,500 +
9 HMS *Hood* British cruiser sunk by the German battleship *Bismarck* in the Denmark Strait, 24 May 1941	1,418
10 *Lusitania* British liner torpedoed off the Irish coast by German submarine *U-20*, 7 May 1915	1,198

BACKGROUND *Titanic*, best-known but seventh worst twentieth-century marine disaster.

THE 10 WORST RAIL DISASTERS IN THE USA

	Incident	Killed
I	9 July 1918, Nashville, Tennessee Two-train collision	101
2	I November 1918, Brooklyn, New York Subway train derailed in a tunnel	97
3=	7 August 1904, Eden, Colorado Train derailed on a bridge during a flood	96
3=	I March 1910, Wellington, Washington Avalanche swept two trains into a canyon	96
5	29 December 1876, Ashtabula, Ohio River bridge collapsed in a snowstorm	92+
6	6 February 1951, Woodbridge, New Jersey Collapse of temporary bridge	85
7	10 August 1887, Chatsworth, Illinois	84
8=	6 September 1943, Frankford Junction, Pennsylvania	79
8=	22 November 1950, Richmond Hill, New York Commuter train rammed rear of another	79
10	16 December 1943, Rennert, North Carolina Two trains collided and derailed	72

THE 10 WORST RAIL DISASTERS IN THE WORLD

	Incident	Killed
I	6 June 1981, Bagmati River, India: A train travelling from Samastipur to Banmukhi in Bihar plunged off a bridge over the river Bagmati. Although the official death toll was said to have been 268, many authorities have claimed that the train was so massively overcrowded that the actual figure was in excess of 800, making it the worst rail disaster of all time.	c 800
2	4 June 1989, Ufa, USSR: Two passenger trains travelling on the Trans-Siberian railway, one of them laden with holidaymakers heading for Black Sea resorts, were destroyed by exploding liquid gas from a nearby pipeline.	600–800
3	12 December 1917, Modane, France: A troop-carrying train ran out of control and was derailed.	543+
4	2 March 1944, Balvano, Italy: A train stalled in the Armi Tunnel, and many passengers were suffocated.	521
5	3 January 1944, Torre, Spain: A collision and fire in a tunnel resulted in many deaths.	500–800
6	3 April 1955, near Guadalajara, Mexico: A train plunged into a ravine.	c 300
7	29 September 1957, Montgomery, Pakistan: A collision between an express and an oil train.	250–300
8	4 February 1970, near Buenos Aires, Argentina: A collision between an express and a standing commuter train.	236
9	22 May 1915, Quintinshill, Scotland: Britain's worst rail disaster. (see below)	227
10	6 October 1972, near Saltilo, Mexico: A train laden with religious pilgrims was derailed and caught fire, with over 1,000 injured.	204

THE 10 WORST RAIL DISASTERS IN THE UK

	Incident	Killed
I	22 May 1915, Quintinshill near Gretna Green: A troop train carrying 500 members of the 7th Royal Scots Regiment from Larbert to Liverpool collided head-on with a local passenger train. The 15 coaches of the troop train, 195 m/213 yards long, were so crushed that they ended up just 61 m/67 yards long. Barely a minute later, the Scottish express, drawn by two engines and weighing a total of 600 tons, ploughed into the wreckage. The gas-lit troop train then caught fire. Since their records were destroyed in the blaze, the actual number of soldiers killed was never established, but was probably 215, as well as two members of the train's crew, eight in the express and two in the local train – a total of 227 killed and 246 injured, many very seriously. An enquiry established that the accident was caused by the negligence of the signalmen, George Meakin and James Tinsley, who were convicted of manslaughter.	227
2	8 October 1952, Harrow and Wealdstone Station: In patchy fog, Robert Jones, the relief driver of the Perth to Euston express, failed to see a series of signal lights warning him of danger and at 8.19 a.m. collided with the waiting Tring to Euston train. Seconds later, the Euston to Liverpool and Manchester express hit the wreckage of the two trains. The casualties were 112 killed instantly, 10 who died later, and 349 injured.	122
3	4 December 1957, Lewisham, South London: A steam and an electric train were in collision in fog, the disaster made worse by the collapse of a bridge onto the wreckage, leaving 90 dead and 109 seriously injured.	90
4	28 December 1879, Tay Bridge, Scotland: As the North British mail train passed over it during a storm, the bridge collapsed killing all 75 passengers and the crew of five. The bridge – the longest in the world at that time	

– had only been opened on 31 May the previous year and Queen Victoria had crossed it in a train soon afterwards. The locomotive was salvaged from the bed of the Tay several months later. Surprisingly little-damaged, it was repaired and continued in service until 1919.   80

5 5 November 1967, Hither Green, South London: The Hastings to Charing Cross train was derailed by a broken track. As well as those killed, 78 were injured, 27 of them very seriously.   49

6 28 February 1975, Moorgate Station, London: The Drayton Park to Moorgate tube ran into the wall at the end of the tunnel, killing 43 and injuring 74 in London Transport's worst rail disaster.   43

7 = 12 December 1988, Clapham Junction, London: The 7.18 Basingstoke to Waterloo train, carrying 906 passengers, stopped at signals outside Clapham Junction; the 6.30 train from Bournemouth ran into its rear and an empty train from Waterloo hit the wreckage leaving 33 dead (and one who died later) and 111 injured.   34

7 = 24 December 1874, Shipton near Oxford: The Paddington to Birkenhead train plunged over the embankment, killing 34 and badly injuring 65.   34

9 20 August 1868, Abergele, Wales: Wagons from a goods train shunted on the main line broke free and hurtled down an incline where they collided with the Irish Mail train. Barrels of paraffin on the goods wagons set the front three carriages on fire, killing 32 passengers who were locked inside them. Amazingly, no one in the rear of the train was injured.   32

10 1 July 1906, Salisbury: The Plymouth to Waterloo express, with passengers from the liner *New York*, was derailed outside Salisbury while travelling at excessive speed and crashed into the rear of the milk train, killing 24 passengers and two crew on the express and two crew on the milk train, with a further eight injured.   28

The 1952 Harrow rail crash remains the UK's second worst.

Transport & Tourism

THE FIRST 10 COUNTRIES TO MAKE SEAT BELTS COMPULSORY

	Country	Date
1	Czechoslovakia	Jan 1969
2	Ivory Coast	Jan 1970
3	Japan	Dec 1971
4	Australia	Jan 1972
5=	Brazil	Jun 1972
5=	New Zealand	Jun 1972
7	Puerto Rico	Jan 1974
8	Spain	Oct 1974
9	Sweden	Jan 1975
10=	Netherlands	Jun 1975
10=	Belgium	Jun 1975
10=	Luxembourg	Jun 1975

Seat belts, long in use in aeroplanes, were not designed for use in private cars until the 1950s. Ford was the first manufacturer in Europe to fit anchorage-points, and belts were first fitted as standard equipment in Swedish Volvos from 1959. They were optional extras in most cars until the 1970s, when they were fitted to all models, but their wearing was not compulsory in many countries until laws enacted during the 1970s and 1980s. The UK introduced its seat belt law on 1 January 1983 – one of the last European countries to do so.

RIGHT The car that broke the bank at Monte Carlo: the 1962 Ferrari 250 GTO sold for a new world record price at Sotheby's 1990 sale.

THE 10 MOST EXPENSIVE CARS SOLD AT AUCTION

Car	Sale	Year	Price (£)
1 1962 Ferrari 250 Gran Turismo Berlinetta Competition GTO	Sotheby's, Monte Carlo	1990	6,307,482
2 1931 Bugatti Royale Type 41 Chassis '41.141'	Christie's, London	1987	5,575,000
3 1929 Bugatti Royale, Chassis '41.150'	William F. Harrah Collection Sale, Reno, USA	1986	4,300,000
4 1957 Aston-Martin DBR2	Christie's, Monaco	1989	2,178,000
5 1934 Alfa Romeo Tipo B Monoposto	Christie's, Monaco	1989	1,971,000
6 1934 Mercedes-Benz 500K Special Roadster	Sotheby's, Monaco	1989	1,956,237
7 John Lennon's 1965 Rolls-Royce Phantom V	Sotheby's, New York	1985	1,768,462
8 1933 Alfa Romeo Tipo 8C 2300	Christie's, Monaco	1989	1,763,000
9 1936 Mercedes-Benz 500K Special Roadster	Christie's, Beaulieu	1988	1,617,000
10 1962 Ferrari 196 SP	Christie's, Monaco	1989	1,607,000

Although these are the highest prices paid at public auction, it was reported in 1989 that the only surviving 1967 original ex-factory team Ferrari 330P4 sports prototype had been purchased privately by a Swiss collector for £5,800,000 and in November of the same year that another 1962 Ferrari 250 GTO, one of only 36 made, had been purchased from a British businessman by a Japanese collector for in excess of £8,500,000.

THE TOP 10 CAR MANUFACTURERS IN THE WORLD

Company	Country	Total car production
1 General Motors	USA	5,605,301
2 Ford Motor Company	USA	4,000,256
3 Toyota	Japan	2,795,964
4 Volkswagen	West Germany	2,337,976
5 Peugeot-Citroën	France	2,300,647
6 Nissan	Japan	2,016,869
7 Renault	France	1,742,474
8 Fiat	Italy	1,674,570
9 Honda	Japan	1,361,645
10 Chrysler	USA	1,186,170

Figures are for 1987 production, amalgamating worldwide production in all companies owned by the manufacturers. The Top 10 car manufacturers are the only firms in the world that produce more than 1,000,000 cars a year, although all of them also produce commercial vehicles, General Motors and Ford each making almost 2,000,000. Mazda of Japan (857,509 cars) comes in at 11th place, with VAZ of the USSR (724,740) a perhaps surprising 12th. The British Rover Group is in 16th place in the world league, just beating both BMW and Volvo.

TOP RIGHT The car park at Renault, the seventh largest car makers in the world.

BELOW RIGHT Following in the tyre tracks of its predecessor, Ford's bestselling Fiesta.

ABOVE The fastest production car in the world: the Lamborghini Diabolo.

*As at April 1990.

This list excludes production models that are no longer available, such as the 317 kph/197 mph Porsche 959 (1987) and the 299 kph/186 mph Aston Martin Zagato (1986) and 'limited edition' cars such as the Ferrari F40.

THE 10 FASTEST PRODUCTION CARS IN THE WORLD

	Model	Price (£)*	Max speed kph	mph
1	Lamborghini Diabolo	155,000	325	202
2=	Ferrari Testarossa	96,795	290	180
2=	Lamborghini Countach S	86,077	290	180
4=	Ferrari 348ts	65,998	277	172
4=	Ferrari 348tb	64,503	277	172
6	Porsche 928 GT	60,792	274	170
7=	Aston Martin V8 Vantage	110,000	270	168
7=	Porsche 928S Series 4	60,792	270	168
9	Porsche 911 Carrera 2	44,058	259	161
10=	Aston Martin V8 Vantage Volante	135,000	257	160
10=	De Tomaso Pantera GT5-S	47,622	257	160
10=	Porsche 911 Turbo	36,874	257	160
10=	TVR 450SEAC	33,950	257	160

THE 10 BESTSELLING FORD MODELS IN EUROPE

Model	Production years	Total manufactured
1 Fiesta	1976–89	4,927,134
2 Cortina	1962–82	4,279,134
3 Escort	1980–	4,091,735
4 Escort	1968–70	4,035,857
5 Taunus	1970–82	2,427,770
6 Sierra	1982–	2,407,821
7 Transit	1965–	2,005,489
8 Granada	1972–85	1,737,428
9 Ford Ten	1932–62	1,303,855
10 Anglia	1959–67	1,284,254

■nternationally, the most successful Ford of all time was the Model T (1908–27), with a worldwide production of approximately 16,000,000, of which more than 300,000 were made in Britain. It is claimed that in the early 1920s over half the cars in the world were Model T Fords.

THE TOP 10 CAR MANUFACTURERS IN THE UK

Company	Total car production
1 Rover Group	466,619
2 Ford Motor Company	382,581
3 Vauxhall Motors	208,333
4 Peugeot-Talbot	107,195
5 Nissan	77,282
6 Jaguar	48,138
7 Rolls-Royce	3,254
8 Carbodies*	2,737
9 Lotus Group	1,061
10 TVR	715

*Carbodies manufacture the traditional 'black cab' taxi.

Car Quiz

1 On which side of the road do the Japanese drive?
2 In what year were driving tests introduced in Great Britain?
3 Who was the author of the children's stories about the flying Paragon Panther motorcar, *Chitty-Chitty-Bang-Bang*?
4 Who wrote Natalie Cole's 1988 No.5 hit record, 'Pink Cadillac'?
5 In the 'Herbie' films (*Herbie Goes to Monte Carlo*, etc), what type of car is Herbie?
6 Who coined the phrase, 'Any colour so long as it's black', and to what car was he referring?
7 What 1953 film starring Kenneth More and Kay Kendall was named after the vintage car in it?
8 What make of car was a Silver Ghost?
9 Where is Britain's National Motor Museum?
10 Who is the only person in the UK permitted to drive a car without registration plates?

THE 10 BESTSELLING CARS IN THE UK

	Make	Model	Total sold (1989)
1	Ford	Escort	181,218
2	Ford	Sierra	175,911
3	Ford	Fiesta	149,358
4	Vauxhall	Cavalier	130,615
5	Vauxhall	Astra	115,294
6	Rover	Metro	99,373
7	Vauxhall	Nova	71,047
8	Ford	Orion	68,598
9	Rover	200 series	68,316
10	Rover	Montego	57,845

Total sales of new cars in 1989 were 2,300,944 – a 3.85 per cent increase on 1988 and the third year running in which they exceeded 2,000,000. Although Ford, Vauxhall and Rover (some of whose models are made overseas) dominate the Top 10, imported cars are hard on their heels in the rest of the Top 20, with the Volkswagen Golf at No. 11 with sales of 56,055, followed by Nissan, Peugeot and Citroën. The total sales of imported cars accounted for 56.95 per cent of the market. Sales by manufacturer were:

	Manufacturer/country	UK-built	Total sold
1	Ford (UK/West Germany/Belgium/Spain/USA)	370,935	608,617
2	GM-Vauxhall Opel (UK/West Germany/Belgium/Spain/USA)	203,038	349,901
3	Rover (UK)	312,306	312,306
4	Peugeot-Talbot (UK/France)	43,326	138,958
5	Nissan (UK/Japan/Spain)	40,141	138,437
6	Audi-Volkswagen (West Germany/Belgium)	0	127,744
7	Renault (France)	0	88,111
8	Volvo (Sweden/Netherlands/Belgium)	0	81,706
9	Fiat (Italy/Portugal)	0	70,173
10	BMW (West Germany)	0	48,910

All the other companies achieving sales in excess of 20,000 are foreign-owned. They are Honda (UK/Japan), Lada (USSR), Mazda (Japan), Mercedes-Benz (West Germany) and Toyota (Japan). 'Prestige' British-made cars such as Jaguar/Daimler and Rolls-Royce/Bentley accounted for relatively small numbers of new registrations in 1989 (14,243 and 1,009 respectively), while two other British companies, Lotus and Reliant, sold just 552 and 111 cars each in the UK.

BACKGROUND RIGHT Tooth loss: though not among the commonest lost property, dentures are often left on London's buses and tubes.

LEFT Ford Escort, the UK's bestselling car of 1989.

RIGHT Based on ticket sales, Waterloo is Britain's second busiest station.

THE 10 COMMONEST TYPES OF LOST PROPERTY ON LONDON TRANSPORT

Type	1986–87	Number 1987–88	1988–89
1 Books	19,013	19,329	19,148
2 'Value items' (handbags, purses, wallets, etc)	21,940	19,868	18,628
3 Umbrellas	21,080	23,250	17,129
4 Clothing	16,497	15,211	14,954
5 Cases and bags	9,222	9,317	9,155
6 Keys	9,923	9,265	8,793
7 Spectacles	5,975	5,754	5,756
8 Cameras, radios and jewellery	5,550	5,304	5,493
9 Gloves (pairs)	5,625	4,402	3,770
10 Gloves (odd)	844	701	576

As we noted in the last edition, there is an inexplicable consistency in the numbers of articles handed in to London Transport's Lost Property Office in Baker Street from year to year, although books, usually in third place, have now moved up to No. 1 (are we reading more, or just losing more?), while umbrellas have dropped from 1st to 3rd place. Hats, once one of the commonest lost items, no longer even warrant a separate category, but expensive electronic calculators and cameras are now lost in large numbers. After the 10 commonest items, the list continues with such articles as 'Smokers' Requisites', 'Perishables' (food items) and nearly 9,000 'Miscellaneous' objects, making a grand total of 112,743 (down from 121,816 in 1987–88). Over the years 'Miscellaneous' items have included such unlikely things as sets of false teeth, a box of glass eyes, an artificial leg, an outboard motor, a stuffed gorilla and an urn containing human ashes. On average, approximately one-third of all lost articles are returned to their owners.

THE 10 BUSIEST RAILWAY STATIONS IN GREAT BRITAIN

1 Glasgow Central
2 London Waterloo
3 London Victoria
4 Leeds
5 London Euston
6 Gatwick Airport
7 Cardiff Central
8 Birmingham New Street
9 Edinburgh Waverley
10 Reading

These are Britain's 10 busiest stations based on ticket sales. However, some London stations may have a greater throughput of commuters who bought their tickets elsewhere.

WATERLOO STATION
1848 A CENTENARY OF UNINTERRUPTED SERVICE DURING PEACE AND WAR 1948
SOUTHERN RAILWAY

THE TOP 10 SHIPPING COUNTRIES IN THE WORLD

Country	No. of ships	Total GRT*
1 Liberia	1,455	47,892,529
2 Panama	5,121	47,365,362
3 Japan	9,830	28,030,425
4 USSR	6,555	25,853,712
5 Greece	1,839	21,324,340
6 USA	6,375	20,587,812
7 Cyprus	1,278	18,134,011
8 Norway	2,304	15,596,900
9 China	1,907	13,513,578
10 Bahamas	724	11,576,891

GRT or gross registered tonnage is not the actual weight of a ship but its cubic capacity (1 ton = 100 cubic feet). Deadweight tonnage is the weight a ship can carry when fully laden. The list includes only ships of more than 100 GRT.

Liberia has held the record for many years, and also has the highest deadweight tonnage – 89,500,943 tons. The UK is in 13th place (after the Philippines and South Korea), with 2,053 ships totalling 7,645,750 GRT/10,251,960 deadweight tonnage. Most of the world's shipping fleets have declined in recent years, and now total fewer than 75,000 vessels with a total GRT of less than 400,000,000 tons, of which about one-third are oil tankers.

THE TOP 10 FERRY OPERATORS IN THE WORLD

Ferry	Country	Total passengers carried (1988)
1 DSB-Danske Statsbaner	Denmark	11,704,022
2 Scandinavian Ferry Lines	Sweden	9,370,689
3 Sealink/British Ferries	UK/International	8,800,000
4 P & O European	UK	8,500,000
5 Stena Line	Sweden	4,286,567
6 Transmediterránea	Spain	3,982,744
7 Viking Line	Finland/Sweden	3,773,616
8 Deutsche Bundesbahn	West Germany	3,036,123
9 Silja Line	Finland/Sweden	2,090,843
10 Brittany Ferries	France	1,811,448

ABOVE International use of its 'flag of convenience' makes Panama the apparent second largest shipping nation in the world.

TOP LEFT Sealink is the third largest ferry operator in the world.

The total number of passengers carried by the Danish ferry operator DSB-Danske Statsbaner is more than double the entire population of Denmark.

THE 10 MOST-VISITED NATIONAL TRUST PROPERTIES

	Property	Visitors
1	Fountains Abbey and Studley Royal, North Yorkshire	289,000
2	Stourhead Garden, Wiltshire	239,000
3	Polesden Lacey House and Garden, Surrey	199,000
4=	St Michael's Mount, Cornwall	185,000
4=	Wakehurst Place, West Sussex	185,000
6	Chartwell, Kent	177,000
7	Corfe Castle, Dorset	169,000
8	Sissinghurst Castle Garden, Kent	166,000
9	Bodnant Castle, Gwynedd	164,000
10	Bodiam Castle, East Sussex	163,000

In 1989 over 10,000,000 people visited properties administered by the National Trust in England and Wales and Northern Ireland (the National Trust for Scotland is a separate organization). Of the hundreds of properties under the Trust's aegis, 75 are visited by 50,000 or more people a year.

TOP Fountains Abbey, the National Trust's most-visited property.

THE TOP 10 TOURIST ATTRACTIONS CHARGING ADMISSION IN SCOTLAND

	Attraction	Annual visitors
1	Edinburgh Castle	1,033,697
2	Magnum Leisure Centre, Irvine	1,010,260
3	Perth Leisure Pool	662,263
4	Edinburgh Zoo	555,000*
5	Mariner Leisure Centre, Falkirk	385,603
6	Palace of Holyroodhouse, Edinburgh	303,811
7	The Old Blacksmith's Shop Visitor Centre, Gretna Green	300,000*
8	Culzean Castle and Country Park, Ayrshire	297,689
9	Stirling Castle	256,218
10	Loch Ness Monster Exhibition, Drumnadrochit, Highland	250,000*

Estimated.

THE TOP 10 TOURIST ATTRACTIONS IN IRELAND

	Attraction	Annual visitors
1	Bunratty Castle and Folk Museum, Cork	179,253
2	Fota Wildlife Park, Cork	163,073
3	Blarney Castle, Cork	158,226
4	Muckross House and Gardens, Kerry	120,734
5	Royal Hospital, Kilmainham, Dublin	120,000
6	Newgrange, Meath	116,916
7	Rock of Cashel, Tipperary	104,088
8	Kilkenny Castle, Kilkenny	92,095
9	Powerscourt Gardens, Wicklow	86,556
10	Aillwee Cave, Clare	80,000

LEFT Edinburgh Castle, a top Scottish tourist attraction.

BACKGROUND Famed as the setting for the TV series, 'The Prisoner', Portmeirion is the fourth most-visited attraction in Wales.

BELOW Glasgow's Botanic Gardens are among the most visited gardens in the UK and top tourist attractions in Scotland.

THE TOP 10 FREE TOURIST ATTRACTIONS IN SCOTLAND*

	Attraction	Annual visitors
1	Glasgow Art Gallery	1,041,401
2	Royal Botanic Gardens, Edinburgh	914,748
3	Museum of Transport, Edinburgh	633,551
4	Burrell Collection, Glasgow	490,572
5	Royal Museum of Scotland, Edinburgh	464,543
6	Glasgow Botanic Gardens	350,000
7	People's Palace Museum, Glasgow	345,559
8	National Gallery of Scotland, Edinburgh	341,337
9	Aberdeen Art Gallery	339,841
10	Museum of Childhood, Edinburgh	261,764

Excluding country parks.

THE TOP 10 TOURIST ATTRACTIONS IN WALES

	Attraction	Annual visitors
1	Coney Beach Funfair, Porthcawl	500,000*
2	Pembrey Country Park	450,000
3	Barry Island Log Flume	424,484
4	Portmeirion, Penrhyndeudraeth	312,711
5	Swallow Falls, Betws-y-Coed	306,626
6	Penscynor Wildlife Park, Neath	290,000
7	Caernarfon Castle	285,789
8	Oakwood Leisure Park, Nr Narberth	270,000
9	Welsh Folk Museum, St Fagans	259,907
10	Padarn Country Park, Llanberis	240,810

Estimated.

There are additionally a number of leisure centres each attracting over 250,000 visitors a year.

ABOVE A Royal tableau at Madame Tussaud's.

BELOW RIGHT York Minster had 2,500,000 visitors in 1989.

THE UK'S TOP 10 TOURIST ATTRACTIONS CHARGING ADMISSION

Attraction	Annual visitors
1 Madame Tussaud's, London	2,609,000
2 Alton Towers, Staffordshire	2,382,000
3 Tower of London	2,214,000
4 Blackpool Tower	1,495,000
5 Natural History Museum, London	1,490,000
6 Thorpe Park, Surrey	1,300,000
7 Chessington World of Adventures	1,236,000
8 London Zoo	1,221,000
9 Kew Gardens, London	1,207,000
10 Science Museum, London	1,121,000

THE 10 MOST-VISITED CHURCHES AND CATHEDRALS IN THE UK

	Church	Total visitors (1989)
1	Westminster Abbey	3,250,000
2=	St Paul's Cathedral	2,500,000
2=	York Minster	2,500,000
4	Canterbury Cathedral	2,125,000
5	Chester Cathedral	750,000
6	Buckfast Abbey, Devon	551,413
7=	Norwich Cathedral	500,000
7=	Salisbury Cathedral	500,000
9	Bolton Abbey	420,000
10	Durham Cathedral	400,000

The number of visitors to St Albans Cathedral is said to be 'confidential' and that for King's College Chapel, Cambridge, is unavailable, so neither is included; both are probably in excess of 500,000. Buckfast Abbey's very precise figure contrasts with the round-figure estimates of the other nine because it uses a sophisticated electronic visitor counter.

THE TOP 10 HISTORIC PROPERTIES IN THE UK

Property	Annual visitors
1 Tower of London	2,214,000
2 Edinburgh Castle	1,033,697
3 Roman Baths and Pump Room, Bath	931,832
4 Windsor Castle, State Apartments	807,880
5 Stonehenge, Wiltshire	681,657
6 Warwick Castle	637,056
7 Shakespeare's Birthplace, Stratford-upon-Avon	571,262
8 Hampton Court Palace	538,838
9 Leeds Castle, Kent	528,529
10 Blenheim Palace, Oxfordshire	523,712

THE TOP 10 FREE TOURIST ATTRACTIONS IN THE UK*

	Attraction	Annual visitors
1	Blackpool Pleasure Beach	6,500,000†
2	Albert Dock, Liverpool	5,100,000
3	British Museum, London	4,670,000
4	Strathclyde Country Park, Motherwell	3,900,000
5	National Gallery, London	3,368,217
6	Great Yarmouth Pleasure Beach	2,475,000
7	Bradgate Park, Leicestershire	1,300,000
8	Stapeley Water Gardens, Cheshire	1,270,000
9	Tate Gallery, London	1,234,000
10	Frontierland, Morecambe	1,200,000

*Excluding churches
and cathedrals.
†Estimated.

LEFT The Roman Baths at Bath, a popular historic property.

TOP Blackpool Beach, the UK's most-visited free attraction.

THE TOP 10 MUSEUMS AND GALLERIES IN THE UK

	Museum/gallery	Annual visitors
1	British Museum, London	4,670,000*
2	National Gallery, London	3,368,217*
3	Natural History Museum, London	1,490,000
4	Tate Gallery, London	1,234,000*
5	Science Museum, London	1,121,000
6	Glasgow Art Gallery and Museum	1,041,401*
7	Victoria & Albert Museum, London	995,986*
8	Jorvik Viking Centre, York	904,483
9	Royal Academy of Arts, London	787,715
10	National Museum of Photography, Bradford	736,444*

Free admission.

ABOVE The British Museum is the most popular in the UK.

BACKGROUND The Pompidou Centre, Paris, is the top French tourist attraction, with over 8,000,000 visitors a year.

THE 10 MOST-VISITED GARDENS IN THE UK

	Garden	Annual visitors
1	Stapeley Water Gardens, Cheshire	1,270,000*
2	Kew Gardens, London	1,207,000
3	Royal Botanic Gardens, Edinburgh	914,748*
4	Walsall Arboretum Illuminations, West Midlands	377,230
5	Glasgow Botanic Gardens	350,000*
6	Trentham Garden, Stoke-on-Trent	250,000
7	Stourhead Garden, Wiltshire	239,000
8	Sewerby Hall, Grounds and Zoo, Bridlington	210,000
9	Birmingham Botanical Gardens	190,744
10	Wakehurst Place Garden, West Sussex	185,000

Free admission.

THE TOP 10 TOURIST ATTRACTIONS IN FRANCE

	Attraction	Annual visitors
1	Pompidou Centre, Paris (cultural centre)	8,129,000
2	Eiffel Tower, Paris	4,668,000
3	Parc de La Villette, Paris (City of Science and Industry, concert halls, gallery of electronic games, etc)	4,000,000
4	Versailles Palace	3,139,000
5	Musée du Louvre, Paris	3,016,000
6	Musée d'Orsay, Paris	2,153,000
7=	La Géode, Paris (film projection auditorium)	1,000,000
7=	Musée Picasso, Paris	1,000,000
9	Les Invalides, Paris (museums, Napoleon's tomb, etc)	905,000
10	Chenonceaux Château, Loire Valley	850,000

Index

Acknowledgements

I would like to thank the following organizations and individuals who kindly supplied me with information to enable me to compile many of the lists in **THE TOP 10 OF EVERYTHING**:

The ADT London Marathon
AGB Research Plc
Agricultural Development and Advisory Service
All England Club
Allergy International Ltd
American Forestry Association
American Kennel Club
Animals in Medicines Research Information Centre
Arbiter Group Plc
The Arts Council
ASH
The Association of the British Pharmaceutical Industry
Association of Comics Enthusiasts
Association of Motor Vehicle Manufacturers & Traders
The Association of Relocation Agents
Audiotex Briefing
Audit Bureau of Circulations Ltd
Automobile Association
BAA
Beefeater Gin, Sponsors of the Oxford & Cambridge Boat Race
BIS Mackintosh
Bookwatch Ltd
The Brewers Society
British Astronomical Association
British Athletic Association
British Broadcasting Corporation
The British Library
The British Museum
The British Olympic Association
British Rail
British Rate & Data
British Tourist Authority
Business Magazine
Cadbury Schweppes Group
Capital Radio Plc
Carbon Dioxide Information Analysis Center
Catfax
Central Statistical Office
The Champagne Bureau
Channel Four Television
Charities Aid Foundation
Christie's
Civil Aviation Authority
Consolidated Gold Fields Plc
The Corporate Intelligence Group Ltd
The Countryside Commission
Dateline International Ltd
Department of Education and Science
Department of Employment
Department of the Environment

Department of Trade and Industry
Department of Transport
The Direct Mail Sales Bureau
Economist Intelligence Unit
Electoral Reform Society
Euromonitor Ltd
Flight International
Food and Agriculture Organization of the United Nations
Football Association
Football League
Football Trust
Forbes Magazine
Ford Motor Company
Foreign & Commonwealth Office
The Forestry Commission
Fortune
French Tourist Office
Gallup
Noel Gay Organization
Generation AB
The Geological Museum
Gill & Duffus Group Ltd
Harrods Ltd
H.J. Heinz Co Ltd
Henley Centre for Forecasting
Major and Mrs Holt's Battlefield Tours Ltd
Home Office
The Imperial War Museum
Independent Broadcasting Authority
Institute for the Study of Drug Dependence
International Dental Federation
International Monetary Fund
International Tea Committee Ltd
Irish Tourist Board
Jacob's Bakery
Kattomeat
KBH Communications
Keep Britain Tidy
The Kennel Club
KP Foods
Lloyds Register of Shipping
The London Coffee Information Centre
London Regional Transport
London Theatre Record
London Theatre Scene
Marks & Spencer Plc
McVitie's Group
MEAL
Meat and Livestock Commission
Meteorological Office
Mintel International Group
Monks Partnership Ltd
Motor Vehicle Manufacturers Association of the United

States, Inc
MRIB
National Aeronautics and Space Administration
National Alliance of Women's Organizations
National Anglers' Council
National Canine Defence League
National Exhibitions Centre
National House-Building Council
The National Maritime Museum
National Opinion Poll
National Park Service
The National Trust
A.C. Nielsen Co Ltd
Nielsen Media Research
Office of Population Censuses and Surveys
Oftel
Olympia Exhibitions Ltd
The Open University
Organization for Economic Research and Development
The Oxford English Dictionary
Penguin Books Ltd
Perrier (UK) Ltd
The Pet Food Manufacturers' Association
The Pet Health Council
The Phobics' Society
The Polytechnic of Central London
Produktschap voor Gedistilleerde Dranken
Proprietory Association of Great Britain
The Ramblers' Association
The Really Useful Group Plc
The Royal Academy
The Royal Aeronautical Society Library
The Royal College of General Practitioners
Royal College of Music
Royal College of Surgeons of England
The Royal Greenwich Observatory
J. Sainsbury Plc
Scottish Tourist Board
Screen International
SGL Corporate
M. Shanken Communications, Inc
Siemens AG
W.H. Smith & Son Ltd
Smithsonian Institution Libraries
Society of Motor Vehicle Manufacturers and Traders Ltd
Sotheby's
Sports Council
The Tate Gallery
D.C. Thomson & Co Ltd

The Times
Trades Union Congress
United Feline Register
United Nations
United Nations Educational, Scientific and Cultural Organization
Variety
The Victoria & Albert Museum
Video Week
WEC International
Welsh Tourist Board
World Association of Girl Guides and Girl Scouts
World Bank
The World Conservation Monitoring Centre
World Health Organization
World Scout Bureau

D'Este Bond
Tony Brown
The late Sir Norman Chester
David Chesterman
Paul Dickson
HRH Prince Edward
Christopher Forbes
Denis Gifford
William Hanham
Dr M. Hutson
Hilary Kay
Dr Benjamin Lucas
Dr Klim McPherson
Hugh Meller
Dr Keith Mumby
Scott Reyburn
Jack Rollin
Eric Syddique
Stephen Wegg-Prosser

It is always invidious to pick out individuals from a list such as this, but I feel the following deserve special mention for their 'beyond the call of duty' work in supplying exceptional data:

Terry Charman
Robert Clark
Ludo Craddock
Luke Crampton
Max Hanna
Peter Harland
Ian Morrison
Adrian Room

I hope **THE TOP 10 OF EVERYTHING** proves that, in a list of 10, last is far from being least, so finally I want to thank the book's picture researcher, Jenny Mortimer, and above all its editor, Lorraine Jerram.

Picture Credits

Action Plus: 218, 218–19
Adams Picture Library: 248TL, 249BL
Advertising Archives: 127
Allsport: 161T, 174T, 219T, 222, 223T, 223M, 226
Amblin Entertainment: 146BR
Andes Press Agency: 196T, 213B
Animal Photography: 36, 37TL
Animals Unlimited: 35B
Associated Press/Topham: 170ML
BBC: 149B
Clive Barda: 137TL
Barnaby's Picture Library: 17, 18ML, 57, 99, 140TR, 244BR
Barnardos: 164
Bodleian Library: 100
Bridgeman Art Library: 27T, 33T, 70BL, 117T, 180, 202T
British Library: 90
British Telecom Telefocus: 168, 170BR
British Tourist Authority: 19BL, 52BR, 77
Burton Retail Ltd: 159L
Camera Press: 12B, 55, 204ML, 211TR
Christie's: 91, 92, 93, 191
Michael Cole: 150, 217TL
Bruce Coleman: 43TR
Collections: 229
Colorific: 89, 194
Columbus Tri Star: 139B
Communist Party: 62–63
Cresswell Studios Limited: 167
Danjaq Sa: 144BL
Zoe Dominic: 133TR
Richard H. Smith/Dominic Photography: 133BL
E.T. Archive: 132
Patrick Eagar: 190–91
Greg Evans: 51L
Mary Evans Picture Library: 35TR, 45, 60TR, 88, 102TR, 103TR, 103BL, 190TR
Ford Motor Company: 241, 242
Forestry Commission: 29TL
Gargling with Jelly, cover reproduced by kind permission of Penguin Books Limited: 111R

Sally & Richard Greenhill: 71, 72TR
Greenpeace: 63
Susan Griggs Agency: 73TR, 78TR
Robert Harding Picture Library: 19TR, 24, 73ML, 80, 84T, 96BL, 97, 153, 162, 199, 238
Harrods Limited, Knightsbridge: 186
Heathrow Airport Ltd: 157MR
Heineken: 193TL
HMV: 149T, 154BL
David Hoffman: 166BL, 195TR
Michael Holford: 200T
Chris Howes: 25
Hulton Deutsch Collection: 61, 68, 81B, 201ML, 217BR, 230, 234–35
Robert Hunt Library: 59TL, 200BR, 203TR, 205MR, 206, 223BR
Hutchison Library: 31BL, 32, 81TR, 112TL, 241TR, 244TL
Illustrated London News: 29BR, 221BR
The Image Bank: 26, 31TR, 66, 67, 86, 95TL, 159, 173, 216BR
Imagine/Irene Lynch: 87
The Kobal Collection: 33BR, 147MR, 151TL
KP Foods: 185T
Landscape Only: 28BR
Frank Lane Picture Library: 15, 20, 43R
London Borough of Hackney: 204BR
Lucas Films: 141BL
Macdonald: 124TL, 124MR, 124BL, 155 ML, 155MR
Raymond Mander & Joe Mitchenson Theatre Collection: 136
Marks & Spencer Plc: 187BL
Matilda, cover reproduced by kind permission of Penguin Books Limited: 111L
John Cleare/ Mountain Camera: 14TR, 16, 22B
National Portrait Gallery: 56BL, 105, 110BL
National Railway Museum: 243B
The National Trust

Photographic Library: 245
NatWest: 85BR
Peter Newark's American Pictures: 28TR, 54, 182
NHPA: 42
Novosti Press Agency: 72BL, 96TR, 203
Robert Opie: 158BR, 181MR, 187BR, 193BR
Oxfam: 163TR
PAN AM: 231BR
Paramount: 146ML
Pavilion Books: 124ML, 124BL
Perrier (UK) Ltd: 188
Phillips Fine Art Auctioneers: 128
Pictor International: 79
Pictorial Press Limited: 58, 60TL, 109ML, 110TR, 135T, 152, 205T, 208T, 240
Popperfoto: 59MR, 120, 201BL, 207, 221ML, 228, 237
Redferns: 117BR, 118TR, 119TR, 118–19, 121, 122, 123, 125, 126MT, 126TR, 126B, 129BR, 130, 131M
Rex Features: 14BL, 38BR, 69, 70TR, 83BL, 84BR, 98, 112BR, 118BL, 126TL, 131BL, 134BR, 135BL, 139TR, 150–51, 154TL, 154MR, 155, 160TR, 161M, 165, 166TR, 172, 174BL, 177, 178TR, 179, 198, 202BL, 212, 216T, 227T, 249T, 250L
Ronald Grant: 138T, 141TL, 141MR, 143, 144T, 145, 146TR, 147TL, 147BL, 148BL
Royal Aeronautical Society: 232
Royal Mail, stamps reproduced by permission of: 163
J. Sainsbury Plc: 157BL, 184
Science Photo Library: 9BR, 10, 11, 12T, 13, 21, 22TL, 44T, 47, 48, 49, 50, 51BR, 52TL
The Secret Diary of Adrian Mole, Aged 13¾, jacket illustration by Caroline Holden, reproduced by permission of Methuen, London: 109MR

Barrie Smith: 250
W.H. Smith: 224BR
Sotheby's: 94, 224L, 225BR, 239
Spectrum Colour Library: 190BL
Tony Stone Worldwide: 27BR, 46, 82, 156
Homer Sykes: 95BR, 213T
Syndicated Features Ltd: 196BR
Syndication International: 18BR, 53, 60BR, 104, 106–107, 108, 113, 134T, 137BL, 171TL, 175, 178BL, 209, 210, 211BL, 227BR
TCL Stock Directory: 192
The Telegraph Colour Library: 23, 30TR, 231ML
Tesco Creative Services: 158TR
Merilyn Thorold: 39BR, 40
Tomy UK Limited: 225T
Topham Picture Library: 83T, 114, 129TL, 243
Touchstone: 138BR, 148M
Universal: 142
Vintage Magazines: 115, 116, 181BR, 185BR, 189TR
John Walmsley: 85BL, 183T
Warner: 140B
Whitbread & Company: 193TL
Wilderness Photographic Library: 74–75
Woodmansterne Ltd, Watford: 246–47, 248MR
ZEFA: 30BL, 38TL, 39T, 44BR, 78B, 160BL, 169, 214, 215, 231TR
Zoo Operations Limited: 43ML

The Publishers have attempted to observe the legal requirements with respect to the rights of suppliers of photographic materials. Nevertheless, persons who have claims are invited to apply to the Publishers.

Quiz Answers

Planets (p.11) 1 Pluto, by American astronomer Clyde Tombaugh in 1930. 2 Mars – *Viking 1* (USA) landed on 20 July 1976. 3 Uranus, by British astronomer William Herschel in 1781. 4 Venus. 5 Mercury – 57,909,200 km/ 35,983,100 miles. 6 10 times – it is 384,399 km/238,855 miles away; the equator measures 40,075 km/24,901 miles. 7 Jupiter – despite being the largest planet, its day lasts only 9 hrs 55 mins. 8 Earth and Mercury – who is the messenger of the gods. 9 164.794 Earth years. 10 Saturn.

Mountains (p.17) 1 In 1865 he was the first to climb the Matterhorn. 2 He had only one leg, yet scaled the Matterhorn and other major peaks. 3 She became the first woman to climb Everest. 4 The Andes, some 7,242 km/ 4,500 miles long. 5 Shirley Bassey. 6 Kilimanjaro, Tanzania (5,894 m/19,340 ft). 7 Australia; it is 2,230 m/ 7,316 ft high. 8 Snowdon. 9 Mount Rushmore, South Dakota. 10 *The Eiger Sanction*.

Trees (p.29) 1 The gallows. 2 Dawn. 3 The ash. 4 The night of 15–16 October. 5 Birnam. 6 Balsa. 7 As an acknowledgement of Britain's role in helping Norway during World War II. 8 Henry Wadsworth Longfellow. 9 The yew (it was a symbol of immortality, and was used to make longbows). 10 Hatfield House, Hertfordshire, on 17 November 1558.

Cats (p.35) 1 Dinah. 2 Garfield. 3 Felix. 4 Mrs Tabitha Twitchit. 5 Orlando. 6 Fritz the Cat. 7 Mog. 8 Sylvester. 9 Jones. 10 Cat (played in the film by a cat called Orangey).

Human Body (p.51) 1 The kneecap. 2 Influenza. 3 The fingerprint. 4 The stethoscope, in 1816. 5 Its first recorded outbreak was among ex-servicemen members of the American Legion at a 1976 reunion. 6 A black eye. 7 Within the ear. 8 It is named after Daniel Salmon, the American veterinary surgeon who first identified it. 9 After Chang and Eng Bunker, born in Meklong, Siam (now Thailand), in 1811, and exhibited in Europe and America. 10 Boring a hole in the skull.

Royalty (p.55) 1 Anne of Cleves and Catherine Parr. 2 Graham Chapman. 3 Humphrey Bogart. 4 Henry I. 5 Angela Marguerite. 6 George I, buried in Hanover, Germany, in 1727. 7 Princess Michael of Kent. 8 William II and Richard I. 9 Beneath King's Cross station, London. 10 Queen Anne.

'Where On Earth?' (p.81) 1 Halifax, Nova Scotia. 2 Chichester, England. 3 Indiana, USA. 4 Wiltshire, England. 5 Los Angeles, USA. 6 Mexico City. 7 Exeter, England. 8 Aix-en-Provence, France. 9 Latvia. 10 Rio de Janeiro, Brazil.

Art (p.93) 1 Giverny, France. 2 El Greco – 'The Greek'. 3 *The Mona Lisa* by Leonardo da Vinci. 4 Ned Kelly. 5 James Whistler. 6 Surrealism. 7 David Hockney. 8 Alexander Calder. 9 Frans Hals. 10 While on loan to the British Museum, it was deliberately smashed by a man called William Lloyd.

Words (p.102) 1 It stands for *Self-Contained Underwater Breathing Apparatus*. 2 Their origins are completely unknown. 3 An aglet, or aiglet. 4 Beards. 5 An exaltation. 6 It comes from a Victorian parlour game of this name invented in the 1880s by British comedian Arthur Roberts (1852–1933). 7 Both can be written using only the top row of letters on a standard 'QWERTY' typewriter. 8 The name of its inventor, Louis Braille (1809–52), who was himself blind. 9 A gnome. 10 Both come from the Latin, *musculum*, a mouse, from the association between a mouse and the movement of muscles and the shape of mussels.

Music (p.131) 1 Madonna Louise Veronica Ciccone. 2 The Monkees and The Kinks both had members called Davey or Davy Jones, and David Bowie's real name is David (Hayward-)Jones. 3 'D.I.V.O.R.C.E.' 4 Bill Wyman, born 24 October 1936. 5 Engelbert Humperdinck. 6 Edward Kennedy. 7 'Happy Birthday To You.' 8 'Don't Go Breaking My Heart' – sung with Kiki Dee, No. 1 in 1976. 9 1965. 10 Cat Stevens.

Theatre (p.137) 1 On a stage – it is a trapdoor. 2 Joe Orton. 3 Lord Olivier. 4 *Hair*. 5 The fedora – from the drama *Fédora* (1882) by French playwright Victorien Sardou. 6 The Japanese classical theatre. 7 J. M. Barrie's *Peter Pan* (1904) – when Mr Darling mistreats the dog-nursemaid, Nana, the Darling children leave home. As a penance, Mr Darling lives in the doghouse until they return. 8 Stephen Sondheim. 9 The Globe. 10 The Savoy.

Film (p.145) 1 David Niven. 2 *The Misfits*; Marilyn Monroe. 3 *Chariots of Fire* and *Gandhi*. 4 An invisible 6 ft white rabbit. 5 Leytonstone, London, on 13 August 1899. 6 *Close Encounters of the Third Kind*. 7 *Cabaret*. 8 Scarlett O'Hara (Vivienne Leigh) in *Gone With the Wind*. 9 John Wayne. 10 Alec Guinness.

TV (p.151) 1 1936. 2 Major Margaret 'Hot Lips' Houlihan. 3 The Swiss spaghetti harvest. 4 1967. 5 E20 – which also does not exist. 6 1960 – 9 December. 7 Outside Broadcast. 8 Sooty: the puppet's show was on BBC television from 1952 to 1968, when it was transferred to Thames, where he has appeared ever since. 9 *All In The Family*; Archie Bunker. 10 *The Avengers* and *The New Avengers*.

Phone (p.169) 1 On 14 February 1876 he was just beaten to the New York patent office by a representative of Alexander Graham Bell, who was thus regarded as the telephone's inventor. 2 1923. 3 Blondie. 4 1 July 1937. 5 E.T. – the Extra Terrestrial. 6 Buckingham Palace. 7 Queen Victoria, on 14 January 1878. 8 Maureen Lipman. 9 Sir Giles Gilbert Scott. 10 846, or its letter equivalent, 'TIM'.

Food & Drink (p.189) 1 1633. 2 Dame Nellie Melba – the Peach Melba and Melba Toast. 3 Seaweed. 4 South African dried meat. 5 The sturgeon. 6 They are all names of varieties of apple. 7 Chicle, a gum extracted from the sapodilla tree. 8 Equivalent to four normal bottles. 9 Mrs Beeton. 10 An illegally distilled Irish spirit.

Prison (p.196) 1 John Bunyan. 2 John Cleland. 3 Miguel de Cervantes. 4 Daniel Defoe. 5 Sir Walter Raleigh. 6 Adolf Hitler. 7 Marco Polo. 8 Oscar Wilde. 9 O. Henry (William Sydney Porter). 10 Richard Lovelace.

Religion (p.215) 1 'A foregone conclusion' – it comes from Shakespeare's *Othello*. 2 Quakers. 3 Nicholas Breakspear, crowned Adrian (or Hadrian) IV on 4 December 1154. 4 The Singing Nun (Soeur Sourire). 5 'And' – it appears 46,227 times in the Old and New Testaments. 6 Eight – Noah, his three sons Shem, Ham and Japeth, and their wives. 7 No one – Cain killed Abel. 8 Joseph Smith. 9 Hinduism. 10 John – there have been 23 of this name, although there was a gap of 624 years between John XXII and John XXIII.

Toys, Sports & Games (p.224) 1 A card game. 2 Five. 3 Lawn tennis. 4 Victorian optical toys. 5 Rubik's Cube. 6 Tobogganing. 7 Windsor Castle. 8 22 – 15 red, 6 coloured and the white cue ball. 9 Tiddlywinks. 10 Lego plastic bricks, from the Danish *leg godt*.

Air & Space (p.228) 1 Kathy Sullivan, from the *Challenger* space shuttle in 1984. 2 *The Spruce Goose*. 3 Laika, the dog in the Russian satellite *Sputnik II*, launched on 3 November 1957. 4 In 1880, in a novel, *Across the Zodiac* by Percy Gregg – where it described the spaceship rather than its occupants. 5 *Telstar*, launched on 10 July 1962. 6 *HAL* – which is one letter in the alphabet back from *IBM*. 7 The jet engine. 8 Neil Armstrong, as the *Apollo XI* lunar module touched down on the Moon, 20 July 1969. 9 It was in 1979 the first man-powered aircraft to cross the English Channel. 10 Both were born in the Far East – Anders in Hong Kong and Lucid in Shanghai.

Cars (p.241) 1 The left. 2 1935. 3 Ian Fleming. 4 Bruce Springsteen. 5 A Volkswagen 'beetle'. 6 Henry Ford, discussing the Model-T Ford. He is said to have remarked 'People can have it in any colour – so long as it's black.' 7 *Genevieve*. 8 A Rolls-Royce (made from 1907–26). 9 At Beaulieu, Hampshire. 10 The Queen.